British culture

British Culture: An Introduction explores the highly varied nature of culture and the arts in Britain today, using a factual approach to locate key elements within a clear, historical context.

Topics include:

- the social and cultural context: politics and society from 1950 to present day, including immigration, feminism, Thatcherism and 'new' Labour, and their effects on the arts
- language and culture: regional accents, minority languages and received pronunciation
- the novel and poetry
- theatre: political drama, comedy, musicals
- cinema: Hammer Horror, Ealing comedies, black British productions, heritage film
- television and radio: crime series, sitcoms and soap operas
- popular music and fashion: The Beatles, punk, BritPop, subculture and style
- art and sculpture: Pop Art, BritArt, Bacon, Freud, Hockney, Hirst
- architecture and interiors: Modernism, post-Modernism, new towns and conservation

Each chapter focuses on key themes and movements of recent years, and gives special emphasis to outstanding artists within each area. The book also strengthens study skills, through follow-up activities and suggestions for further reading.

David Christopher works for the British Council and has lectured on English and British Studies at the Universities of Edinburgh, London and La Rioja in Spain.

British culture

An introduction

David Christopher

London and New York

First published 1999
by Routledge
11 New Fetter Lane, London EC4P 4EE

Simultaneously published in the USA and Canada
by Routledge
29 West 35th Street, New York, NY 10001

Routledge is an imprint of the Taylor & Francis Group

© 1999 David Christopher

Typeset in Sabon by Routledge
Printed and bound in Great Britain by Biddles Ltd, Guildford and
King's Lynn

British Library Cataloguing in Publication Data
A catalogue record for this book is available from the British Library

Library of Congress Cataloging in Publication Data
Christopher, David, 1958–
    British culture: an introduction / David Christopher.
            p.   cm.
    Includes bibliographical references and index.
    1. Great Britain – Civilization – 20th Century. 2. Popular culture –
    Great Britain – History – 20th century. I. Title.
DA566.4.C46   1999
941.082–dc21   99–36124
                                                              CIP

ISBN 0–415–22053–X (hbk)
ISBN 0–415–14218–0 (pbk)

Contents

Illustrations

Figures

Acknowledgements

This book describes some of the most significant features of cultural and artistic life in modern Britain. Such a work is necessarily indebted to a wide variety of descriptive and analytic texts, and some of those used in the compilation of each chapter can be found in the further reading sections.

A large number of people have made this book possible in different ways and I would like to thank Rawwaida Baksh, G. Elisa Bussi, Dale Gunthorp, Ellen Frivold, Ana Halbach, Oddvar Holmesland, Joyce Pederson and Timothy Whitton, who all provided criticisms of earlier drafts.

Among the many I pestered for information and advice, I would particularly like to thank Carol Wallace and Terence Morris. I am also extremely grateful to all at Routledge for their commitment to the book and to Heather McCallum for her patience and encouragement.

Finally, I would like to express my gratitude to those who tolerated me while I wrote it, especially Carmelo Cunchillos, Rosamaria Lombardo and my parents.

Photo credits

Photo illustrations are courtesy of:
Arcaid/Alex Bartel (4.2), Arcaid/Martin Jones (9.2), Arcaid/Richard Bryant (9.3), BBC (6.3, 6.4), Hulton Getty (6.1, 6.2), Lamplight, Wakefield (9.1), Redferns/Paul Fenton (7.2), Redferns/Val Wilmer (7.1), Ronald Grant Archive (5.1, 5.2), Simon Kemp (4.1), Stephen White (8.2), Tate Gallery/David Hockney (8.1)
Every effort has been made to obtain permission to reproduce copyright material. If any proper acknowledgement has not been made, I would invite copyright holders to inform me of the oversight.

Introduction

For the student of British Studies or merely the interested reader, there are many textbooks, journals and articles which analyse and comment on different aspects of cultural life, for example the feminist novel, ethnicity in television soap opera, or the standing of BritArt. However, without carrying out extensive background research, it is often difficult to acquire the basic knowledge on which the debates are founded. After teaching English at all levels for some time, I became convinced of the need for an introductory text which would provide a compressed survey of the most significant and studied areas of cultural and artistic interest for the non-specialist reader. This book aims to meet that need by exploring those aspects of the arts which, at the time of writing, are some of the most discussed and debated in a critical context, and which are often indicative of broader tendencies within society as a whole.

Precise definitions of the terms 'culture' and 'arts' have always been elusive and frequently elitist. But current trends point towards a more inclusive notion of culture which embraces a broad range of texts and practices. This is reflected in the renaming of the government's own Department of Heritage (with responsibility for the arts) as the Department of Culture, Media and Sport, headed by its own Culture Secretary. Similarly, arts comment and reviews within the British media frequently appear under the heading of 'culture', and vice versa.

Any text about 'British culture' must immediately recognise the problematic nature of a concept containing numerous differences as well as similarities. Since the 1950s the expression and experience of cultural life in Britain has become fragmented and reshaped by the influences of gender, ethnicity, class and region. Moreover, as we enter the third Millenium, with the gradual devolution of power to Scotland, Northern Ireland and Wales, it seems likely that regional cultural identities will be expressed more distinctively. This will inevitably lead to greater investment in regional arts and a stronger expression of locality in cultural life.

Furthermore, selection of material for this book does not recognise the misleading and dated distinction between 'high' and 'low' culture. It is certainly true that in a secular society at a time of mass communication and increasingly individualised attitudes, values and beliefs, much cultural material is clearly created more for entertainment than for moral and spiritual guidance. But 'good' and 'bad' examples exist within both categories, and while some elements are more easily accessible than others, this does not imply their inferiority.

However, the choice of material is obviously bound by a degree of subjectivity: the most commercially popular works are not necessarily the most critically praised or commented upon and many are excluded on these grounds. At the same time, trends do not change simultaneously and any particular 'scene' is always plural and varied, with many earlier styles co-existing with more recent ones. But it is hoped that the reader will be aware of these inevitabilities and will go on to consider the cited works, and to read some of the suggested texts at the end of each chapter. In this way they can form an opinion about different types of material, and the areas of critical and cultural interest to which they relate.

Aims of the book

The main aim is to provide readers with a map of the terrain: to offer signposts and co-ordinates to the people, places and events which make up substantial and evolving areas of cultural life, from where they may go on to examine the broader, theoretical issues involved in their research.

A subsequent concern is the study of change. Many textbooks consider aspects of cultural life as if they were inert or static. But as the rhythms of social and cultural change continue to quicken, it is possible that, on entering the third Millennium, we stand before a period of transition as fundamental as those of the late eighteenth and nineteenth centuries. This book reflects on the main changes which have taken place in the recent past and identifies the major developments taking place in Britain today.

Third, the book recognises the need to provide a historical context for its subject matter. This involves more than just a chapter on the cultural context created by recent social and political events. Such information is certainly necessary, given that students' knowledge of even relatively recent history may be limited. But it is also included because an important development in the recent study of culture has been the resurgence of historical analysis, which contributes to our understanding of society and the arts in the present. Therefore, the accounts and interpretations offered within most of the separate chapters are located within a historical framework.

A fourth aim is to give particular attention to changing expressions of ethnicity and gender in culture and the arts. The period under review has coincided with the break-up of the British Empire and an expansion in the Commonwealth, which has led to the immigration of people of numerous nationalities, languages, cultures and heritages. The gradual globalising of life in Britain, to which this phenomena has contributed, has produced a multi-ethnic society, a plurality of cultures and identities, whose expression increasingly contributes to the themes and tendencies found in its cultural and artistic life. Similarly, the second wave of the feminist movement, which started in the 1960s, has brought about fundamental changes in the position of women in society and their relations with men. This period has therefore witnessed the impact of social movements of race, ethnicity, multi-culturalism and feminism, and their subsequent transition into the mainstream from the margins of cultural expression.

To the British reader, a fifth aim is to keep alive the increasingly short popular memory, to provide a 'defence against forgetting' where this is due to the regular inundation of images and news through the popular media, such as television, radio, newspapers and the internet. For readers outside Britain, the study of another culture may provide a useful comparison with one's own. It should be a liberating experience which improves under-standing and imagination, and helps to provide new perspectives and thoughts.

The book is also intended to strengthen study skills, through follow-up activities and suggestions for further reading provided at the end of each chapter (see also 'Using this book'). Finally, the reader should note that it does not aim to offer an introduction to the study of cultural theory, with its attendant perspectives and methods of analysis. Instead, students may take up and explore these issues, depending on their needs and interests.

Using this book

The book is designed to be flexible, for use either at home or in class, and can easily be adapted to the needs of particular courses. Chapters can be studied in a different order or omitted, as each one is written as an inde-pendent unit. However, the reader may find the first chapter on social and political change particularly relevant to an understanding of thematic chapters, since it provides a context for their study.

For classroom use, it is suggested that teachers assemble their own archive of material to supplement the text, which can be developed and exploited according to the aims of the course, the level of the class, students' interests and so on. Material might include video recordings of films, plays and television programmes; audio recordings of music, radio news and reviews; as well as books, pictures and other visual aids. Photocopies of old newspapers also make interesting documents for exploitation in and out of class, and BBC television's Learning Zone offers another good audiovisual resource. Almost all the material mentioned in the text is available on video or sound recordings and is often broadcast on terrestrial and satellite television channels. Other material may be obtained from literary or pictorial sources (see below for more information). The internet is also a useful tool which can be used to consult a variety of topics and terms.

At the end of each chapter are six discussion topics and activities, which can be chosen and dealt with in class according to students' particular interests or needs. They may be used for subsequent projects or essays. Alternatively, it may be necessary to obtain more information before beginning a longer piece of work and some suggestions on further reading are provided in each relevant section.

Sources of information in British Studies

For the student beginning to explore a particular topic related to the study of Britain, there are a number of useful sources. Major encyclopedias, such as the *Encyclopaedia Britannica*, contain many relevant entries. Similarly, modern dictionaries and reference texts provide useful sources, and both usually supply short lists of books and articles to guide further reading.

Students may wish to prepare a longer piece of work such as a dissertation, which requires more in-depth research. For British Studies, newspapers offer a mine of information, especially the Sunday ones which contain many articles and reviews of cultural interest. The *Guardian*, *Independent*, *Observer*, *Telegraph* and *The Times* newspapers are the most important in this respect, and each produces an annual index of topics and names that have appeared in its pages that year. Newspapers from previous years are often held on microfilm or compact disc in many university and public libraries, and computers now allow rapid searches to be made.

With regard to other sources, such as books, films, plays and music, most if not all are easily obtainable from university or public libraries in Britain, or from larger bookshops. Films, television series and sound recordings are also available in video and compact disc format from many stockists, or on loan from the British Library (which incorporates the National Sound Archive), the British Film Institute, the BBC or the British Council. The scripts from many plays are also available from good bookshops.

Students should also become familiar with the main journals relevant to their field of interest. They usually appear three or four times a year, and the information and debates which they contain are usually more up to date than those in books, which take longer to write and publish. Although journal articles can be technical and difficult to understand for someone new to the field, many of the leading ones publish articles of general interest which are accessible to those with only a limited knowledge of the subject.

Finally, for selected statistical information on many aspects of cultural and social life in Britain, *Social Trends* and the *Annual Abstract of Statistics* are good starting points. They are both available from the government's publisher (HMSO) and appear every year.

1

The social and cultural context

Introduction

Since the 1950s Britain has experienced a period of accelerated social and cultural change. This has coincided with the disintegration of the British Empire, an expansion of the Commonwealth and the immigration of people of numerous nationalities, languages and cultures. The gradual globalising of life, to which these phenomena have contributed, has produced a multi-ethnic Britain, with a plurality of identities and heritages.

One of the most powerful forces for change during this period has been the women's movement. The entry of women into the labour market and their increasing independence has brought about fundamental changes in their position in society and their relations with men. Similarly, the emergence of youth as an identifiable group with a very different lifestyle to members of an older generation, has contributed substantially to the changing social and cultural profile.

Between 1948 and 1978 the impact of ethnicity, feminism and youth in Britain was felt across the arts, as successive governments provided funds through the Arts Council to encourage new styles of expression. This continued until the election of the Conservative Government in 1979, which marked an important turning point. State subsidies and benefits for the arts were replaced with a 'culture' of individualism, private enterprise and the values of the market-place in almost every area of society. Cultural life suffered greatly, as funding was reduced or disappeared in all areas. The arts were treated as any other business, so that plays, films and exhibitions were seen as products for consumption by consumers in a competitive market-place.

'Thatcherism' marked the greatest political, economic and cultural shift in Britain this century. But by the mid-1990s the Conservative Government was suffering from weak leadership and profound internal divisions. There was enthusiasm for change and the victory of New Labour in May 1997 provided the country and its cultural life with a new sense of self-confidence, with promises of moral rectitude and social inclusion in public life, plus subsidies and support for the arts.

New society (1945–60)

Economics and politics

In 1945 Britain was ready for change. After six years of fighting fascism, industry was in ruins, homes were destroyed and many people struggled to survive. In 1948 the Labour Government led by Clement Attlee introduced new plans for a 'brave new post-war world' with the creation of the welfare state, the nationalisation of key industries and a meritocratic, open society. The granting of independence to India announced a gradual dissolution of the British Empire. But despite the reforms it was a time of austerity, with shortages, queues and inconveniences.

The generation which had won the war also wanted fun and consumerism which the government had failed to deliver, and in 1951 Labour lost the election to the Conservatives led by Harold Macmillan. The same year marked the centenary of the Great Exhibition of 1851, held in London's Hyde Park to celebrate imperial greatness. To commemorate the event, the Festival of Britain was organised with parties, parades, speeches and optimism. It was a modest beginning to a decade in which crime rates were low, production rose and consumerism increased. During 1955–60, average industrial earnings rose by 34 per cent. With their new prosperity, many ordinary people were able to discover cars, fashions and foreign holidays.

Britain's economic growth created high levels of demand for manual labour in low-paid areas of work such as transport, health and catering. There was a labour shortage and the British municipal authorities began to offer jobs to Commonwealth citizens in the West Indies, India, Pakistan, Africa and Hong Kong. Enoch Powell and other Conservative MPs went to the Caribbean territories to actively recruit local people and on 21 June 1948, the ship *Empire Windrush* docked at Tilbury, to the east of London, bringing 492 Commonwealth citizens to Britain.

Their arrival marked the beginning of a migration which continued through the 1950s and 1960s and brought nearly half a million West Indians to the UK. Many established communities in Birmingham and the West Midlands, in London, in the textile towns of Bradford and Leeds in the north, and in other poor urban areas of cities around Britain. It was a strange, cold, alien country compared to the ones they had left behind.

Throughout the 1950s around 20,000 per year arrived in a country which was almost exclusively white. Immigrants were given the right of permanent residence, but many people from the poorer districts (to which the immigrants gravitated) began to resent it. Almost one third of the Commonwealth immigrants made their homes in London's East End, where local communities and daily lives began to change.

As immigration increased, race became a source of social conflict. There was competition for jobs and accommodation, and many were forced into overcrowded, unsafe housing. Attitudes became hostile and in 1958 local black communities were attacked during riots in Nottingham and in London's Notting Hill.

While immigration was mostly a working-class concern, many of the middle class were worried about the increasing danger of nuclear war. Britain had successfully tested a nuclear bomb in Australia in 1953, but there was a strong feeling among the political left that Britain would be safer without nuclear arms. A group of writers, musicians, artists and others formed the Campaign for Nuclear Disarmament. Some of the founder members included the philosopher Bertrand Russell, the composer Benjamin Britten, the sculptor Henry Moore, the historian A.J.P. Taylor, and the novelists E.M. Forster and Doris Lessing.

At Easter in 1958, 5,000 protesters marched from London to Aldermaston, the site of a nuclear research establishment. Bands and folk singers accompanied a mixture of pacifists, Christians, trade unionists, young parents and children. The movement became increasingly influential and the following year some 50,000 took part. It became an annual event and popular protest movements have since become a common feature of the political landscape.

Society and culture

During the Second World War (1939–45) many women had gone to work in the fields and factories, but afterwards they were encouraged to return to their domestic roles as wives and mothers. The birth rate rose sharply and large families became fashionable. But at the same time there were indications of domestic unhappiness. Divorces quadrupled from 8,000 per year pre-war to 32,000 in 1950, and continued to rise. More and more women began seeking the services of psychiatrists and marriage guidance counsellors. Many wanted to return to work and by 1957 one third of married women were in employment, even though the majority of jobs open to women were low-paid, part-time and monotonous.

Worries about women's independence intensified following the publica-tion in Britain of an American study called *Sexual Behaviour in the Human Female*, better known as the second Kinsey Report (1953). It revealed that women could enjoy sex as much as men, and that discontent and adultery in marriage were common. The findings caused public shock and disbelief, but initiated public and private debates about the differences

3

between the sexes and marked the beginnings of a new sexual openness in Britain and America.

The more relaxed attitude towards sexuality had implications for the content of numerous artistic works. Previously, certain books by authors such as D.H. Lawrence and James Joyce could not be published because of their erotic content, and some sculptures by Jacob Epstein were said to be obscene. But within three years of the Kinsey Report, the limits of censorship in the arts and entertainments became more relaxed and many films, plays and books began to include sexually explicit material.

In American and European cinema, the depiction of women gradually changed as Marilyn Monroe and Brigitte Bardot became famous for their projection of an innocent, child-like sexuality. In Britain, Diana Dors began her career as a cinematic sex symbol. In their roles they defined a 'third way' for women which was neither submissive nor whore-like. They were shown as fun-loving girls who were independent, sexually confident and happy. However, for many young British women of the 1950s, this was still not an option, and a life of dependence and child-rearing remained the reality.

Due to the post-war 'baby boom', by the late 1950s the average age had dropped sharply and by 1959 there were over four million single people aged between 13 and 25. Society was younger; it was also richer and more image-conscious. With full employment, it was easy to achieve financial independence at an early age. Businesses began to market their products to teenagers who now had enough money to create a new world of their own. Fashionable new clothes, hair styles and records were among the most popular items. Coffee bars and 'melody' (music) bars opened, providing meeting places for a generation with money to spend on leisure and pleasure.

Although unemployment was low, juvenile crimes by offenders under 21 rose from around 24,000 in 1955 to over 45,000 in 1959. There were frequent debates about the relationship between affluence and violence. The influence of television was often blamed, especially the content of commercial television, and the suggestive sounds and lyrics of rock'n'roll music. One of the most visible signs of change among the younger generation could be seen around 1953 with the appearance of 'Teddy Boys', urban working-class gangs dressed in colourful suits. Their behaviour was said to be threatening and brutal, and there were frequent newspaper reports of violent confrontations. The mass media began to report incidents involving the 'Teds', and presented a shocking image which frightened people and sold many newspapers.

The exaggerated images of advertising and mass culture were opposed by a tendency in the arts to confront and expose the real and the authentic in society. Many works engaged with major social issues of the time, such as criminality, punishment, poverty, family tension and racism. In literature, theatre and film, the strident works of radical new writers reflected the lives of the industrial working class in a realistic way. On television too, new series of plays and documentaries brought realistic dramas and factual reports into millions of homes. In art, the St Ives school painted simple everyday scenes in natural colours. In architecture, cool, clean minimal forms demonstrated the purity of rational design, with a conspicuous absence of decoration or artifice.

The new movements were often received by the public with shock and disdain. But they brought to the stage, screen, novel and canvas the concerns and problems of ordinary people, and not just those of a better-educated, affluent minority, which had been the case before the war. They introduced dissent into the arts, which reflected the growing dissent in society and helped establish a critical, influential tradition of social realism. This had not been done before and has since become a characteristic feature of the arts in Britain.

The debate about popular culture

During the 1950s electronic goods such as televisions, small radios and record players became cheap and widely available, and by 1960 most homes contained at least one of these. Cultural material was increasingly created for mass audiences in the form of television programmes, popular music and films. The sale of popular novels, women's magazines, sensational newspapers and comics also increased to meet demand for light entertainment.

But some social commentators and academics were concerned about the mass consumption of films and music which had been created simply to make profits. They believed that standards and quality in the arts would fall. Like many earlier critics, such as Matthew Arnold and T.S. Eliot, F.R. Leavis believed that great works of art carried a moral, civilising message, which was educational, and a means of social and self-improvement. But the mass-produced forms of music, art and popular entertainment did not and could not do this, and only encouraged individualism, hedonism, laziness and decadence.

Several influential books were written expressing the probable consequences. In *The Uses of Literacy* (1957), Richard Hoggart studied the consequences for the individual. He believed that the absence of moral content in popular literature and the arts made it more difficult for the ordinary person to become educated, wise and cultured. In *The Long Revolution* (1961), Raymond Williams considered the social consequences. He thought it would lead to an increase in materialism, self-interest, a reduction in the importance of the social services (such as education and health) and a less radical, more individualist Labour Party. But he also believed that the negative effects could be combated with a strong left-wing government and better standards of education.

In spite of the worries about moral decay and cultural decline, by the end of the 1950s the consumer society had become firmly established.

British society was about to be transformed. Its ethic of individualism and pleasure-seeking contrasted sharply with the collectivism which marked the beginning of the decade.

Progress and pop (1960–70)

Economy and politics

In spite of the material gains of the 1950s, by the mid-1960s there was a feeling of disappointment with a Conservative Party which had been in power for thirteen years. The country and had changed greatly, developing into a dynamic consumer society, but the old-fashioned speech, manners and dress of the figures of authority identified them with a much earlier age. It had also begun to appear disorganised and out of touch with politics and people. In the mid-1950s there were stories of top civil servants defecting to Russia. In 1956 there was a major government failure in the handling of the Suez Canal crisis, which resulted in a brief war and an embarrassing retreat. Later, in 1963, the Minister for War John Profumo resigned from government after admitting he lied to Parliament about his affair with a prostitute. The public was beginning to lose respect for the government, its institutions and the ruling class.

In 1964 a Labour Government won the election with Harold Wilson as its leader. With the rapid advances in science and industry, the Prime Minister famously spoke of 'the white heat of the technological revolution' and, with a television in nearly every home, the new revolution could be seen by all. There was a consumer boom and rising aspirations. Demand grew for secretarial, clerical and administrative skills, creating posts which were frequently taken by women. A commercial mass media, supermarkets and tall, modernist apartment blocks all became part of everyday life.

But in spite of material improvements in the quality of life, dissent flourished. Numerous groups demanded freedoms – political, economic and personal – as rights. The government responded with a retreat from strict social controls and punishments, many of which had been introduced in the Victorian era. Capital punishment was abolished in 1965 and criminal law was reformed in areas affecting private morality (such as obscenity, homosexuality, abortion and gambling). In 1960 gambling was legalised and many betting shops, bingo halls and clubs appeared. Homosexuality was legalised in 1967 and in 1969 18-year-olds were given the right to vote.

But the most significant advance was in the position of women. The style and ideology of the British women's movement was modelled on the movement in America, which in turn had modelled its style on the tactics of the American black liberation movement. Tactics included marches, sit-ins and strikes. But legislation was gradually introduced giving women the equality and rights for which they had fought. In 1967 the Abortion Act permitted legal terminations for social and health reasons. The same year, the Family Planning Act enabled women to obtain contraceptives through the National Health Service. These included the oral contraceptive known as 'the Pill' which became available free of charge from 1974. Before this time, women had to rely on men with condoms or simply trust their luck. Divorce was also made easier with the Divorce Reform Act of 1969.

Before the advances of the 1960s many women's lives were conditioned by their reproductive abilities. But on taking control of their fertility, they could begin to control their lives. They could decide if they wanted to become wives and mothers, or if they wanted to plan or postpone family life to fit in with their jobs. These measures helped to ensure that another 'baby boom' similar to that of the late 1940s would be unlikely.

As well as demands for more personal independence, the 1960s also witnessed demands for greater regional autonomy. Scottish, Welsh and Irish nationalists all began to demand freedom from British rule. In 1968 there were riots in Northern Ireland where the Civil Rights Association demanded equal treatment for Catholics and Protestants. In 1969 the British government sent troops there to keep order on the streets, where they have remained ever since.

But not everyone approved of the changes which the decade brought. The Church of England, other Protestant churches and the Roman Catholic churches remained firmly traditional, but their influence gradually declined. However, the political right remained firmly opposed to liberal reform and when economic growth began to slow down around 1966, immigration was made a controversial issue. In 1968, Conservative MP Enoch Powell warned that uncontrolled immigration could lead to violence. In an inflammatory, emotive, infamous speech he quoted lines from an epic poem by Virgil, about the River Tiber foaming with blood. His performance made him simultaneously hated by the left and admired by racists, who found support in his speech. Although he was sacked from the Shadow Cabinet by the party leader Edward Heath, it was a sharp warning of the increased polarisation of society which would characterise Britain in the 1970s.

Society and culture

The early years of the decade saw rising affluence, full employment and increasing optimism. As the children of the post-war years became young adults, there were new generational attitudes. An early indication of change came in 1960, when the publishers Penguin Books won against a charge of obscenity for the publication of the D.H. Lawrence novel *Lady Chatterley's Lover*. On the day of the victory 200,000 copies were sold.

The material affluence and the new freedoms in law contributed to young people's growing self-confidence to choose not only their own fashions and music, but also politics, religion and sexuality. With the freedom to protest, consume and create their own lifestyle, all sections of society which had previously been ignored became visible: workers, blacks, women, provincials. In the words of the American pop artist Andy Warhol, everyone would be famous for fifteen minutes.

The popular music and fashion industries saw that a numerically significant section of the population had money to spend on an alternative, 'pop' culture, and there was a boom in spending on music and clothes. Many of the period's cultural innovators were young musicians. They often came from provincial towns and spoke with regional accents. They had little or no formal training, but enough natural ability and charisma to capture public attention. The Beatles and the Rolling Stones were discovered and marketed to a mass teenage audience. The Beatles often wrote songs using the informal slang of their young fans, while the Rolling Stones were more influenced by black American blues singers. They became highly influential and many other groups copied their style.

In fashion, the 'canon' of the couturier was largely abandoned and ready-to-wear clothes appeared in daring new styles. Recycling, mixing and matching of clothes from an earlier time became common, while the miniskirt seemed to affirm the new confidence of women in their sexuality. The skinny model known simply as Twiggy became the fashion yardstick and promoted a new look, as a girl who was both thin and desirable.

Across the cultural spectrum, new, exciting, distinctive styles and movements appeared, inspired and amplified by the reflections of writers, novelists, playwrights, film-makers, architects and artists. Pop art, modernist and 'plug-in' architecture, 'swinging' London films and nudity on the stage became symbols of the decade, while James Bond, George Best, the Avengers, Twiggy, the Beatles and the Stones, became some of its most fashionable figures.

But some young people rejected consumerism and became involved with alternative or 'underground' culture. New magazines appeared, such as *Black Dwarf*, *Oz* and the *International Times*, which helped to circulate information on alternative politics and lifestyles. The expansion of higher education had encouraged many young people to think critically about politics and society, and there was a growing interest in subjects offering fresh critical perspectives, such as sociology. Ideas were often radical and diverse, but there was a general belief that progressive, libertarian groups could create a new, unified society based on peace and co-operation, to replace the competitive, materialist Western model.

Towards the end of the 1960s and throughout the 1970s alternative ideas began to find expression in the arts, with the appearance of small-scale, non-profit making co-operatives in art, drama, film, writing and music. Many of their works carried themes which the commercial mainstream found unacceptable, such as racial oppression, women's liberation and gay rights. But at the same time, other young people were rejecting both politics and consumerism, in favour of spirituality and enlightenment.

The attraction was not the traditional Church of England, but the exotic possibilities offered by cheap overseas travel along the 'hippy trail' to India.

Opinion over the changes of the 1960s was divided. Some regarded the reforms as positive, while the supporters of traditional moral standards spoke of the increasing decline and commercialisation of culture. They blamed law reforms in divorce, abortion and the wide availability of contraceptives for increases in juvenile crime, violence and sexual promiscuity. However, studies showed that the sexual behaviour of young people changed very little, and that changes in attitudes and in law concerning sexual behaviour benefitted men more than women. But nothing seemed stable as a new popular culture displaced the old traditions of the past, resulting in confusion and anxiety among many older members of the public.

Anger and division (1970–9)

Economy and politics

In 1970 the Conservative Party won the election, with Ted Heath as its leader. In contrast with the optimism and hedonism of the 1960s, it was the beginning of a dark decade marked by social division, strikes, high inflation, unemployment and political violence. In 1974, with inflation at 25 per cent and prolonged strikes by the mineworkers' union, the lights went out in a series of power cuts, which forced an election. The result indicated a victory for the Labour Party, with a minority government. Its leader Harold Wilson was able to settle the miners' strike and in a second election the same year Labour won with a small majority.

But high oil prices left the economy depressed. The unions were strong and well organised, and as the economic crisis worsened there were rumours of a Communist plot to take over the Labour Party. Political tension increased as International Marxists became more numerous and various anarchist groups were visible. On the political far-right, the National Front was winning more votes in local elections and for a short time became the third party in British politics, beating the Liberal Party in several local elections. Another far-right group, the National Association for Freedom, was formed in 1975, but one of its organisers was killed by the IRA less than one month later. Then the IRA began a bombing campaign in several British cities. Support for Irish, Scottish and Welsh nationalism was at its peak, and political and social fragmentation across Britain was increasingly obvious.

Economists debated the reasons for persistent economic failure. The long-term decline of mining, shipbuilding, steel production and motor vehicle manufacture were all seen as significant factors. These heavy industries were no longer competitive in global markets. The resistance of the trade unions to industrial change, the tendency of management to think and plan only for the short term, inflation and the oil crisis of the mid-1970s were all blamed. No government could govern effectively and towards the end of the 1970s there was a growing sense of desperation. The forceful personality of Margaret Thatcher and the simplicity of her free-market solutions began to appear an attractive alternative.

Society and culture

The women's movement continued to make progress in their search for equal opportunities. In the field of employment, the Equal Pay Act was introduced in 1970, although this did not become law until five years later. The Sex Discrimination Act of 1975 made it illegal to discriminate between men and women most areas of employment. With these measures, women had access to levels of economic independence which were unimaginable to the previous generation.

The achievements of the women's movement were not only in the field of law: during the 1970s it became increasingly politicised. A modern, untheoretical expression of its beliefs arrived with Germaine Greer's *The Female Eunuch* (1970). When the first National Women's Liberation March took place in London in 1971, there were already signs of a division within the movement. Radical feminists demanded feminism based on lesbian relationships, insisting on their superiority. In 1971 the first Gay Pride march had been held in London, and a lesbian one took place soon after. But many other women insisted on a less radical feminism, one which combined equality with family life and relationships with men.

Departments of Women's Studies opened in many universities and departments of language, literature, anthropology and history began to develop feminist perspectives. Women's writing became an established literary genre and publishing houses (such as Virago) opened to promote writing by female authors. New, non-commercial 'underground' magazines such as *The Shrew* and *Spare Rib* gave coverage and support to women's liberation. Then, in 1972, a colourful new American publication became available in Britain: *Cosmopolitan* dealt with feminist issues such as rape, sexuality, abortion and contraception, but ignored the radical politics and sexuality of the underground press. It was not popular with militant feminists, but many other women found its approach more compatible with their chosen lifestyles.

In spite of the legal reforms to ensure equal opportunities for women and black people, in many areas of the arts and mass media their representation remained firmly traditional. In popular television series, from the music show *Top of the Pops* to the sitcom *Steptoe and Son*, working women were often shown as sexually provocative and available. Similarly, tabloid newspapers such as the *Sun* were frequently criticised by women's groups for their stereotyped presentation and treatment of women as sex objects. The representation of immigrant groups and individuals also suffered. In television series such as *Till Death Us Do Part* and *Love Thy Neighbour*, blacks were frequently the target of racial jokes and stereotyping in programmes which were among the most popular of the 1960s and 1970s.

Although television had introduced some brave new dramas during the previous decade, during in the 1970s programming became increasingly bland. Many programmes were created to comfort and reassure audiences rather than challenge or provoke them. Historical adaptations and trivial sitcoms were among the most popular programmes of their time and provided light relief from the turbulence outside.

As unemployment rose, so did the number of strikes, and towards the middle of the decade inflation reached 25 per cent. Numerous social groups were demanding rights denied to them, as society became increasingly confrontational. Racial tension increased in the cities, where the National Front had begun to openly provoke black communities and their supporters. Conflict intensified following the 'Spaghetti House siege' in 1975, when three Afro-Caribbeans attempted a robbery and took hostages in a restaurant in the London suburb of Brixton.

Acts of vandalism were frequent, and there was public hostility towards the oppressive severity and frequently dysfunctional modernist architecture. Many felt threatened by the presence on the streets of numerous young vandals, skinheads and football hooligans. Popular newspapers such as the *Sun* and *Daily Mirror* carried sensational stories of social problems and crimes, such as racial violence, robbery, football hooliganism, pornography and rape. Punks appeared on streets around Britain. Their shocking appearance reflected a sense of disgust with a society which seemed to have abandoned its youth and its future.

In many areas of the arts, fantasy and reality were mixing freely in a kind of dream-like disorder. Films such as Stanley Kubrick's *A Clockwork Orange* (1971) reflected the ugly mood of the times. It is filmed as a type of documentary about a declining society in which aggressive, drug-crazed youths rob and rape their way through the city. In a similar style, Derek Jarman's *Jubilee* (1978) showed London as a city full of nightmares. In the theatre, it was a time of highly politicised dramas which addressed Britain's resistance to change. Plays by David Hare, Howard Brenton and David Edgar shocked their audiences with frank depictions of sexuality and violence in a decade marked by division and decline.

All change (1979–97)

Economy and politics

Following the defeat of the Conservatives in the 1974 election, Margaret Hilda Thatcher, a greengrocer's daughter from the market town of

Grantham in Lincolnshire, was elected as the new leader. She went on to lead the Conservatives to victory in the election of 1979 and the party remained in power until 1997. The period opened optimistically, with Thatcher quoting St Francis of Assisi, a medieval saint who made a virtue of poverty:

> Where there is discord, may we bring harmony,
> Where there is error, may we bring truth,
> Where there is doubt, may we bring faith,
> Where there is despair, may we bring hope.

Her early publicity depicted her as a happily married suburban housewife, cheerfully washing up in her suburban semi-detached house. But at the same time she was developing economic ideas which were guided by the fashionable theories of monetarism. These involved reducing inflation with high interest rates and submitting all aspects of the economy to free-market theories and the laws of supply and demand.

But in the early 1980s Britain's economic crisis became even worse. The government became deeply unpopular, as factories closed and unemployment rose to over 13 per cent, with more than three million out of work. Manufacturing declined and the shipbuilding, mining and steel industries practically disappeared. The regions of Scotland, the north of England, Wales and the West Midlands had traditionally depended on this kind of industry and were economically devastated.

There was civil and industrial conflict in many areas, and in April 1981 rioting broke out in London, Bristol, Liverpool, Nottingham, and other cities around Britain. It was spontaneous and anarchic, directed against the police and the local environment. On 2 April the following year, Thatcher led Britain into war with Argentina over the occupation of the Falklands Islands (Islas Malvinas) and emerged victorious on 14 June.

In spite of record unemployment, riots and a war, the Conservatives emerged victorious in the General Election of 1983, and the economic and political ideas which came to be known as 'Thatcherism' began to be fully expressed and implemented. These included an even greater reduction of public spending and measures to privatise industries in the public sector (such as gas, steel, transport and telecommunications). The measures were highly unpopular with the working class and unemployed, and resulted in more violent industrial disputes. They were also expensive to implement, being of great cost to the welfare state, but the discovery of oil in the North Sea in the 1970s helped to finance Thatcher's project.

Next she addressed those she called 'the enemy within.' These consisted of powerful trade unions, the miners, left-wing local governments, the IRA, illegal immigrants, the Greens and 'unreliable' members of her own party. The most notorious confrontation with these was the Miners' Strike of 1984–5, which Thatcher saw as part of her plan to break the power of the unions. She became known as the 'Iron Lady' and passed legislation to permanently weaken the unions' power.

Early opposition focussed on the stationing of nuclear weapons in Britain. This began to be forcefully expressed with the establishing of a women's 'peace camp' outside Greenham Common airbase in 1981. There were also concerns over the environment and membership of Green parties such as the Ramblers, Friends of the Earth, Greenpeace and Hunt Saboteurs increased.

The government found new opposition in 1987 when the Local Government Act was introduced. Clause 28 of the Act prohibited state schools from promoting homosexuality or teaching that it is acceptable. As a result, campaigning for gay rights and equality intensified, with greater participation in the annual Gay Pride march, and in the activities and profile of pressure groups such as Stonewall, Act Up and Outrage. Some tactics involved exposure in the media ('outing') of homosexuals and lesbians, and high levels of public interest.

During 1985–6 there were more riots in cities around Britain. Burglary, car theft and vandalism all increased. Football hooliganism became a serious social problem. Relations between the police and public were tense. Commentators on the left blamed high unemployment (almost four million), homelessness (around one million) and the loss of community, which an ethos of economic individualism had promoted. Those on the right blamed the permissive society of the 1960s, which had allowed the young to grow up with no respect for the police, teachers or authority.

But after the government removed restrictions on money-lending and dealing in shares, the financial sector boomed. Credit was easy to obtain and taxes were cut, and share prices rose quickly when newly privatised public industries such as British Airways, British Steel and all the public utilities (such as gas, water and telecommunications) were floated. The dominant economic influences changed from heavy industry and manufacturing to financial services and North Sea oil revenues.

Government policies had severe consequences for the poorly educated and least skilled, who were unable to obtain manual work as they had done in previous generations. Many were women, who transferred from manufacturing work to low-paid, part-time service industries in which there were no pension or union benefits. But on a different social level, women were beginning to occupy posts in traditional male-dominated areas such as business, law and banks. Many could enjoy the benefits of increasing financial and sexual freedom, and were postponing marriage and children.

By 1986 the economy was strong and house prices were rising sharply. There was an air of enterprise and optimism as a new society emerged. Britain became more affluent, competitive and more interested in cash than class. There was a new generation of aspirational, stylish and image-conscious consumers, and spending on restaurants, clothes, cars, homes and holidays reached record levels.

Advertising and publicity became fine arts. The Conservatives employed the services of the Saatchi and Saatchi advertising agency to promote the party. Its logo was a flaming blue torch, a symbol closely associated with the Oscar-winning film *Chariots of Fire*. Meanwhile, Labour adopted a red rose as their logo and hired the services of Hugh Hudson, the director of *Chariots*, to make a publicity film of the leader Neil Kinnock.

Following her third election victory in 1987, Thatcher claimed she had cured Britain of its strikes, low productivity, low investment and 'winters of discontent' forever. But the same year the economy began to stagnate when share prices crashed. At the same time, house prices and inflation continued to rise dramatically. The unemployed and sick suffered greater poverty and insecurity through the reduced levels of social services. Increasing numbers of homeless beggars appeared on the streets, the use of illegal drugs increased, while the numbers of AIDS and HIV sufferers also grew alarmingly.

But the government ignored a gradual deterioration in many people's quality of life. For several years Britain lived a kind of 'American Dream'. Its dominant attitudes, values and beliefs were openly approved of by the majority, even if they were excluded. But towards the end of the decade the public began to realise that what the politicians said about Britain was very different from the reality of living in it.

Society and culture

For many years the arts had been insulated from the realities of commercial life. The Arts Council, created to support the arts in 1946 under the chairmanship of the economist John Maynard Keynes, did not interfere with the work of artists and performers. Its ideology survived changes in government and helped to support the wealth and variety of British theatre, music and the visual arts. But during the early 1980s the free market became the only source of information for social, economic and political ideas. The Council's funding was sharply reduced, as the arts were treated as any other business.

The effects of the cuts were widely felt. For the first time, many museums and galleries began to charge admission prices. To attract subsidies, arts productions had to become less adventurous and more populist, for example by showing Shakespeare's plays in ways which removed their social content and stressed their sentimental aspects. But some writers were still prepared to write brave dramas which critically engaged with modern society. Numerous works by Howard Brenton, David Edgar, David Hare and Caryl Churchill continued to depict a growing amorality and a loss of liberal values. Many works of literature reflected similar sentiments. Martin Amis, Ian McEwan and Graham Swift wrote novels about a disordered, chaotic country, and showed their disgust with the replacement of liberal values by those of the market-place.

14

In television, all channels including the BBC became more conscious of the need to compete in a commercial world. During a brief period of eighteen months, television programming was transformed. Previously, broadcasts had begun around early afternoon, but in 1983 the BBC and ITV both began transmissions from dawn. Channel 4 started transmitting in 1984, the same year as the privately owned station Sky television. Sky marked the introduction of satellite television in Britain and for many households a 'dish' antenna on the outside wall became a fashionable accessory.

Some of the most successful serials of the early 1980s were traditional reconstructions of the past such as *Brideshead Revisited* and *The Jewel in the Crown*, which were both popular and critically praised. But there were still notable series which bravely commented on modern themes. The loss of the dignity of work was memorably expressed the drama series *Boys from the Blackstuff*, while *A Very British Coup* showed how the conservative nature of Britain's institutions, in particular the civil service and press, could conspire to bring down any socialist government of the future. *Edge of Darkness* and *The Monocled Mutineer* were brave, highly praised series which contrasted the government's view of nuclear conflict and of war with the realities of life as perceived by the public.

The arrival of Channel 4 provided programmes for minority groups and often radical, permissive plays. It also began to sponsor critical films, such as *My Beautiful Launderette* and *A Letter to Brezhnev*, which expressed their opposition to the loss of tolerance and liberal values. These and others such as *The Ploughman's Lunch*, *Britannia Hospital* and *Defence of the Realm* promoted a lively political critique of the mass media, society and defence under the Conservative Government. The new possibilities open to many women were depicted with humorous vitality in films such as *Educating Rita* and *Shirley Valentine*, in which the heroines abandon the security of their domestic 'prisons' for romance, excitement and a new life.

But some of the most commercially successful of the decade were 'heritage' films. They were often based on successful novels, such as E.M. Forster's *Room with a View* and *A Passage to India*, which reconstructed an elegant, upper-class, imperialist Britain. *Chariots of Fire* also enjoyed huge commercial success. Its themes of competing, winning and British superiority coincided with the wedding of Prince Charles to Diana in 1981, victory over Argentina in the Falkland Islands (Islas Malvinas) in 1982 and the victory of the ruling Conservative Party in the election soon afterwards. It became the film of the moment and won four Oscars.

In architecture, there were few advances during the early 1980s. The construction industry was at a standstill due to a lack of investment and low economic confidence. But the renovation of older buildings frequently provided cheaper, more attractive solutions, and started to become a common practice. Later in the decade when credit restrictions were lifted,

15

there was a period of accelerated growth. New high-technology office blocks were built in a fashionable post-modern style. One of the most outstanding developments was Docklands in east London, where glamorous, futuristic buildings announced a booming economy.

The individualism and commerce promoted by the Conservative Government were embraced by many young British artists. Traditionally, they had depended on the patronage of gallery owners, but now began to look for empty warehouses and other buildings where they could show and sell their work more independently. At the same time they introduced a variety of challenging new styles which often made use of living and organic material, such as the installations of Damien Hirst. Warehouses also became the location for the dominant musical force of the decade. High-energy dance music was played at maximum volume in fiestas of apolitical hedonism or 'raves', illegally held in large unoccupied buildings around Britain where thousands of young people danced defiantly through the years of Tory rule.

The Blair Revolution (1997–)

Economy and politics

Until the early 1990s, the Labour Party was divided and in chaos. It was committed to policies such as leaving the Common Market, big tax rises, nuclear disarmament, the restoration of trade unions' privileges and returning privatised industries to state control. Michael Foot had replaced James Callaghan as Labour leader, but was dominated by the militant left-wing in his party, which was firmly rejected in the election of 1983. After another change of leader, the party's symbol of the red flag was rejected and the red rose introduced. With new leader Neil Kinnock, the party was given a less militant, more centrist and popular appeal.

In 1981, a new party had been formed by MPs from the other major parties: the Social Democratic Party. In the late 1980s, under its new name of the Liberal Democrats, it won many seats from Labour, attacking the problems of poverty, homelessness and unemployment. But after the 1987 election, many political observers suggested that it had prevented the Labour Party from winning power by dividing the opposition vote.

There were more serious disturbances in 1990 with rioting in London during demonstrations against a new tax known as the 'poll tax'. Margaret Thatcher also became increasingly hostile to the idea of an integrated Europe. The issue divided her cabinet and eventually contributed to her rejection by the party in 1990. John Major was elected as the new leader. But political commentators saw a divided party governing a divided, disillusioned nation. He managed to briefly reverse the Conservative's fortunes with an unexpected victory in the 1992 election, bringing a record fourth consecutive election victory for the Conservatives.

But later that year there was humiliation when Major faced opposition and internal rebellion from those opposed to the Maastricht Treaty and closer monetary union with other European countries.

Divisions over European integration and the decline in popularity of the Conservatives gave the Labour Party an opportunity to reorganise. John Smith was elected as the new leader. But after his sudden death from a heart attack, Tony Blair was chosen. He transformed the party, leaving behind the traditional socialist ideas about stronger unions and state ownership of the major industries. Many were concerned that the party was becoming too much like the Conservatives and not enough like the traditional Labour Party, with its commitments to nationalisation and redistribution of wealth. But he stuck to his message about principles being futile without power, which alienated some traditional labour supporters.

For much of the 1990s there was an overwhelming sensation of disillusion. Studies repeatedly showed that public confidence had fallen in all the major institutions, especially in Parliament, the legal system and the press. And throughout the decade the monarchy, like the Church, was appearing increasingly fragile and irrelevant, amid the devolution of power to Scotland, the plans of the Labour Government to abolish the House of Lords and increasing demands by the Republican pressure group Charter 88.

Meanwhile, the Conservative decline continued, and there were more internal divisions about weak leadership, an uncaring attitude towards weaker sections of the community and doubts over closer European integration. There were also allegations of financial and moral impropriety within the party, commonly known as 'sleaze'. The opinion polls were high in favour of the opposition Labour Party and in May 1997 it gained a historic electoral victory, with a majority of 179 MPs. There was a record number of 101 women Labour MPs and three openly gay men and one lesbian. But public interest in politics seemed to have declined, especially as the manifestos of the two parties appeared to resemble each other so closely. Instead there was increasing tendency to take direct action, especially on environmental issues, such as opposition to road-building schemes and support of animal welfare. In a decade marked by confusion and uncertainty, politics became the least convincing of the performing arts.

Demands increased for regional autonomy and, within several months of its 1997 election victory, the Labour Government began to introduce a devolution of power to Scotland, an assembly to aid regional autonomy for Wales and made a peace treaty with Northern Ireland.

The death of Diana, Princess of Wales, at the end of August 1997 threw the nation into a period of mourning and emotional introspection. Some of the public said her death had affected them more than the death of their own loved ones and, on the day of her funeral, hundreds of thousands were on the streets to throw flowers at the funeral car. The Prime Minister called her the 'People's Princess' and almost provoked a crisis when the public took this as a signal to turn against the formal, old-fashioned Royal Family. Instead, Labour's publicity department came to their aid and helped organise the funeral, which became a national event of unique emotional impact. The Royal Family began to change, characterised by less formality, less protocol and a closer relationship with the people, in an attempt to restore their diminished popularity.

As the nation publicly mourned the loss of Diana, the rest of the world could watch every detail of the ceremony. Telecommunications and the internet had increasingly become part of people's daily lives, and a globalisation of news, politics and the economy meant that events could be watched as they happened almost anywhere in the world. These, together with a greater understanding of genes and how to manipulate them in humans and animals, were among some of the most significant technical developments of the decade.

But at the same time there was a growing suspicion of science and medicine. There were reports of fatal new diseases, such as CJD, and threats to nature, such as global warming, forcing many to believe the environment needed protection not exploitation. There were few signs that this would happen soon and many intellectuals were pessimistic about the future. Health become a political as well as a personal issue, as people were retiring earlier, living longer and were often in child-free households, which all imposed a greater burden on public health provision. Traditional pleasures became suspect, as food, drink, sex, smoking and sunshine were all said to carry substantial health risks.

In a move which seemed to represent a loss of confidence in science, there was increasing interest in the paranormal and less conventional forms of religion. In 1997 some 70 per cent of Britons professed religious faith but not necessarily the traditional Christian one, and 90 per cent did not go to church regularly. Some social commentators argued this was due to the personal insecurities which life in the 1990s had produced. Moreover, that growing interest in 'alternative' religion showed a public lack of confidence in traditional authorities such as government, science and the Christian church, and their ability to provide answers to modern problems.

Society and culture

In spite of the progress made by the women's movement since the 1960s, Britain's institutions have remained largely male-dominated. Within Parliament there are still relatively few female MPs, with 24 in 1945, 41 in 1987 and 141 of 650 MPs after the election of 1997. In 1990 there were no female Law Lords and only 1 in 80 was a High Court judge. Within the Church of England, women could not be ordained until 1992 and continue to be excluded from the orders of bishops, deacons and priests. In 1990 less than 10 per cent of businesses were owned by women, only 21 of the

top 200 companies had women in their boardrooms, and of 401 profes-
sors at the Universities of Oxford and Cambridge, only 12 were women.

Although some women have made considerable advances in their
chosen careers compared with twenty years ago, most are white, middle-
class university graduates. They also earn approximately 20 per cent less
than men in business, industry and government, even when doing similar
types of work. Within the domestic sphere, divorce rates have continued to
rise and in 1994 some 40 per cent of marriages ended in divorce, leaving
many women in single-parent households. But in the 1990s debates about
equality began to move from economic to social issues, such as political
correctness in language and behaviour, sexual harassment and male
violence, in what became known as a 'post-feminist' era.

With regard to the ethnic composition of British society, in March 1995
just under 6 per cent (3.2 million) of the total population of Great Britain
considered they belonged to a 'non-white group'. 1.6 per cent (891,000)
were Afro-Caribbean, 1.5 per cent Indian, 0.9 per cent Pakistani, 0.3 per
cent Bangladeshi, 0.3 per cent Chinese, while 0.9 per cent belonged to
other ethnic groups. Although half the 'non-white group' (around 1.5
million) were born in Britain, many are unwilling or unable to integrate
fully into British society and continue to live in the same urban areas as in
the 1950s and 1960s where the concentration of immigrants is much
higher. According to the national census of 1991, 25.6 per cent of the
population of inner London considered themselves as belonging to some
ethnic group. This contrasts with 14.6 per cent of the West Midlands and
approximately 1 per cent of the rural parts of Scotland and Yorkshire.
While the culture and lifestyle of many non-whites is often quite different
to other British citizens, it often has little in common with those living in
their country of origin. Years spent living in a different culture have
resulted in the appropriation of different social and artistic influences to
generate new styles of language, literature, music and other arts. The result
is the creation of new cultural spaces, which help to sustain a lively and
imaginative multi-cultural Britain.

Compared with only ten years ago, the gay community has emerged as
another significant minority group. In 1999 programmes were created
specifically for gay audiences on BBC2, Channel 4 and on Radio 5. There
were several newspapers for the gay community and many bookshops
carried a large selection of gay literature. With an increasing understanding and acceptance of homosexuals and lesbians, more 'came out'
and publicly declared their homosexuality. The age of consent was reduced
from 21 to 18 in 1994 and in the near future this is likely to be lowered to
16, the same as for heterosexual relationships. However, homosexuality is
still seen as a sensitive area surrounded by ignorance and prejudice, and
while it is openly represented in literary and theatrical works, in other
areas of the arts, such as television and film, it remains relatively rare.

Following the change of government in 1997, there was a powerful sense of cultural confidence and renewal which extended across the arts. In the same year, the Department for National Heritage was replaced by the Department of Culture, Media and Sport, with responsibility for government policy and expenditure on museums and galleries; the Arts Councils of England, Scotland, Wales and Northern Ireland; plus regulation of the film industry, broadcasting and the press.

Decisions were taken to advance plans for the Millennium celebrations at Greenwich in London, which included the construction of an enormous dome, whose architecture seemed to be a physical, permanent demonstration of a new national optimism. Numerous other new projects also began in the public sector which embraced arts buildings, sports stadiums and transport schemes. Many were assisted with funds from the National Lottery, which began in 1995.

Although new public architecture often appeared imaginative and futuristic, the most fashionable new domestic housing continued to be traditional in appearance and modern in convenience. Taking an attractive traditional design and making it practical, relevant and usable, has been common in architectural practice for over a century. But in the late 1990s the practice had become frequent in many other areas of cultural life. 'Makeovers', 'reworkings' and reinventing traditional plays, stories, styles and songs were frequent in literature, in film adaptations and in popular music.

Elsewhere in the arts, the influence of realism was overwhelming, with frequent attempts to find drama in authentic daily life, rather than create it in works of fantasy and imagination. In television, many 'reality' programmes brought viewers true-life experiences from a variety of settings, from cruise ships and airlines to modelling agencies and animal hospitals. The public found them entertaining, but critics saw them as merely cheap and populist. Broadcasters had become more cautious, offering more populist programmes which were guaranteed to attract large audiences. This was due to acute competition in the television 'business' of the late 1990s, as the terrestrial channels faced challenges from satellite television and a proliferation of new channels from digital services. The realist influence extended to many new works by young British artists. These were often personal and confessional, and sometimes involved the use of organic or bodily matter combined with modern technology. The public often found them confusing and controversial, but many younger spectators found them provocative and original.

For the first time in many years, the cultural scene appeared to renounce any American influences and stood proud and alone in its splendid isolation. The media spoke enthusiastically of 'Cool Britannia' which coincided with recent international successes in film with *The English Patient* and *The Full Monty* and in pop with bands such as Oasis. But 'BritFilm', 'BritPop' and other 'BritArts' are phenomena which were overwhelmingly made in England, indicating a clear trend towards the centralisation of creative activity. London continues to be pre-eminent for the presentation of almost any production. The presence of all the national media and the opportunity to give their works maximum exposure, often to an international audience, has attracted many creative professionals, who feel the need to live and work there to develop their careers.

But in the theatre, which was once a source of the most radical and original cultural productions, the majority of performances staged around Britain were musicals and interpretations of historical plays, and for the first time in a decade, it was rare to find a political drama on the London stage.

Not for the first time, some critics complained of a spiritual emptiness in modern culture. But traditional debates about 'high' and 'low' forms were rarely heard. Diversity and variety in the arts had inhibited the making of such distinctions. Moreover, increased educational opportunities and fewer social distinctions had created broader, more diverse and generally better-educated audiences.

Although many of Raymond Williams' predictions of 1961 had come true, so did his wish for a broader education in schools and universities, which included studies of society, the press, film, television and drama. Instead of debates between proponents of 'elite' culture and 'popular' culture, academics began to ask difficult, theoretical questions about how great works have emerged and how they are maintained; how distinctions between 'high' and 'low' emerge, and whether absolute aesthetic standards can exist. By the mid-1990s, cultural and media studies had become one of the most popular subjects in British universities.

Discussion topics

1   Briefly summarise the most important political and social changes in Britain since 1945. Which period do you find the most interesting from a cultural point of view?

2   Use the text and other sources to explain the following terms: immigration and multi-cultural Britain / the women's movement / the permissive society / Thatcherism / the Arts Council / New Labour / regional autonomy.

3   Think of a distinctive period in your country's recent history. What cultural elements and symbols, such as songs, books, films and popular music, do you associate with it?

4   What changes can you see in the arts of your country compared to ten or fifteen years ago? What has caused those changes? Have they been positive?

5   Should the government subsidise the arts or should they exist independently like any other commercial enterprise?

6   'The value of the arts is not merely in their worth as imaginative constructs, but in their relationship to political events and history.' Discuss.

Suggested further reading

Books

Booker, C. (1969) *The Neophiliacs* London: Collins.

Booker, C. (1980) *The Seventies: The Decade that Changed the Future* New York: Stein & Day.

Britain 1998: An Official Handbook (1998) London: The Stationery Office.

Burston, P. and Richardson, C. (1995) *A Queer Romance: Lesbians, Gay Men and Popular Culture* London: Routledge.

Caterall, P. and Obelkevitch, J. (eds) *Understanding Post-War British Society* London: Routledge.

Chambers, I. (1986) *Popular Culture: The Metropolitan Experience* London: Routledge.

Gascoigne, B. (1993) *Encyclopaedia of Britain* Basingstoke: Macmillan.

Lewis, P. (1978) *The Fifties* London: William Heinemann.

Melly, G. (1970) *Revolt into Style* Harmondsworth: Penguin.

Mirza, H.S. (ed.) (1997) *Black British Feminism: A Reader* London: Routledge.

Hall, S. (1988) *The Hard Road to Renewal: Thatcherism and the Crisis of the Left* London: Verso.

Oakland, J. (1998) *British Civilisation* London: Routledge.

Phillips, M. and Phillips, T. (1998) *Windrush: The Irresistible Rise of Multi-Racial Britain* London: HarperCollins.

Rowbotham, S. (1997) *A Century of Women: The History of Women in Britain and the U.S.* London: Viking.

Strinati, D. and Wagg, J. (eds) (1992) *Come On Down? Popular Culture in Post-War Britain* London: Routledge.

Thorne, T. (1993) *Fads, Fashions and Cults* London: Bloomsbury.

Wambu, O. (ed.) (1998) *Empire Windrush: 50 Years of Writing About Black Britain* London: Gollancz.

Whitehead, P. (1985) *The Writing on the Wall: Britain in the Seventies* London: Michael Joseph.

York, P. and Jennings, C. (1995) *Peter York's Eighties* London: BBC Books.

Young, H. (1989) *One of Us: A Biography of Margaret Thatcher* London: Macmillan.

Journals

The daily and weekly quality newspapers provide an excellent source of material to follow cultural trends.

2

Language in culture

Introduction

The ocean of the English language is sustained around the world by people as varied as the language itself. The past 400 years have seen an exponential growth and it is now spoken by around one in five of the world's population. Over 1.4 billion people live in countries where English has official status. It is not only an international language but is also commonly used in such diverse fields as science, sport, advertising, diplomacy, pop music, space and cyberspace.

Within Britain, English is spoken by 95 per cent of the population (some 52 million). However, the British Isles is also home to many dialects and speech varies considerably from region to region. In addition, there are several minority languages, such as Welsh, Irish, Scottish-Gaelic and Scots, which have long histories and considerable literatures. Numerous other languages are also spoken by Britain's ethnic communities. The most common are from the Asian subcontinent, such as Urdu and Hindi, which each have over 100,000 speakers and are widely spoken in the larger cities.

A brief history of English

Like many of the world's languages, English is a hybrid, a linguistic 'stew' which has absorbed varied elements of speech brought by ancient conquering tribes and nationalities. Almost 2,000 years ago the Romans introduced Latin to Britain. Today numerous English towns still bear names of Latin origin, such as London (Londinium), and its use in formal ceremonies by the Church and at the Universities of Oxford and Cambridge persists in the twentieth century.

Although Latin was the official language of church and government for several centuries, people around Britain spoke in a variety of dialects. Around 450 AD Englisc was commonly used in parts of the east and south of England. This was based on the dialects of Angle, Saxon and Jute invaders, who came from lands across the North Sea which now form part of Holland, Germany and Denmark. Englisc gradually became more widely spoken around England and became known as Old English.

To the modern reader, Old English appears rather like an exotic foreign language. But around 1150 it began to change, and over the next three centuries it expanded and evolved. This was the period of Middle English. During that time, dialects from around the country mixed with each other and with French, which arrived in England with the Norman conquest of 1066. Thousands of new words were absorbed into English in all areas of civil and cultural life, such as government, Church, the law, the military, education and the arts. The introduction of printing presses in the fifteenth century and a greater organisation of society, both promoted a standardisation of written forms and by 1500 it had evolved into a language much closer to the English of today.

Over the next three centuries English was exported to the continents of North America, Africa, Asia and Australasia, on voyages of trade, discovery and imperial expansion. In their splendid isolation on four continents, different varieties began to emerge, such as American English and Australian English. Elsewhere in the world, for example in the Caribbean islands of the West Indies, English mixed with African dialects to form exotic hybrids known as 'pidgins' and 'creoles'.

But in spite of its variation, both national and international, English has never had an academy to regulate its use. During the seventeenth and eighteenth centuries, numerous poets and authors (including Pope, Swift, Dryden and Defoe) regularly discussed proposals for one. However, these were gradually abandoned when substantial, authoritative dictionaries began to appear, such as Dr Samuel Johnson's. Unlike earlier works, these included many everyday words and used literary quotations to illustrate current usage and word-meaning. This technique is still used in the compilation of authoritative English dictionaries today.

Speech and social background

Although English is widely spoken around the world, far more variety is found among the regions of Britain. Among the most distinctive are the dialects of Glasgow, Liverpool, the West Midlands, Northern Ireland, Yorkshire, Newcastle and East London. They contain many non-standard words and the distinctive pronunciation of their vowels and intonation make them easy to recognise. In Liverpool the dialect is known as Scouse –

a mixture of Lancashire, Irish and Welsh – while the vernacular speech of east London is Cockney, a dialect known for its rhyming slang.

A different form of speech is used by some Afro-Caribbean immigrants and their descendants. This mixes dialect speech from the West Indies (Caribbean creole) with an English accent of the locality. It is known as black British English or black English vernacular.

Both accent (pronunciation) and dialect (words and grammar) can give clues about people's geographical and social background. Numerous regional features are commonly used by people who have had little formal education, and who have spent most or all their lives in the same locality. Moreover, these speakers tend to be male rather than female. Since the eighteenth century this characteristic has often been exploited by novelists and dramatists who used dialect to create characters and make social comment. In his novels of London low-life, the Victorian storyteller Charles Dickens made frequent attempts to recreate Cockney, as did American novelists Herman Melville and Jack London during their time in Britain. The classic novels of Thomas Hardy (Dorset), William Wordsworth (Cumberland), and later D.H. Lawrence (Nottingham) are all well known for their explorations of the relationship between social class and dialect speech.

Paradoxically, while dialect literature was becoming established during the nineteenth century, there was a growing interest in establishing common standards of spoken and written English. This was related to public demand for formal education and schooling. Moreover, the expansion of the British Empire required clear standards of language which would be intelligible to all foreigners. The Education Act of 1870 helped to meet this need. It made education compulsory for all children up to 11 years old. As class sizes grew, the demand for a more exclusive private education increased and the number of public schools expanded.

Rich and upper-class children from around Britain were brought together in the new public schools, where they were taught a standard of written English. This was based on a variety used around the mid-fifteenth century in government documents of the period. But educators also wanted to introduce a pronunciation standard to eliminate the cacophony of regional accents. Grammarians recommended the speech of London and the court as the most correct and desirable. This carried many regional features found in speech of the south-eastern counties of England, as far north as Cambridge and as far west as Oxford. But it was selected because it was spoken by the ruling class – by the aristocracy and its court – and therefore carried authority. It was sometimes called 'Queen's English' and later became known as 'received pronunciation' (often abbreviated to RP) because it was 'received' – that is, understood – by everyone.

The expansion of the British Empire and its army, Church, government and administrators all absorbed the products of the British public schools and many former students went on to occupy positions of power and influence within it. As a result, RP became not a regional accent, but a social one: the voice of authority and synonymous with the power, prestige and education of the speaker.

Speech in cultural life

The main consequence of RP is that a high degree of social significance is attached to English speech. RP's prestige and authority implied the inferiority of regional accents and vocabulary, which became socially stigmatised as a mark of ignorance and poverty. Linguistic differences came to be seen as linguistic errors and the socially ambitious had to modify their speech towards that of their betters. This was famously exemplified in George Bernard Shaw's play *Pygmalion* (1913), in which Professor Higgins, a language teacher (originally based on the British scholar of phonetics, Henry Sweet), convinces Eliza Doolittle, a poor flower-seller, that with pronunciation lessons he can make her appear sophisticated and aristocratic. The play was later adapted into the classic Hollywood musical *My Fair Lady* (1964).

The arrival of public broadcasting in 1922 helped to extend RP's social prestige. Although it was spoken by only 2–3 per cent of the population, it was preferred by the BBC because it was widely understood and respected. An advisory committee was appointed to resolve any doubts about pronunciation, which included the writer George Bernard Shaw, the Poet Laureate Robert Bridges, the art historian Kenneth Clark and Alistair Cooke, a young journalist. Their judgements on correctness helped to make the BBC an unofficial authority on language and led to the expression 'BBC English'.

Moreover, RP's clear vowel sounds and exaggerated intonation aided voice projection in large theatres, and it was later adopted in drama schools as a standard for teaching purposes. When 'talkie' films arrived in Britain during the 1920s some actors had to retire because their accents were unsuitable.

The dominance of RP meant that for many years non-standard regional speech was rarely heard on television, radio or at the cinema, except in the roles of 'characters': players and performers who were spontaneous and open, but usually marginalised as poor, uneducated and either comic or deviant, such as backward rural farmworkers or petty criminals. In popular entertainment, the success of 'figures of fun' such as Tommy Trinder (Cockney) and George Formby (Lancashire) largely depended on the comic effects produced by their strong regional accents. During the Second World War these were even used to fool the enemy. For a brief period the BBC radio news was read by Wilfred Pickles, whose strong Yorkshire accent could not be easily understood by German Intelligence.

However, with the social changes of the post-war decades, prejudice over regional accents gradually decreased. A number of post-war education reforms, in particular the Butler Education Act of 1944, greatly improved educational opportunities for a generation of working-class and lower-middle-class children. There was an expansion of the university sector and improved access for children from all social backgrounds and regions. With the expansion of higher education and growing social mobility, divisions between the classes became less rigid and movement between them easier. In this way, the old associations between accent and background began to be lost.

The arts of the late 1950s began to show more realistic representations of speech and society. Plays by writers such as Harold Pinter and Joe Orton accurately represented regional dialects in a variety of characters and provided a more authentic theatre of social experience. The mid-1950s also saw the arrival of new television drama series such as *Armchair Theatre*, which brought realistic, regional stories into the nation's living rooms. These, together with soap operas such as *Coronation Street* from Manchester and *Z Cars* from Liverpool, all helped to present a more realistic and complete representation of British accents to audiences around the country.

In the cinema of the early 1960s, several film adaptations of 'realist' novels and plays, such as *Saturday Night, Sunday Morning* and *The Loneliness of the Long-Distance Runner*, showed realistic portrayals of working-class life, and well-known actors such as Albert Finney and Tom Courtney had to rediscover the northern accents they had lost at drama school in order to play the leading characters. Later in the decade, Sean Connery (Scottish), Richard Burton (Welsh) and Michael Caine (London) became some of the most popular actors of the time, playing glamorous, sophisticated roles with non-RP accents.

The emergence of popular culture also encouraged a wider acceptance of regional speech in the public sphere, where it was suddenly possible for relatively uneducated individuals to obtain social advancement in new professions such as photography, music, art, fashion and design. The Beatles and others from Liverpool, the Rolling Stones and the Who from London, together with numerous American groups, all attracted intense media interest. New popular music radio stations, such as BBC Radio 1, and television shows such as *Ready Steady Go!* provided new stages for the amplification of accented speech in interviews and comment. The talent, status and self-confidence of popular culture's new heroes helped remove the stigma attached to regional speech, which became fashionable and frequently imitated, especially among the young.

With changing social attitudes and greater movement between the social classes, the RP accent has become less influential and today it is not possible to say that it is regarded by everyone as the 'best' pronunciation. Although it is still widely used as a pronunciation model for teaching English to foreign students, it is still only spoken by 2–3 per cent of the population (a figure which corresponds approximately to the number who have attended a public school) which sometimes causes comprehension problems for overseas visitors to Britain. The RP accent is even rejected by some young people who see it as an unfashionable symbol of traditional authority. Instead new speech styles are often preferred, such as Estuary English (or Estuarine). This is a popular variety of London speech which mixes Cockney with RP and is commonly spoken among the young of the south-east.

While a variety of regional accents is often heard in public broadcasting and the arts, a standard English grammar and vocabulary is retained for most types of public communication. This is the variety which is taught and examined in British state schools. However, in recent years this has been opposed by some regional pressure groups, who argue that children who speak a regional variety of English are educationally handicapped if they have to learn a different variety when they enter school. Instead, they demand the introduction of regional vocabulary and grammar on the syllabus.

In spite of the recent social changes and a greater tolerance of regional speech, there is evidence that some varieties may still carry negative connotations in the public sphere or, to put it another way, some accents may carry more positive connotations than others. For example, advertisers on most local radio and television stations rarely choose local accents to advertise their products. Instead, RP or an American accent is generally preferred, unless the goods have strong traditional or regional associations, such as beer or bread. This is because they feel that the public will be more attracted to their products if they are advertised by someone with an RP accent, than someone with a non-RP accent. The present situation is thus a complex, unstable one for students of English, in which differences in pronunciation reflect differences in region, social background and generation.

Minority languages

It is often imagined that Britain is a linguistically homogeneous country, but in 1980 at least twelve languages could claim more than 100,000 speakers. Many of these, such as Urdu and Hindi, were spoken in families of immigrants from the Indian subcontinent who have settled in Britain since the late 1950s. But there are also several others which have been present in Britain for over 2,000 years: most of these are varieties of Gaelic.

Gaelic is a separate language from English and has a long history in the British Isles. Its origins are obscure, but most accounts begin around the fourth century BC when the islands were invaded by Gaelic-speaking Celts known as Gaels. They came from central Europe and settled in Ireland, Scotland, the Isle of Man, and later in southern England and parts of Wales. Some 800 years later, around the fifth century AD, Britain was again invaded (this time in the east) by Anglo-Saxon tribes from northern Europe. They forced British Celts to go west and north, to the safety of the hills and mountains of Wales, Cornwall, Devon and Scotland, and to the Brittany region of France. The geographical separation of groups of Gaelic speakers led to linguistic and cultural differences, as Welsh, Irish and Scottish-Gaelic all developed independently. Others existed too: Cornish was spoken in the counties of Cornwall and Devon, and Manx in the Isle of Man. Although there are current attempts to revive them, the last speakers of Cornish as a living language died in the early nineteenth century and the Manx language disappeared during the late 1940s.

Welsh

The Anglo-Saxon invaders' name for foreigners was *wealas*, from which 'Wales' is derived. Today, of a population of around 2.7 million, about 0.5 million are Welsh speakers. This makes it the most widely spoken minority language in Britain. Its literature is among the oldest in Europe and is celebrated each year during a national festival of music, literature and drama known as the Royal National Eisteddfod, an event which originated in the twelfth century. It is held alternately each year in North and South Wales, during the first week of August, and is open to the public. An international festival of music and folk dancing is also held in Llangollen each year and is known as the International Music Eisteddfod. It attracts people from all over the world to recite poetry, sing and dance in this colourful spectacle.

For almost 1,000 years until the Act of Union with England in 1536, Welsh was the only language spoken in Wales. But then English gradually became the language of government, education and trade, while Welsh was only spoken in the home and at church. The number of speakers slowly declined and in the nineteenth century was hastened by the influx of English workers to the industrial areas of the south. But some Welshmen were unwilling to adopt English ways and in 1865 a party of 165 Welshmen and women emigrated to Patagonia in Argentina, where Patagonian Welsh is still spoken by their descendants.

The use of Welsh continued to decline until the 1960s when an increase in political nationalism led to a rediscovery of Welsh identity through language. The British government was responsive to the nationalists' demands for projects to promote the language and in 1964 the government established BBC Radio Wales, the first regional service in Britain. Support for Welsh was secured in legislation with the Welsh Language Act of 1967, which ordered that all official documents be written in both languages. The country is now comparatively well-served by a Welsh-language mass media. Local newspapers in Welsh appeared in the 1970s and numerous radio stations now broadcast in Welsh. In 1982 the television channel S4C (Sianel Pedwar Cymru – Channel Four Wales) began. A significant part of its programme-making is in Welsh and one of its most popular programmes is a soap opera *Pobl y Cwm* (People of the Valley).

Official support for the Welsh language was firmly established with the Welsh Language Act of 1993, which stipulated that Welsh and English should be considered as equal languages in public affairs and the administration of justice. In all schools, the study of Welsh is now compulsory and several offer a Welsh-medium education. Welsh is now widely used for official purposes, in most place names, road signs, job advertisements and public-information documents.

Irish

In Ireland, language and politics have always been closely related. The Irish language is a variety of Gaelic and was widely spoken in a united, independent Ireland until it became part of the United Kingdom with the Act of Union of 1803. Then its use in urban areas began a rapid decline, although it was still widely spoken in rural areas until the 1840s. However, following the death and emigration of millions during the tragic famine of 1845–8 there were even fewer speakers. But towards the end of the nineteenth century, a Republican movement for independence from Britain emerged, whose supporters adopted Irish (Erse) as a distinctive symbol of their culture and identity.

In 1921 Southern Ireland gained partial independence from Britain and its new government began to organise a revival of Irish. It is now taught in all schools as a second language and there is a small Irish media. Of some 3.5 million inhabitants, over 1 million speak both languages. But the use of Irish for everyday communication is declining. Only around 5,000 monoglot Irish speakers remain and most are elderly inhabitants of remote, Gaelic-speaking areas in the west of Ireland, known as *Gaeltacht*. However, Irish remains the first official language of the Irish Republic.

Irish literature has a long tradition going back to the sixth century. But since the eighteenth century some of its most prestigious authors, such as Swift, Sheridan, Wilde, Yeats, Shaw, Joyce, Beckett and Heaney, have expressed themselves in English and become leading figures of British literature. Some critics argue that the idiosyncratic style found in their novels, poetry and plays is the result of the imposition of English on Irish. This can produce an unconventional use of language similar to the dream-like 'magic realism' found elsewhere in contemporary literature.

In Northern Ireland, use of the English language remains strongly politicised. Since the Act of Union of 1803, the use of Irish has been linked with Irish nationalism. However, because Irish has no official status, reliable data on the number of speakers is difficult to obtain. But the British government recognises its importance, and provides some financial support for activities to promote it. In the capital Belfast there are bilingual schools, while the BBC and independent stations broadcast television and radio programmes in Irish. After the agreements reached with the Labour Government in 1997/8, such projects seem likely to increase in number. Paradoxically, as interest in Irish has grown in the north, it has declined in the more prosperous south.

Scottish-Gaelic and Scots

Around the fifth century AD, tribes of Gaels arrived in the Highlands and Western Isles of Scotland from both Ireland and the north of England. Five hundred years later, their geographic isolation resulted in a separate variety of Gaelic from that spoken in their former lands. But their remote situation made the language uninfluential and it has been in steady decline from 250,000 speakers in 1891 to fewer than 70,000 today (1.4 per cent of the Scottish population), of whom some 5,000 are monoglot Gaelic speakers. However, Gaelic is supported by the British government: it is taught in schools and is present on television and radio. But its literary corpus remains small and is most noted for its tradition of verse during the eighteenth century, a tradition which is continued today with the poetry of Sorley MacLean and others.

Another language of Scotland is Scots, which is closely related to a dialect of Old English. It was widely spoken in the north of England and in many non-Gaelic parts of Scotland until the sixteenth century. But after the abolition of the Scottish Parliament in 1707 and the transfer of power to London, English became the dominant language of the educated and merchant classes, and the number of Scots speakers declined.

As with Irish and Scottish-Gaelic, Scots acquired a negative image which was closely associated with the poor rural areas where it was spoken. However, during the eighteenth and nineteenth centuries it found support among prestigious literary figures such as Robert Louis Stevenson, Robert Burns and Walter Scott, who all wrote frequently in Scots. In their romantic view, Scots was an authentic and natural language, the genuine voice of the oppressed poor.

Robert Burns remains one of its best known historical figures. In many pubs around Britain his birthday is celebrated each year with Burns' Night (25 January), an event characterised by readings of his poetry and a haggis supper. His song 'Auld Lang Syne', written in Scots about nostalgic reunion, is sung not only in Scotland, but by people throughout Britain at midnight on 31 December, and has become one of the most traditional of British anthems.

In the twentieth century, the literary use of Scots can be found in the poetry of Hugh MacDiarmid, who wrote in Lallans, a mixture of Scots dialects past and present. Today, writers like poet Tom Leonard and playwright Robert McLellan continue to write in various forms of Scots and to promote the language. But in spite of attempts to maintain it, its position is precarious. Some critics argue it is a dialect of English, while others claim it an artificial language which is only exploited for literary purposes. Because it is not recognised as an official language it is not recognised in censi. Therefore, data about the number of speakers is unreliable and few funds are available for its support. Moreover, there are few demands for the protection of either Scottish Gaelic or Scots from Scottish nationalists, who appear to have enough confidence in the country's independent identity and culture without the support of minority languages.

Non-indigenous languages

Britain is a predominantly Anglo-Saxon country, but ethnic diversity is a major characteristic of many towns and cities. During the past 500 years there has been a steady flow of immigrants to Britain, although during the twentieth century it has become more pronounced. Since the 1930s Jews, Russians and Italians have settled in Britain following persecution, war and poverty in Europe. During the 1940s and 1950s the government invited Commonwealth citizens to fill job vacancies in the major towns and cities. Waves of immigration followed, mainly from the countries of West Africa, the Caribbean, India, Pakistan and Hong Kong. Immigrants settled in the areas where work was plentiful and housing cheap. The central areas of Leicester, London, Slough and Birmingham, and the major ports of Bristol, Cardiff and Liverpool soon had large established ethnic communities.

In 1995, 3.2 million (almost 6 per cent of Britain's population) belonged to an ethnic community. Some 2.5 million were of West Indian or Asian origin and of these approximately 1.3 million were born in Britain. The most widely spoken foreign languages are those of the Asian subcontinent, such as Urdu from Pakistan, and Hindi, Bengali, Punjabi and Gujarati from India. These are well-protected by an educational policy which provides tuition in the native language and an established mass media of newspapers, radio and television programmes.

But at the same time, many British Asians have a complex relationship with English, which often varies according to age. The inner London borough of Tower Hamlets is 25 per cent Bangladeshi, but less than two-thirds of the community speak English. Most of the proficient English speakers are children. The majority grow up bilingual: they study the community language at school and practice it at home, but use English in all other contexts. In contrast, the community elders often have a poor command of English. Among Bangladeshi women, only one in ten between the ages of 50 and 74 speaks English.

The cultural distance between many younger immigrants and British society often provides the inspiration for new forms of creative expression. Novels, films, plays and music by British Asians and Afro-Caribbeans frequently propose a complex new British identity, one composed of varied cultural, political and historical influences. This is amply demonstrated in the works of numerous artists and writers who appear on the following pages, whose presence helps to make cultural life in Britain among the most diverse and dynamic in the world.

Discussion topics and activities

1   Use the text and other sources to explain the following: accent and dialect / RP / minority languages.
2   There has never been an academy to regulate the English language. What do you think are the advantages and disadvantages of such an authority?
3   Should regional speech forms be allowed in the classroom, or should children be encouraged to use the 'prestige' dialect of the south-east, as they are at present?
4   Which is the 'most correct' or 'prestige' accent in your country? What attitudes do people have towards speakers of regional accents and minority languages? Are they found in advertising, the mass media and certain types of role in films and plays? Why or why not?
5   How has your language been affected by English in recent years? Is change and diversity good for a language?
6   Listen carefully to the varieties of speech you hear spoken in buses, bars and other public places. Does language-use vary according to the region, social background and educational level of the speaker? If so, how?

Suggested further reading

Books

Baugh, A. and Cable, T. (1993) *A History of the English Language* 4th edn, London: Routledge.

Blake, N.F. (1996) *A History of the English Language* Basingstoke: Macmillan.

Bryson, B. (1990) *Mother Tongue* Harmondsworth: Penguin.

Coates, J. (1986) *Men, Women and Language* London: Longman.

Crystal, D. (1987) *Cambridge Encyclopaedia of the English Language* Cambridge: Cambridge University Press.

Crystal, D. (1997) *English as a Global Language* Cambridge: Cambridge University Press.

Honey, J. (1997) *The Story of Standard English and its Enemies* London: Faber & Faber.

Kay, B. (1993) *Scots: The Mither Tongue* Darvel: Alloway Publishing.

Leith, D. (1983) *A Social History of English* London: Routledge.

Montgomery, M. (1995) *An Introduction to Language and Society* London: Routledge.

Sutcliffe, D. (1982) *British Black English* London: Blackwell.

Wells, J.C. (1982) *Accents of English* Cambridge: Cambridge University Press.

3

The novel and poetry

Introduction

Within Britain, literature enjoys a reputation as the most prestigious of arts. Some of the world's most illustrious authors, such as Chaucer, Shakespeare, Charles Dickens, Jane Austen and Virginia Woolf, have established a long and distinguished tradition which is internationally recognised and widely praised. Their works are extensively studied in schools, colleges and universities in Britain and around the world. They are also the subject of frequent adaptations into films, television series and plays for theatre and radio.

Reading and writing are also popular spare-time activities, and Britain has (with Denmark) the joint highest literacy rate in the world. Public lending libraries are free and Britain has more than any other country. There are also many private literary societies dedicated to the discussion of a variety of authors' works. But for those more interested in creative writing, several centres offer specialised courses. One of the most famous is at the University of East Anglia in Norwich, where contemporary authors such as Ian McEwan and Kazuo Ishiguro have studied.

The publishing and retailing of classic and modern works have become major industries, and over 6,000 new fiction titles appear each year. There are numerous awards for new books and authors, such as the Whitbread Prize and the Guardian Fiction Prize. But the most prestigious for English fiction by a British or Commonwealth author is the Booker Prize. It ensures wide publicity for the winning author and has been offered annually since

1969 by Booker McConnell Ltd; the winner is chosen by a panel of publishers, novelists and critics.

Some of the most highly praised works of recent years have been produced by overseas authors from Commonwealth countries, such as Salman Rushdie (India) and Ben Okri (Nigeria). Britain's gradual loss of Empire, the arrival of immigrants, increasing cultural diversity and the emancipation of women, have all produced new waves of literary energy. At the same time, techniques of storytelling have also changed. These frequently involve the creation of fantasy styles to communicate new experiences, identities and realities. This is a common characteristic of many authors with overseas ties, whose writing often mixes historical fact and contemporary reality with fantasy and fable. It is sometimes described as 'phantasmagorical' writing or 'magic realism' and has become highly influential in English literature.

Early influences on English literature

Until the late 1800s religious belief exerted a powerful influence over the literary world. Christianity had traditionally provided the principal system of values which supported literary ideas. But towards the end of the century its influence gradually declined. There was a reaction against the traditional certainties which it offered and an enthusiasm for the exploration of new subjects and experimentation with new forms.

A growing knowledge of the natural and social world provided important new influences and many writers believed that with knowledge, progress and understanding, Earth could be like heaven. This optimistic view was amply reflected in works by the novelist and poet Rudyard Kipling, who took inspiration from the achievements of the British Empire and the creation of a rich, new civilisation. His work earned him a reputation as 'Poet of Empire' and in 1907 he became the first English author to win the Nobel Prize for Literature.

Kipling's optimism was shared by George Bernard Shaw and H.G. Wells. They wrote enthusiastically about the benefits of progress and increased knowledge of the scientific and social world. But some authors were pessimistic about the future without state intervention to prevent exploitation and suffering. George Orwell's novels frequently expressed the need for socialism, although later in his career his views became closer to those of E.M. Forster, whose novels stressed the importance of individual freedom over collective, social demands.

In contrast, other authors were more sceptical about the ability of scientific progress and political doctrine to create a better world. Oscar Wilde was sustained by natural beauty, hedonism and decadent living. Thomas Hardy preferred the simplicity and authenticity of rural life and nature, believing they were important sources of human happiness. D.H. Lawrence and Aldous Huxley felt modern civilisation had a dehumanising effect on man. For them, personal fulfilment lay within, and could only be achieved by exploring the senses and obeying the instincts.

As literary themes changed, so did ways of storytelling, and during the early twentieth century many writers began to experiment with different techniques. Some found traditional descriptive methods too conventional, such as James Joyce and Virginia Woolf. They wanted a more liberating style of expression and developed a technique known as 'stream of consciousness'. This consists of a mixture of verse and prose without traditional grammar or logical sequence, which creates the sensation of a dream or interior monologue. This seemed a more natural, authentic way to represent human thoughts and impressions, and was given full expression in Joyce's *Ulysses* (1921). This was initially received as a novel of radical experimentation, but has since become one of the most original and highly praised works of English literature.

New techniques of expression extended to poetry. One of the most influential works of the twentieth century is T.S. Eliot's *The Waste Land* (1922). It explored what Eliot saw as the sterility of modern life and used an innovative style of free verse. This consisted of references to earlier literature, myth and religion. Its compilation of broken images introduced a new style of poetry, which influenced many other modernist poets and became a literary landmark.

New arrivals: working-class youth, immigrants and teenagers

In the late 1940s Britain was exhausted by the losses of war. The public looked not for brave new ideas and styles, but comfort and reassurance in literature. Many highly respected authors, such as William Golding, Graham Greene and Evelyn Waugh, continued to write inspired by their religious beliefs. But some began to question the old values and certainties which religion and nation had traditionally provided. The experience of war, the expansion of education and the welfare state, and increasing affluence had given birth to a new society, and by 1955 a new generation of critical young playwrights, novelists and artists was emerging.

Playwright John Osborne and novelists Colin Wilson, John Wain, Stan Barstow, Alan Sillitoe, Keith Waterhouse, Kingsley Amis and others were mostly aged under 30. They were critical of convention, dissatisfied with modern life and shared an impatience with tradition, authority and the ruling class. Many were from the north of England and promoted a new style of storytelling about the lives of ordinary working people. Together with their resentful literary characters, they became known as the 'angry young men'.

John Waine's *Hurry on Down* (1953), Kingsley Amis's *Lucky Jim* (1954), Colin Wilson's *The Outsider* (1956), John Braine's *Room at the Top* (1957) and Alan Sillitoe's *Saturday Night, Sunday Morning* (1958) are some of their most representative works. Many stories are set in working-class areas of depressed cities of the industrial north and contain sexually explicit scenes. Dialogue is often in regional dialect, giving a strong sense of the characters' identity and social background. The protagonists of these novels were 'outsiders'. They did not identify with modern society. They were impatient, dissatisfied and critical of conventional morality and behaviour. They felt isolated and powerless, and were sometimes violent.

Although the style was simple and unadventurous, the content was new. It was considered provocative and subversive to write on themes of frustrated ambition, sexuality and class conflict. The creation of uneducated, undisciplined heroes was a departure from literary convention and angered many critics. However, it introduced anger and dissent into the arts, and also helped establish a tradition of social realism in literature, theatre, television and film.

However, as their fame and reputation grew the authors became more conservative and individual, and the group gradually disintegrated. Sillitoe (Nottinghamshire) and Barstow (Yorkshire) continued to write with a strong regional emphasis, while Kingsley Amis became regarded as a fine comic novelist. His first novel, *Lucky Jim* (1954), deals with a young, philistine university lecturer who drinks heavily, hates classical music and is critical of the cultural pretensions of academia. It was the first satirical examination of university life, which later became an established genre known as the 'campus novel.'

Amis's early works indicate his support for the political left, but in the 1960s he became closer to the right. His later novels began to reveal the attitudes and mentality of middle-class, middle-aged men. *Jake's Thing* (1978) and *Stanley and the Women* (1984) were notorious for their politically incorrect depictions of women as mad, bad and dangerous. His conservative views also made him critical of avante-garde literature. He believed that writers should concentrate on entertainment more than experiment. But he gained critical respect for his prose style, precise descriptions and naturalistic dialogue.

The new currents of content and style in the novel of the 1950s also extended to poetry. In 1956 Robert Conquest edited *New Lines*, a collection of poems by young authors who were united by their hostility to the cultural pretensions and elitism of contemporary writing. Many used an ironic, anti-Romantic style to write satirically about modern suburban life. Thom Gunn contributed 'Fighting Terms' about motorcycle gangs of the time, a literary act seen as daring and provocative in Britain of the mid-1950s. The contributors to *New Lines* became known as 'the Movement', and included John Wain and Kingsley Amis, who later became better known for their novels and plays.

One of the most significant contributors to *New Lines* was Philip Larkin. He ignored stylistic experimentation and wrote clear, economical observations about daily life in Britain. His three major collections, *The*

Less Deceived (1955), *The Whitsun Weddings* (1964) and *High Windows* (1964), established his reputation as a major poet, containing what the poet and critic Peter Levi once called 'eighty-five perfect poems'. Many tell a story in which the subject is carefully described and satirised in an ironic, witty style. In *Whitsun Weddings* (1964), Larkin describes a train journey from Hull to London and comments on a sad England of false merriment, cheap fashions and joyless weddings. His style and subject matter were a revelation and created new territory for English poetry. Larkin was also a fan of jazz music and in *All What Jazz?* (1970) presented a collection of reviews criticising the freedom and experimentation of modern styles.

Jazz music has always had a following in Britain. This was still quite small in the mid-1950s when a steady flow of Afro-Caribbean immigrants began to arrive in Britain from the West Indies. They had been invited to cover a shortage of labour in poorly paid, manual sectors of the economy, such as transport and the health service. For many, Britain offered an exciting new world of freedom and adventure, a view captured in Samuel Selvon's humorous novel *The Lonely Londoners* (1956), which also gives insights into post-war English attitudes to differences of race and nationality.

Another early portrait of immigrants' experiences is drawn by Colin MacInnes, in the nostalgic *City of Spades* (1957). MacInnes grew up in Australia, but in *Absolute Beginners* (1959) and *Mr Love and Justice* (1960) he depicts a newly emergent youth culture of coffee bars, jazz clubs, teenage fashions and conflict with authority in London of the 1950s. The three novels together form the *London Trilogy*. They were the first to recognise the emergence of a new popular culture and showed how it provided a young generation with a sense of identity and belonging. *England, Half-English* (1961) is a fascinating collection of MacInnes' essays which successfully capture the atmosphere of the period.

Literature of the 1960s and 1970s

During the 1960s some of the most highly praised authors of recent times began to receive critical recognition as major writers. However, their themes are diverse and have little in common. Many still did not openly identify with the new intellectual currents of feminism, although some were sympathetic to its messages in their work.

One such author is Muriel Spark, who was born into a Scottish family of Jewish descent and later converted to Catholicism. Her stories are short, funny and stylish, and often emphasise the roles of the female characters. Her best-known work is *The Prime of Miss Jean Brodie* (1961), a story set in her native Edinburgh. It features a charismatic teacher who is proud, cultured and romantic. She begins to transform a group of young girls into an elite, but demands almost total control over them. Power and authority are themes of central importance which are also explored in *Girls of Slender Means* (1963) and *Public Image* (1968).

Themes of individual freedom and control are also explored in the novels of John Fowles. He made his debut with an exciting psychological thriller *The Collector* (1963), about a butterfly collector who kidnaps an attractive young art student. Later, the more ambitious *The Magus* (1966, revised 1977) involves a young English teacher in an adventure of distorted reality and sexual licence on a Greek island. In this and several other works, heroines feature prominently. They have deep and varied characters, but all combine femininity with inner strength to conquer their circumstances.

Fowles' novels are also noted for their detailed observation of the natural world, such as *The Maggot* (1985). But *The French Lieutenant's Woman* (1969) is his most famous. It is based on a Victorian story, but Fowles plays with the narrative, verbally reminding the reader of his tricks. He provides three endings to demonstrate the possibilities available. In this way, he gives the reader a freedom and responsibility to finish the story, which becomes almost interactive. It later became a highly successful film and Fowles is one of the few British authors who has written serious, experimental fiction while remaining on the bestseller list.

Like those of Fowles and Spark, Iris Murdoch's novels are read for entertainment as well as by critics and academics. They frequently analyse human freedom and question how goodness can triumph over evil. These issues are often reflected in her characters' problems and are examined more formally in her philosophical studies of Sartre and Plato. She was known as a brilliant academic and her novels frequently combine philo-sophical questions with detailed observations of middle-class life and academic intrigue.

The first of her many successful works was the comedy *Under the Net* (1954), while one of her finest – *The Bell* (1958) – looks at a declining reli-gious community. The humour and surprises in stories such as *A Fairly Honourable Defeat* (1970) and *An Accidental Man* (1971) have also received critical praise and popular acclaim. All her novels are noted for their intense descriptions of her characters, who are often possessed by fantasies of erotic love. These are mixed with unexpected and bizarre inci-dents which sometimes involve cats, dogs, mice and spiders to create comic effect. During a prolific career she has won numerous awards, including the prestigious Booker Prize for *The Sea, the Sea* (1978).

Like Iris Murdoch, Anthony Burgess's novels are frequently concerned with moral issues. During a long and prolific career he wrote many novels, of which the most critically admired is *Earthly Powers* (1980), a complex work concerned with the choices which men have between good and evil. His experiences as an English teacher in Malaya and Brunei provided inspiration for his early writing, such as the *Malayan Trilogy* (1972), later reissued as *The Long Day Wanes* (1982). But it was *A Clockwork Orange*

(1962) which brought him fame. The main theme is morality, in which both totalitarian and liberal humanist approaches are satirised. It is set in a future England, where an aggressive gang of young delinquents rob, rape, torture and murder. The gang speak *nadsat*, a private teenage slang, an 'inhuman' language invented by the author to emphasise the gang's collective identity and their distance from conventional society. Eventually, their leader is captured and treated, but begins to produce mechanical, robotic responses to those things which should humanise him: sex, violence and the arts. In 1971 the story was made into a highly successful film by Stanley Kubrick (see p. 85).

Burgess also wrote non-fiction, journalism, memoirs, music and several comic stories, such as his four Enderby novels (1963–84). These are set in England, Rome, Tangiers and New York, and describe the humorous adventures of Enderby, a middle-aged poet and lecturer. The liberal, progressive, permissive atmosphere of the university campus, with its own petty problems and jealousies, provided many other writers of the 1970s with material for humorous tales. They became known as 'campus' novels and helped to establish the careers of several modern authors, among them Malcolm Bradbury and David Lodge.

One of Lodge's most successful is *Changing Places* (1975), a comical story about an academic exchange between the imaginary universities of 'Euphoria State' in America and 'Rummidge' in the English Midlands. But the story is also technically playful and offers a strong satire of contemporary literary and critical ideas. *Small Worlds* (1984) is a humorous tale of intrigue at an academic conference, while *How Far Can You Go?* (1980) is both a serious and comic exploration of the moral dilemmas of young British Catholics growing up in a secular, permissive society. Lodge is a former professor of English literature who is also well known for his extensive work on literary criticism.

In *Stepping Westward* (1965) Malcolm Bradbury also makes a humorous comparison between American and British university life. But *The History Man* (1975) is a cynical tale of hypocrisy and jealousy set on the British university campus. It features a young sociology lecturer who manipulates his colleagues, students and family for his own ambitious ends. Apart from his novels, Bradbury will be remembered for the creation of Britain's first course in creative writing at the University of East Anglia, where between 1970 and 1995 he was Professor of American Studies.

The permissive youth culture of the early 1970s also found expression in popular literature. Richard Allen wrote stories based on the imagined lifestyles of teenage gangs. *Boot-Boy*, *Suedehead*, *Glam* and others depicted closed, mean, brutal worlds of teenagers with no future. Allen's books included many detailed descriptions of vandalism and violence, and critics complained that they encouraged imitative, 'copycat' behaviour. But they remain energetic, romanticised accounts, which were popular reading material with many teenagers of the period and have been rediscovered in recent years as popular artifacts of early 1970s youth culture.

The work of the Mersey Poets from Liverpool indicated that poetry could also be made more accessible to a younger, non-literary audience. The success of the Beatles and other Liverpool groups helped to generate interest in the local popular culture and during the mid-1960s poets such as Roger McGough, Adrian Henri and Brian Patten were pioneering a new style of verse. Unlike many poets they were funny, irreverent and streetwise. They wore fashionable clothes and mixed with pop stars. Theirs was pop poetry: poetry with a performance, pop music without the music. A flavour of their work is captured in the anthology *The Mersey Sound* (1967).

Feminism and fiction

In the politics, law and social life of the mid-1960s, the impact of feminism was widely felt. Traditional attitudes towards women's sexuality, marriage, work and many other aspects of their lives began to change and there was a new recognition of women's role in society. Germaine Greer's *The Female Eunuch* (1970) gave literary expression to feminist ideas. Its provocative and outspoken text offered a clear, untheoretical manifesto which all women could understand. Its impact was enormous and soon afterwards a significant new body of women's literature emerged. This contained powerful descriptions of women's experience and feminist writing quickly became an influential new genre.

Literature had been a male-dominated field, but new feminist publishing houses opened to energetically encourage women's writing. Virago, the Women's Press and Pandora contracted many feminist authors and began promoting others, such as Stevie Smith, Storm Jameson, Rebecca West, Rose Macaulay, Barbara Pym and Jean Rhys, whose work passed largely unnoticed earlier in the twentieth century. There were also important changes in the universities. Departments of Women's Studies were established and departments of literature began to study themes and imagery in women's writing.

The position of women in society, social injustice and their search for equality with men were some of the challenging themes in the early novels of many new authors. Fay Weldon's robustly feminist novels deal with female resentment, anger and revenge in a way which is detached and often ironic. *Down Among the Women* (1971) draws attention to the repetitive nature of most women's lives, spent cooking, cleaning and looking after children. Told in a colloquial present tense, the narrative produces a realistic, documentary effect, as if something is actually taking place. Her early work is close to social realism, but her later novels are less conventional, reflecting her interest in experimental styles of women's writing. For example, both *Praxis* (1978) and *The Cloning of Joanna May* (1989) suggest the presence of multiple realities in the same individual.

The former tells the story in the first and third person, and the latter considers the life of a girl with four identical sisters.

More conventional themes of social injustice and oppression are found in the highly praised novels of Margaret Drabble. These often have female protagonists and detail their education, careers and family relationships. Their experiences are part-autobiographical. In *The Millstone* (1965) the heroine has to fight against various distractions to gain her independence. Then she has an unplanned baby daughter which both helps and limits her development. But *The Ice Age* (1977) is considered by many critics to be her finest work. It deals not only with women's liberation, but also social deprivation, and in particular the weaknesses of the health-care system in mid-1970s Britain, where the public services were seriously failing. The trilogy *The Radiant Way*, *A Natural Curiosity* and *The Gates of Ivory* (1980) in which three women look back on their younger selves, also provides a clear description of a desperate decade.

While many early feminist writers focussed on themes of social inequality, others were more concerned with women's domestic lives and their relationships with men. The fiction of Edna O'Brien portrays women as having a frustrating choice between either loneliness or slavery to men and the family. This is apparent in her early trilogy *The Country Girls* (1960–3), in which sexual desires conflict with the heroine's Catholic upbringing. This uncertainty again finds expression in *Casualties of Peace* (1966), a story told with wit and pace. The eroticism of her stories brought to the novel a frank exposure of women's sexual needs and amplified the spectrum of women's writing.

Doris Lessing

Doris Lessing (b. 1919) is among the most highly respected of contemporary British writers, the author of prolific and varied works. As well as many novels she has also written short stories, poetry and travel writing. At the beginning of her career, her left-wing politics and sense of realism identified her with the social realists of the 1950s. But she later adopted a more imaginative style of writing, characterised by fantasy, interior monologues and multiple realities.

Lessing grew up in South Africa. This was the setting for her early stories and novels, which include the five-volume *Children of Violence* (1952–69), critically praised as one of the finest works in English literature about childhood and adolescence. The story begins in Rhodesia, where the first volume, *Martha Quest*, tells the story of women's 'absence' from history. The setting later moves to England and forward to the year 2000. The novels aim to present the arguments of feminists who witnessed the bigotry and apartheid of South African politics of the 1960s. But the author also expresses her cynicism about Communism, doubting it could provide a more equal society for both men and women.

The Golden Notebook (1962) is a work of politics and psychology, in which heroine Anna Freeman Wulf suffers a crisis in her personal life and eventually has a nervous breakdown. After recovering, she takes an American lover and becomes involved in socialist politics. The novel explores in different sections her feelings as a socialist liberated woman, private individual and author. This novel, especially the section 'Free Women', is seen by many critics as one of the most significant contributions to the literature of women's emancipation this century.

Lessing's interest in experimental storytelling extends into her work in the 1980s as a writer of science fiction. *Canopus in Argos: Archives* (1979–83) is an allegorical story which tells how fantastic beasts on distant planets affect life on earth. It is both subtle and feminist, but its argument is not that women are superior to men. Instead, she convinces the reader that traditional feminine qualities are repressed or ignored by society and that many contemporary problems could be solved if they were given greater expression.

Women's writing since 1980

At a time when women's writing was becoming increasingly diverse and experimental, several highly regarded authors such as Penelope Lively and Anita Brookner continued to write about women's issues in a simple, direct way. Before she became a respected author of feminist novels, Penelope Lively wrote children's fiction. A rediscovery of the past is a common theme, for example a child finding an object or place which brings memories of the past in *A House Inside Out* (1987). Her adult novels began with *The Road to Lichfield* (1977) and in 1987 she won the Booker Prize for *Moon Tiger*.

Anita Brookner's style of writing is simple, elegant and funny. She began her career as an art historian specialising in eighteenth-century painting, but later she began creating literary portraits. These are frequently of a lonely, intellectual, single woman who lives unhappily. *A Friend from England* (1987) and *Fraud* (1992) share a common theme of an intelligent heroine who is too shy to get what she wants from life. Instead of rebelling against society, her characters accept their situation and cannot be described as feminists. But in *Hotel du Lac* (1984) the heroine makes the brave decision not to get married on her wedding day. *Hotel du Lac* won the Booker Prize in 1984 and was later made into a successful television series.

While authors such as Maureen Duffy, Penelope Fitzgerald, Penelope Mortimer and Rose Tremain continued to write about women in a similar conventional manner, others began to explore new, experimental styles of language and storytelling. There was a belief that, because society was dominated by men, women had to learn male habits of thinking and feeling. Therefore, to find a more natural, authentic voice, women had to free themselves from traditional, established practices in thought, language and literary style.

The novels and short stories of A.S. Byatt demonstrate her interests in both imaginative experimental literature and factual history. Early in her career the heroines of her novels suffered from family and literary rivalry. These mirrored her own experiences in life (Margaret Drabble is her sister). However, her later works became more fictional and fantastic, and her novel *Possession* (1990) is part fairy tale, part journal, part academic essay, part verse, which together tell the story of an imaginary poet of the nineteenth century. It was awarded the Booker Prize in 1990.

A more vigorous attack on accepted notions of reality is found in the works of Angela Carter. Her works are an energetic mixture of fairy tales, eroticism and transsexuality, in which characters regularly change role and sex, in a way which challenges conventional types of storytelling. This is a characteristic of magic realism, a technique associated with South American writers such as Gabriel García Márquez, whose stories mix extravagant fantasy and fable with everyday events.

The writing of Jean Rhys and Eva Figes used a gentle, poetic, impressionist style to project a feminine sensibility. But their main characteristic was the frequent use of split narrative, in which the story is sometimes told in the first person and sometimes in the third. This creates the sense of a divided self and of fantasy. Rhys wrote her early novels during the 1920s, but was 'rediscovered' during the 1960s. Her novel *The Wide Sargasso Sea* (1966) was published when she was aged 72. It is set in the 1830s and is a highly imaginative, tragic story about Rochester's mad wife, a character from Charlotte Brontë's *Jane Eyre* (1847). This technique of 'reworking' a traditional story has become a distinctive characteristic of many novels of recent years. It involves the changing of numerous details to create an imaginative and accessible story with contemporary relevance. Some examples include Fay Weldon's *The Cloning of Joanna May* (1989), a reworking of Mary Shelley's classic tale *Frankenstein* (1818), and Emma Tennant's *Tess* (1993), in which she took Thomas Hardy and his women as her subjects.

Jeanette Winterson has also explored these possibilities in several of her novels. *Boating for Beginners* (1985) is based on the biblical story of Noah's Ark, but is given a modern emphasis by presenting Noah as a businessman who builds boats. *Sexing the Cherry* (1989) is a mixture of history and fiction, set between the English Civil War of the seventeenth century and present time, while *The Passion* (1987) is set in Venice, as well as in Russia during Napoleon's march on Moscow. One of the main characters is Napoleon's chef; another is a bisexual woman who walks on water. Her imaginative fiction is often cited as magic realism, in which her sentimental, intense style is frequently used to explore lesbian sexuality. *Oranges Are Not the Only Fruit* (1985) analyses the conflict between her traditional, evangelical Pentecostal upbringing and her own lesbian inclinations, while *Written on the Body* (1992) is a love story, about an anonymous narrator whose female lover has a terminal illness. Gay and lesbian writing became increasingly established in the late 1980s in the work of authors such as Alan Hollinghurst, Adam Mars-Jones and others. However, unlike in the United States, it has been slower to gain recognition amongst a conservative literary establishment and readership.

Since the late 1970s, women's writing has continued to be distinctive, influential and increasingly diverse. The tendency to experiment with the form of women's fiction has been widely developed in the work of Angela Carter, Zoë Fairbairns, Marina Warner, Sara Maitland and others. It indicates that modern women's writing is both feminist and feminine: women expect material equality in law, employment and in their relations with men, but they also want to develop a more liberated and natural way of expressing the world, one which is extensive in its narrative range and varied in its technique.

New directions

The breaking of social barriers during previous decades led to a vigorous expansion of literary themes in the 1980s and techniques of storytelling continued to diversify. Some writers looked to the past and took inspiration from earlier traditions, while others began to combine different narrative styles, such as fact and fiction, the past and the present in the same story. The new styles were often imaginative and escapist, but often in a dark, sinister way. Fantastic, grotesque scenarios were created, in which the corruption of innocence and 'paradise lost' were common themes.

One of the most representative novelists of this trend is Martin Amis. The son of Kingsley Amis, he is a satiric, witty author and sharp social commentary is a characteristic of all his novels. His two early works *The Rachel Papers* (1973) and *Dead Babies* (1975) deal with decay, deprivation and sexuality in a declining Britain. Later titles, such as *Success* (1979) and *Money* (1984) ironically reflect the spirit of the times. For Amis, the prosperity enjoyed by some during the 1980s appeared to extinguish all moral obligation to others, as people became more selfish, envious and greedy. He writes of a class system based on money and privilege, in which the spirit is starved and an ecological disaster is imminent. War is another of Amis's preoccupations, which finds expression in *Einstein's Monsters* (1986), a collection of short stories about nuclear war. *Time's Arrow* (1991) narrates the story of the Second World War and describes its effects on the present. Its imaginative technique tells the story in reverse, beginning in the present time and regressing chronologically.

Like Amis, Ian McEwan's early work seemed to demonstrate a wish to shock. In his two collections of short stories *First Love, Last Rites* (1975) and *In Between the Sheets* (1977), McEwan uses precise, elegant prose to write about dark, sinister themes such as incest and infanticide, earning him a reputation as the *enfant terrible* of British fiction. During the 1980s he wrote several television plays and the screenplay for the film *The Ploughman's Lunch* (1983), a critical view of news and media presentation during the Falklands War. Although his later novels remain intensely dark, they are less shocking. They often begin with realistic descriptions of everyday life, before entering into a disordered world of macabre fantasies and chaos. *Enduring Love* (1997) is a complex story about Joe, a science journalist, who is having a picnic with his girlfriend Clarissa, when they see a hot-air balloon going out of control. Together with some strangers, they try to stop it. But they fail and one of them is killed; another begins to pursue Joe. This highly praised novel was followed by *Amsterdam*, which won the Booker Prize of the same year.

Dark themes, including the effects of abortion and murder during adolescence on the writer as a grown man, are found in Graham Swift's *Waterland* (1983), a story set in the Fenlands of Cambridgeshire. Swift's theme is that people often live in the shadow of a suspect past, a corrupted history. This is developed through Tom Crick, a history teacher, who explores with his pupils the history of the regional area through his own life story. *Out of this World* (1987) is also concerned with memories of history and place. Swift's style of writing and his preoccupations with memory and the past have been compared to the magical realism of South American writers, and *Waterland* was critically praised as one of the decade's finest novels.

Concerns with history and place are also found in Peter Ackroyd's *Hawksmoor* (1985), a novel about the London architect (1661–1736) who worked with Sir Christopher Wren. Chapters are alternately set in London of the eighteenth century and the city today, each in the language and style of the period. London was also the setting for his first work *The Great Fire of London* (1982), which deals with the making of a film of Dickens' *Little Dorrit*, and his second novel *The Last Testament of Oscar Wilde* (1983) was a convincing story of the last four months of the dramatist's life, as recorded in his own diary. Ackroyd is considered to be one of the most original writers of the 1980s and is also well known as a poet, biographer and reviewer.

Julian Barnes is a witty, self-confident author whose stories contrast strongly with the dark, macabre works of many other authors of the time. Several reveal an interest in France and its culture. His first, *Metroland* (1980), is set during the Paris riots of 1968, and *Flaubert's Parrot* (1984) is a realistic tale of an elderly doctor's fascination with Gustave Flaubert (1821–80) the French novelist who famously worked with a stuffed parrot on his desk. However, Barnes abandons a conventional way of storytelling for biography, fantasy and intimate conversations with the reader. His later *Cross Channel* (1996) is a collection of short stories set in France, but

England, England (1998) is a humorous novel set in a Britain of the near future, in which England has became an enormous theme park for overseas visitors, who happily pay to enter a country in which everything is presented as traditional and typical, but nothing is authentic. As well as his fictional novels, Barnes has also written several crime novels under the pseudonym of Dan Kavanagh.

Regional English literature

A literature with significant regional characteristics is much less well developed in Britain than in many other European countries. The extent to which English is spoken in the British Isles and around the world means that most writers use it in order to reach a wider audience. However, in Wales there is a strong tradition of writing in the Welsh language. This has been maintained for centuries in the annual cultural festival of the Royal Eisteddfod, and since the 1960s Welsh has been supported as a 'living language' by the British government.

In Scotland, Scots-Gaelic and Scots also have long histories. But today they are used more to conserve an ancient literary tradition than as living languages. However, in recent years the English language novels of several Scottish authors have become more prominent.

Humorous comparisons between the Scots and the English are found in Alasdair Gray's best-known work *Lanark* (1981). It describes the author as a young Glaswegian and is told in a dual style, both fantasy and reality, indicating a split nature or identity. Similar complexities are also found in works by Ron Butlin and Brian McCabe. Iain Banks is another Scottish novelist who has written varied stories in which fantasy and reality become mixed. Several are science fiction stories, but he is more widely known for his novels. *The Wasp Factory* (1984) contains detailed descriptions of horrific violence, but was critically admired for the author's distinctive style, which was further developed in novels such as *The Bridge* (1986) and *The Crow Road* (1992).

Irvine Welsh's popular books *Trainspotting* (1993) and *The Acid House* (1994) exposed a darker side to the elegant city of Edinburgh, although the cycles of violence, drug addiction and boredom are lifted by the author's lively, humorous style. Black humour and disturbing descriptions are also features of novels by Scottish author James Kelman. His urban realism often deals with the hard life on the streets of Glasgow and is written in local dialect with numerous expletives. His rejection of standard English prose have made him controversial and sometimes difficult to evaluate, but his novel *How Late It Was, How Late* (1994) was highly praised and won the Booker Prize the same year.

In Ireland as in Scotland, most novels are written in English. Some of the most highly praised of recent years have incorporated realist themes found in the work of several other British novelists. One of the most warmly received of the late 1980s was Roddy Doyle's *The Commitments* (1988), about a white soul band. Together with *The Snapper* (1990) and *The Van* (1991), they form a comic trilogy about working-class life in Dublin, and are told in a humorous, colloquial style. In *The Van*, two Dublin friends invest their redundancy money in a fish'n'chip van. The World Cup football tournament is on television and the Irish team is doing well. Meanwhile, Jimmy and Bimbo make a fortune from frying sausages before success begins to change their lives. In 1993 *Paddy Clarke Ha Ha Ha* won the Booker prize, making Doyle one of the most successful Irish authors of recent times.

The continuing tensions in Northern Ireland between the violent demands for independence and the maintenance of union with Britain have provided the basis for several novels of the 1980s and 1990s by Bernard McLaverty, Alan Judd and others. There is also strong tradition of verse, maintained by poets such as Tom Paulin, Paul Durcan, Paul Muldoon and Derek Mahon, whose works have examined the problems and pressures of life in the Northern Counties.

One of the most highly praised Irish poets of recent years is Seamus Heaney (b.1939). He was born in Northern Ireland, but later moved to the Irish Republic. His early collections *Death of a Naturalist* (1966) and *Door into the Dark* (1969) describe his familiar childhood environment of farmers and fishermen with an accuracy which won him immediate praise. However, his later collections *Wintering Out* (1972), *North* (1975) and *Fieldwork* (1979) bring together local politics and history. *North* is his clearest political statement, which examines Irish history and the current 'troubles' in the northern counties. *Seeing Things* (1991) is another imaginative work in which the past and present, imagination and reality are brought together. As well as poetry, Heaney has also written several volumes of prose, such as *The Redress of Poetry* (1990). He is seen by many critics as the most talented writer of verse since W.B. Yeats and, together with Ted Hughes, as a leading British poet. His international stature was acknowledged when he received the 1995 Nobel Prize for Literature.

Ted Hughes was born in a country village of West Yorkshire in the north of England and is considered by many critics to be the finest poet of his generation. Unlike the poems of many of his early contemporaries in the Movement of the mid-1950s, his work frequently deals with the natural world. The birds, beasts, insects and fish of his native countryside provide the inspiration for many of his poems. They are written in rapid, simple, imaginative verse from the point of view of a detached, disinterested observer. They reflect an aggression and violence in both the natural and the human world, which is both objective and unsentimental.

His early collection *The Hawk in the Rain* (1957) announced the arrival of a major British poet. Since then he has written volumes of poetry for children, verse plays for radio and several works of criticism. In 1984 he succeeded Sir John Betjeman to become Poet Laureate. This is a title held by an 'official' poet to the Royal Household, a position created in 1616 so that poems would be written for important state occasions. His collection *Rain Charm for the Duchy* (1992) contains his Laureate verse, but some of his finest work appeared later in his career, such as *Birthday Letters* (1995), in which he described his troubled marriage to the American poet Sylvia Plath, who committed suicide in 1963.

The cry of the colonies

In 1969 the Booker Prize for Fiction was awarded for the first time. Because it was open to foreign authors who wrote in English, it drew attention to the fiction being created outside Britain. It received widespread support from publishers and recent overseas winners have included Salman Rushdie from India (1981, 1993) for *Midnight's Children*, Thomas Keneally from Australia for *Schindler's Ark* (1982), Keri Hulme from New Zealand for *The Bone People* (1985), Peter Carey from Australia for *Oscar and Lucinda* (1988), Kazuo Ishiguro from Japan for *The Remains of the Day* (1989), Ben Okri from Nigeria for *The Famished Road* (1991) and Arundhati Roy from India for *The God of Small Things* (1997).

As Britain became a multi-cultural society, the voices of writers of different nationalities and origins became louder, and what Salman Rushdie has called 'migrants' tales' became a significant area of English literature. For some writers, the memory of British rule in their country is as much part of their history as their independence. Other writers come from families who were early immigrants to Britain. But a shared characteristic of their writing is that they are frequently concerned with the search for identity, which is often complicated by the presence of numerous cultural, political and historical influences. Their varied experiences have brought a new perspective to creative writing, which involves an 'outsider's' view of the world: the expression of someone in it, but not of it. Some critics see this as comparable with feminist writing of recent years.

Some recent examples of immigrant writing include Caryl Phillips' *The Final Passage* (1985) about the Caribbean community in London during the 1950s and the life that Leila, a young woman, finds when she arrives. Suburban London is also the setting for David Dabydeen's *The Intended* (1991), which depicts a young man from Guyana trying to understand his different heritage as he grows up. Dabydeen and his compatriot Fred d'Aguiar have also written poetry on race relations in Britain.

Some of the liveliest and most colourful accounts of modern, multi-racial Britain are found in the works of Hanif Kureishi. These frequently draw on race relations and his childhood experiences in the suburbs of London. His highly praised *Buddha of Suburbia* (1990) is part-autobiographical and tells the humorous story of a young Pakistani growing up in Britain and learning about his heritage, wondering how he can successfully integrate it with his London life. His later novel *The Black Album* (1995) is a thriller set in London in 1989 and tells a story of drugs, religion and sexual passion. As well as writing novels, Kureishi has also written screenplays and television dramas which include the film *My Beautiful Launderette* (1985).

Impressions of life in Britain from an Anglo-Oriental perspective are found in the works of both Kazuo Ishiguro and Timothy Mo. Ishiguro arrived in Britain from Japan as a small child. In *An Artist of the Floating World* (1986) he looks at an ageing painter's detachment from political and cultural developments in modern Japan. But his later and most successful novel, *Remains of the Day* (1989), uses precise and detailed observation of an elderly butler in an English country house to present a portrait of British life and society in the mid-twentieth century. His fine observations of class distinctions and social behaviour won the Booker Prize of the same year and later became a successful film.

The Anglo-Oriental roots of Timothy Mo are also given expression in his novels. In *Monkey King* (1980) he observes the ancient and modern traditions of his native Hong Kong, while *Sour, Sweet* (1982) describes the closed, distant character of the Chinese community in the London district of Soho. Two of his later works look more closely at the politics of the former British territory: the origins of Hong Kong form the subject of *Insular Possession* (1986), which examines its the history from different points of view and uses letters, newspaper reports and drama to create an authentic sense of communication with the reader; the Far East is also the setting for *Redundancy of Courage* (1991), which describes how the Far Eastern island of East Timor was abandoned by the Portuguese colonial power, leaving it in chaos and anarchy.

V.S. Naipaul and Derek Walcott are two of the finest writers the Caribbean region has produced. Naipaul's long and prolific career began with satirical novels set in Trinidad in the 1950s and 1960s, which included the comical *A House for Mr Biswas* (1961). His later works included travel writing, which expressed concern about the negative effects of imperial rule. Two works were set in England: *Mr Stone and the Knights Companion* (1963) about life in the city, and *The Enigma of Arrival* (1987) about the countryside. Others include novels about the Caribbean, the American South, India and the Islamic world. Derek Walcott's career as a poet and playwright began in the early 1960s and since then it has covered a wide range of themes. *Sea Grapes* (1976) and *Midsummer* (1983) were influenced by religious themes, while *Omeros* (1989) and his play *The Odyssey* (1992) make parallels between the writing of Homer about the Aegean Sea and Walcott's own Caribbean. He received the Nobel Prize for Literature in 1992.

Political change and struggle are common themes to many writers from Africa. One of the most highly praised novels of the early 1990s was Ben

Okri's *The Famished Road* (1991). His novel gives a colourful description of his Nigerian childhood and is supplemented by an account of political turbulence as Nigeria becomes an independent country. Although it is told simply, it is expressed through a fantastic, magical narrative, in which tales and rumours captivate and entertain the reader. The magic realism follows the conventions of Nigerian fables and, as with the novels of his compatriot Chinua Achebe, fantasy is used to communicate new levels of human experience. His later novel, *Dangerous Love* (1996), is a more conventional, realist story of corruption in Nigeria.

The politics and society of South Africa are prominent themes in the novels of Nadine Gordimer. Her long and prolific career began in 1949 with *Face to Face*, a collection of short stories. Later she began to write novels which mirrored her view of progress towards the removal of apartheid in South Africa. *Burgher's Daughter* (1979) is about the daughter of strict Afrikaner Marxists, while *My Son's Story* (1990) is a novel about a young coloured man who tries to understand his history and identity in modern South Africa. In 1991 she was awarded the Nobel Prize for Literature.

Salman Rushdie

One of the most critically praised writers in the English language is Salman Rushdie (b.1947). He was born into a Muslim family in Bombay, India, and emigrated to Britain in 1965. His homeland provides the setting for *Midnight's Children* (1981), whose title refers to a new generation of Indians who are born at midnight on 15 August 1947, when India became an independent republic. The story is a mixture of fantasy and magic, and is widely acclaimed as original, clever and observant. It twice won the Booker Prize: once in 1981 and again in 1993 (as the best novel during the first twenty-five years of Booker awards).

His next works included *Shame* (1983), about Pakistan, and *The Jaguar Smile* (1987), a travel book about life in Nicaragua under the Sandinistas. But it was *The Satanic Verses* (1988) for which the author became renowned. The 'satanic verses' of the title are verses from the Koran, the Muslim holy text. Set in Arabia, India and Britain, it is a complex, imaginative story about the act of storytelling. But some Muslims found it a blasphemous abuse of their religion and Ayatollah Khomeini of Iran demanded that the author be killed. An Italian translator of the book was subsequently attacked and a Japanese translator murdered.

In Britain, the book was publicly burnt by Muslims and because they feared attack, many bookshops withdrew it. Thousands of authors pledged their support for Rushdie, who made only very rare public appearances. However, he has continued to produce a variety of books which have included children's stories *Haroun and the Sea of Stories* (1990), collected essays in *Imaginary Homelands* (1991) and a volume of short stories *East,*

West (1994). In September 1998, on the tenth anniversary of the publication of *Satanic Verses*, the death threat was finally withdrawn by the Iranian government.

The new populism: English literature today

During the early years of the 1990s, harsh economic and social policies intensified a deep economic recession. This mirrored the depression of many critics over the state of modern fiction. They complained about the absence of political voices or moral direction in modern writing, frustrated at a growing inability to distinguish serious literature from sensational novels or 'pulp' fiction and the absence of any clear sense of British identity in the novel.

The role of the novel in society was changing. Earlier in the century it was generally seen as a contribution to thought on a particular subject. The erudite views of respected authors were regularly read and discussed, and this was frequently made possible by a shared morality between author and readers. However, during the second half of the twentieth century, morality, attitudes, values and behaviour gradually became more personal matters, as people had less confidence or belief in authority of all kinds: political, religious or scientific. At the same time, television, radio and quality newspapers all carried accessible, apolitical features on topical matters, which helped provide information on major issues. Consequently, as the novel came to be read more for entertainment than for inspiration or influence, its traditional role diminished.

This has led to an expansion of popular interest in reading. Publishing became one of the few growth industries of the early 1980s and, by the late 1990s, some 6,000 new fictional works were published each year. The number of chain-store bookshops in the high street increased, and the marketing and publicity of new books became fine arts. There was much comment in the media about new works, as well as gossip about the size of writers' commissions. Some became public figures, and occasionally vice versa. For the first time, works of literature and popular fiction began to compete with each other in the bestseller lists and the novel became a popular, fashionable object. Several university departments began to offer courses in creative writing; one of the most prestigious is at the University of East Anglia in Norwich.

The role of poetry has also changed. Like many 'classical' art forms, for many years it was neglected. Most people believed it as had little to say about modern themes. But in recent times there has been a steady growth of interest as popular new styles appeared, such as 'performance poetry'. This is verse which is written to be read aloud. In previous years the Mersey Poets had pioneered such a style and during the 1970s and 1980s it was exploited by the punk poet John Cooper-Clarke. It involved elaborately dressed performers reading their dramatic poems about topical urban themes such as sex, drugs and fame, to an appreciative, youthful, non-literary audience.

In a new development during the 1980s, black musical styles were incorporated into poetry. A leading exponent is the British Rastafarian poet Benjamin Zephaniah whose 'rap' verse is performed in a rapid, spoken monologue. In the early 1980s, when punks and Rastafarians were protesting about high unemployment, homelessness and the National Front, his poems could be heard at demonstrations, outside police stations and even on the dancefloor. His collections include *Pen Rhythm* (1980), *The Dread Affair* (1985), *Inna Liverpool* (1988) and *Propa Propaganda* (1996). In 1998 he was a shortlisted candidate for the prestigious post of Poet Laureate, following the death of Ted Hughes.

A related type of performance poetry is 'dub', a verse-form with the distinctive rhythms of reggae but without the music. Linton Kwesi Johnson has written several volumes of 'dub' poetry. He was born in Jamaica, but came to Britain in 1963. His poems are set in urban areas, and are often dark and violent. *Inglan is a Bitch* (1980) is one of his best known collections. He has also made records of his poetry, including *Bass Culture* (1980) and *Making History* (1984).

Attitudes towards the new verse varied. While younger readers found them accessible and enjoyable, many older critics claimed such poetry was shallow, populist and had little substance. They argued that its impact on the page is lost when the 'imported' rhythm of the author's voice is absent. However, other poets continued to work in a more conventional way. Andrew Motion, Tony Harrison, Geoffrey Hill, Tom Paulin and James Fenton all write highly praised poetry about contemporary themes with rich, anecdotal narrative.

The strength and vitality of novel writing has produced an increasing number of genres and sub-genres of literature. Women's writing in particular has continued to grow and diversify. The influence of magical realism provided a fresh stimulus, and both male and female authors began to incorporate elements of fantasy into their works. There was also a growing number of gay and lesbian fiction writers who were inspired by the new perspectives offered by 'queer' literature in America. However, this has been slow to develop among British authors, for whom sexuality is often a personal matter more than an issue of public or political importance.

The kind of women's writing which still has the largest women's readership is escapist, romantic writing. Traditional romances and historical dramas with their carefully observed speech, manners, and dress style are consistently appreciated by British readers and authors such as Jilly Cooper and Catherine Cookson are popular with the public. As well as romance, astrology, health and alternative medicine are among the most popular types of writing, in which the contribution of women authors is consistently greater than that of men.

Biography is another genre which has grown in popularity. Many public figures have written about themselves or employed a 'ghost writer' to assist them. This may be due to the growing appetite for personal details, trivia and information about different lifestyles. Interest has been encouraged by the type of reporting found in popular newspapers and magazines, particularly since the mid-1980s. Paradoxically, books about famous people often sell more than books by them, perhaps because the former are more critical and revealing.

A related area or sub-genre is the 'confessional' biography, in which intimate details are revealed about the subject's private life. One of the most critically praised is Nick Hornby's *Fever Pitch* (1992). Set in the 1970s, this is the autobiographical story of a young man from suburban London whose complex emotions are expressed in his passionate obsession with Arsenal Football Club. It became a bestseller and one of the most talked about novels of the mid-1990s. His subsequent novels are part-autobiographical. *High Fidelity* (1994) and *About a Boy* (1997) are similar explorations of suburban youth culture of the 1970s and 1980s. Helen Fielding's *Bridget Jones' Diary* (1997) is the female sequel, which humorously details the anxieties of a young, single, suburban female of the 1990s.

As levels of crime increased sharply in the 1980s and 1990s, so did interest in crime and detective novels. The tradition began during the 1890s with Sir Arthur Conan Doyle and his fictitious sleuth Sherlock Holmes. But during the twentieth century it has been largely maintained by women authors, such as Agatha Christie with her detective heroes Miss Marple and Poirot. Stories were set in a remote country house and involved an affluent, middle-class group in a type of intellectual puzzle popularly known as a 'whodunit'. It projected a morality which everyone could agree with and created a psychological tension through suggestion and subtlety. In the 1990s this popular tradition is continued by P.D. James (with her sleuths Adam Dalgleish and Delia Gray), Ruth Rendell (Inspector Wexford), Colin Dexter (Inspector Morse) and many of their stories have been adapted for television series.

A related type of novel is the spy 'thriller', a genre which was especially popular during the years of the Cold War. Graham Greene, John Le Carré, Len Deighton and Ian Fleming were among the most acclaimed. In the 1970s they provided some critical commentary on the condition of British institutions, such as their secrecy, inefficiency and resistance to change. But as the Cold War disappeared, interest in the spy novel declined.

Declining interest in spy stories has contrasted with the growth in popularity of science-fiction novels. Technological advances, space exploration and fantastic military capabilities have all increased worries about the present and led to dark speculation about the future. The freedom of 'sci-fi' to create time, place and plot exposes some of the limitations of the more conventional novels and has provided authors, such as J.G. Ballard, Brian Aldiss, Ray Bradbury, Michael Moorcock and others, with limitless possibilities for creative writing. But the scenarios of the next century and beyond are often represented as sad, bad, uneasy places, with an absence of community or values. Pessimistic speculation about life in space has begun to mirror that of life on Earth.

Discussion topics and activities

1   What do you consider to be the most distinctive aspects of English literature since the mid-1950s? Which kind would you prefer to read?
2   How do the themes and style of the literature of your country differ from those of English literature? Think about women's writing, immigrants' and regional writing.
3   Refer to the text and other sources to explain the following: women's writing / migrants' tales / immigrant writing / magic realism / performance poetry.
4   Imagine you are a book critic for a popular magazine. Write a critical review of a novel which you know well, explaining what you like or dislike about it.
5   Does a serious novelist have an obligation to entertain the reader?
6   Imagine a theme for your own novel. Using approximately 150 words for each part, write the beginning and end of it.

Suggested further reading

Books

Bradbury, M. (1992) *The Modern British Novel* Harmondsworth: Penguin.
Breen, J. (1990) *In Her Own Write: Twentieth-Century Women's Fiction* London: Macmillan.
Cairns, C. (1987) *The History of Scottish Literature*, vol. 4, *The Twentieth Century* Aberdeen: Aberdeen University Press.
Carter, R. and McRae, J. (1997) *The Routledge History of Literature in English: Britain and Ireland* London and New York: Routledge.
Connor, S. (1996) *The English Novel in History* London and New York: Routledge.
Dabydeen, D. (ed.) (1985) *The Black Presence in English Literature* Manchester: Manchester University Press.
Munt, S.M. (1994) *Murder by the Book: Feminism and the Crime Novel* London: Routledge.
Sanders, A. (1994) *The Short Oxford History of English Literature* Oxford: Oxford University Press.
Stevenson, R. (1993) *A Reader's Guide to the Twentieth-Century Novel in Britain* Hemel Hempstead: Harvester Wheatsheaf.
Thieme, J. (ed.) (1996) *Post-Colonial Literatures in English* London: Arnold.
Wallace, G. and Stevenson, R. (eds) (1993) *The Scottish Novel since the Seventies: New Visions, Old Dreams* Edinburgh: Edinburgh University Press.

Waugh, P. (1995) *Harvest of the Sixties: English Literature and its Background 1960–90* Oxford: Oxford University Press.

Journals

Granta, the *Literary Review*, the *London Magazine*, the *London Review of Books*, *Strand* and the *Times Literary Supplement* all carry up-to-date information, news and comment on current developments. The British Council has a regular newsletter *Literature Matters* which includes recent information on academic conferences, publications and so on, as well as analysis of the latest trends in English literature.

4

Theatre

Introduction

British drama is consistently admired for its variety and vitality. Traditional productions, novel reinterpretations, brave new works, lively musicals and pantomime are all elements of contemporary theatre. Creativity and evolution are highly valued and the work of young play-wrights is strongly encouraged.

Plays are performed in many different places. Settings vary from the intimacy of a small room above a village pub to the formality of the Royal National Theatre in London, whose company of actors and staff is among the most prestigious in the country. There are approximately 300 theatres in Britain and more than forty have resident companies of actors, play-wrights and other staff. These are known as repertory or 'rep' theatres, and offer a variety of plays for short periods. They generally receive a subsidy from the Arts Council, which enables them to be more creative and free from commerical pressures.

Repertory theatres are found in all the major cities. Some of the largest are Glasgow Citizens', Sheffield Crucible, Bristol Old Vic and the Liverpool Playhouse. They have a reputation for original, varied and high-quality plays, and the most successful often transfer to London. This is a priority for any director seeking a larger audience and national publicity. Some are even exported abroad, where there is always strong demand for traditional works. However, foreign productions on the British stage are rare.

London has around one hundred theatres, of which fifteen are occupied

59

by subsidised companies. The large commercial ones, such as the Theatre Royal in Drury Lane, are situated in the West End, the capital's focal point for night-life. These theatres generally offer a familiar programme of light entertainment, such as musicals and comedy shows, while plays with more individual themes are offered in smaller, more compact theatres, such as the Donmar Warehouse or the Tricycle, which are situated off-West End. But the most innovative and experimental work is usually found in the 'fringe' theatres. These are smaller, simple stages which specialise in small-scale works of quality and are found in all parts of the city.

Drama schools offer specialised training for the stage. Among the best known are the Royal Academy for Dramatic Art (RADA), the Central School for Speech and Drama and the London Academy of Music and Dramatic Art. Numerous other colleges, art schools and universities also offer courses in drama, theatre design and related subjects, as well as training for technicians and directors. Afterwards, many actors go to work in 'rep' before working in film and television, where for the lucky few, the fame and financial rewards can be much greater.

Drama is also a popular spare-time activity. Many provincial towns and cities have amateur dramatics societies which put on an annual play for the local community and, of course, for their own enjoyment. Schools, colleges and universities also have drama societies where students can exercise their dramatic talent and where many famous actors begin their careers.

Figure 4.1 Shaftesbury Avenue, at the heart of London's West End

Historical influences

Since the seventeenth century, London's West End has been the home of 'theatreland', where many of the country's most prestigious establishments are packed into a maze of narrow streets. But many of today's grand old establishments were built around 1900, often on the sites of much older ones, such as the Theatre Royal and the Royal Opera House. Modern theatres include the National, on London's South Bank, and the Barbican Centre, situated to the east of the city. The latter is home to the Royal Shakespeare Company, which also has a base in the West Midlands town of Stratford-on-Avon, Shakespeare's birthplace. The RSC is dedicated to interpreting Shakespeare's plays and presents works throughout the year.

Although British theatre is often considered to be synonymous with Shakespeare, most contemporary dramas have their origins in the

Figure 4.2 The Barbican Centre, London

mid-nineteenth century. Until 1843, the moral and political content of theatre plays was strictly controlled by the government. In London, only three theatres had a licence to show plays: the Drury Lane, the Covent Garden and the Haymarket. Theatres without a licence could only offer musical shows and, to avoid problems with the law, lively dramas of crime, violence, sadism and seduction were combined with background music. For their combination of melody and drama, these popular spectacles became known as 'melodramas'.

In 1843 the government introduced the Theatre Regulating Act which allowed small theatres to offer a variety of plays. The new freedoms encouraged the writing of many new works, but there were few dramatists of quality. However, later in the century some of the most popular and talented playwrights of recent history emerged, such as the Irish playwright Oscar Wilde. His imaginative, witty plays were based on sharp social observation, the best-known being his comedy of manners *The Importance of Being Earnest* (1895). W.S. Gilbert and A. Sullivan combined lyrics and music in numerous comic operas, for example *H.M.S. Pinafore* (1878) and *The Mikado* (1885).

The political and social themes of Henrik Ibsen (1828–1906) had a great impact on British theatre. Ibsen was a Norwegian playwright whose 'problem plays' examined controversial themes, such as the effects of the social environment on the individual, and the situation of women in marriage. Plays such as *Hedda Gabler* (1890) shocked audiences and critics, but he was supported by the influential dramatist George Bernard Shaw, who proposed that British drama should be influenced more by social ideas than by spectacle and comedy.

Shaw was an Irish playwright and a master of language. He often mixed different styles, for example colloquial and biblical, to great dramatic effect in works which were witty, provocative and political. At a time when it was unfashionable and even eccentric, he was feminist, vegetarian and abstemious, and his inventive works, such as *Man and Superman* (1903) and *Pygmalion* (1913), frequently attacked conventional morality and ideas. Shaw's influence has been enduring and in 1925 he received the Nobel Prize for Literature.

Social realism

Drama of the late 1940s and early 1950s was generally undistinguished and was dominated by weak thrillers and comedies set in country houses. However, during the mid-1950s changing social conditions provided new playwrights with a fresh stimulus. Although the economy was slowly beginning to improve after the devastation of the war years, there was dissatisfaction with the government, which was seen as old-fashioned and remote from society. There was also a feeling among the young that the new society was only concerned with material benefits. Many felt discontented, and looked for causes and values in their spiritually empty, materialist lives.

By 1955 this discontent had found expression in a new wave of cultural activity across the arts. Young authors began to write plays and novels which spoke from the heart. They criticised the ruling class of government, church and business-leaders. They became known as the 'angry young men', a description originally used in the publicity for John Osborne's *Look Back in Anger* (1956) at London's Royal Court Theatre, a stage known for its adventurous and experimental plays.

Osborne's play tells the story of Jimmy Porter, a university graduate who lives in a small Midlands town. Porter is nostalgic for the past and angry with the modern world, which he sees as dull and false. His concerns are those of many young people at that time: a desire for social change and the need for new values and causes. Much of the action takes place in his cheap, untidy bed-sitting room and centres on his chaotic marriage.

The play was highly successful. It caught the mood of the times and was immediately influential. Young audiences crowded to hear the new voices speaking from the heart. Forceful plays followed which expressed the discontent, frustration and anger of the post-war young. These included Irish playwright Brendan Behan's *The Quare Fellow* (1956) and *The Hostage* (1959), two witty accounts of life in Dublin. Shelagh Delaney's *A Taste of Honey* (1962) and Ann Jellicoe's *The Knack* (1962) both dealt with unmarried couples living together, a subject considered taboo in the Britain of the early 1960s.

In many plays the story takes place in a small, scruffy room, with the double bed, ironing board, table, fireplace and sink. These became such common props that the plays and stories were nicknamed 'kitchen sink dramas' after an earlier term for a style of painting with similar subject-matter. They were often received by audiences with bemusement, shock and disdain. But the new movement put on the stage the concerns and problems of ordinary people and not just those of a better-educated, affluent minority, which had been the case until before the war. It introduced dissent into the arts and provided a more complete theatre of social experience.

Samuel Beckett

Beckett was born in Ireland in 1903. He studied in Dublin before travelling widely in Europe, where he began to write novels and short stories. These usually depicted a pessimistic view of modern humanity, showing them to be isolated and powerless. But his works are also witty and contain much wordplay with thoughts and objects.

His play *Waiting for Godot* (1955) is his most famous work. In the play, the two main characters (Vladimir and Estragon) appear dressed as tramps. For Beckett, they represent the two sides of human beings: one represents their thoughts and the other represents their feelings. The two tramps chat and argue about life while they wait for Godot. But Godot never appears, nor is identified. Vladimir and Estragon continue to wait and pass the time repeating daily actions and conversations.

Waiting for Godot is recognised as one of the greatest plays of the twentieth century and has had a lasting effect on British drama. In common with several other new dramas of the mid-1950s, its theme was the absence of causes and values to give any real meaning to life and immediately found favour with audiences. In the early 1960s the play was identified as a work belonging to the 'theatre of the absurd' after the title of a study by the writer and critic Martin Esslin. In this context, 'absurd' means 'out of harmony'. It referred to a group of playwrights who drama-tised the strange, meaningless nature of life, in which people have no religious roots and have to suffer to survive. For them, life has no certain-ties or purpose and communication between people fails because they have nothing in common.

Plays belonging to the 'theatre of the absurd' have no conventional plot. They offer no moral lessons and no story. Instead, they present the situa-tion of characters faced with the meaninglessness of their life. The works of Beckett and Harold Pinter regularly express such a view, along with several other European playwrights such as Ionesco and Genet.

After the success of *Godot* Beckett settled in France, where he produced several short novels and dramatic works for the stage, cinema and televi-sion. These were even more austere and minimal in their presentation. *Krapp's Last Tape* (1958) featured a man alone with a tape recorder. In *Happy Days* (1961) the protagonist is buried up to her neck in sand and in *Not I* (1973) only the actress's mouth is visible, which verbally vomits the performance. During his lifetime Beckett became a major dramatist and his works frequently reinterpreted. In 1969 he was awarded the Nobel Prize for Literature.

After the influence of social realism and Beckett, a third significant and lasting influence on modern British drama is that of the East German play-wright Bertolt Brecht. Plays such as *Mother Courage* (1941) and *The Caucasian Chalk Circle* (1948) introduced new ideas about production and acting. For Brecht, stage design was minimal, because decoration distracted the audience from the script and the performance. Instead, his productions involved the audience more directly: either through participa-tion or by changing the auditorium, bringing it into the stage. He also introduced a strongly political element into drama: the rebel individual not as bad or deviant, but as someone fighting against corruption in society. Brecht has influenced many British playwrights, who often incorporated his radical political insights and elements of his presentational style into their works.

Harold Pinter

The late 1950s was a fertile period for British drama and several new writers emerged who would go on to have long and successful careers. One such playwright is Harold Pinter, the longest established among prominent dramatists, who is regarded by many critics as Britain's finest living playwright.

His first major play was *The Birthday Party* (1958), in which the two protagonists are forced into a situation which they cannot control. It has humour, sex and menace. *The Homecoming* (1965) is one of his best-known works. It is about a divided family in which the father does not get on well with his sons. One of them works at an American university and returns home with his new wife Ruth, who has strong views on women's equality and liberation. But the family expect her to be a traditional mother and wife, and attempt to dominate her. The action in Pinter's plays often takes place in one room, where the characters attempt to express their internal feelings, irrational thoughts and ideas.

One of Pinter's most notable contributions to drama is in the writing of dialogue. Earlier playwrights wrote it in an extravagant and impressive manner. But Pinter's is naturalistic and includes many pauses, hesitations and changes of subject, as in real life. He allows the audience to use their imagination, to create meaning from the text and decide what the play is about. This was considered radical in the 1950s, but since then it has become a characteristic of dialogue in many British plays and films.

His later works often deal with questions of self-identity and knowledge of others, for example *Old Times* (1971) and *No Man's Land* (1975). But since the late 1980s his works have become more explicitly political. *Mountain Language* (1988) is set in an unnamed dictatorial, totalitarian state where people are imprisoned for using their indigenous but prohibited language. The play warns of the dangers of a centralised culture and authority where local differences and identities are not merely ignored, but are actively repressed. *New World Order* (1991) is a short play based on the Gulf War, in which Pinter expresses his doubts about the conflict.

Pinter is a prolific writer who has written extensively for film, radio and television, and won several awards. The uniqueness of his style led to the adoption of the term 'Pinteresque', commonly used to describe dark threatening situations in which people become victims of their own internal feelings, desires and guilts, even though their lives seem superficially normal.

Shocks of the new: theatre in the 1960s and 1970s

At the beginning of the 1960s, a highly original and entertaining new comedy show *Beyond the Fringe* appeared at the Edinburgh Festival. The team of Peter Cook, Jonathan Miller, Alan Bennett and Dudley Moore wrote and performed in a series of irreverent, satirical sketches. Their principal targets were English manners, eccentricities and the government of the time. In 1961 the show transferred to London where it continued until 1966. It was an immediate success and marked a new beginning for political satire on stage and later on television, with *TW3* and *Monty Python's Flying Circus*.

Drama was becoming more provocative and Joe Orton was a leading exponent of the new trend. Orton disliked authority and control by the state, and his works were created to alarm respectable, bourgeois audiences. Although his works were comedies, they also had a dark side to them. *Loot* (1966) deals with murder and robbery; *What the Butler Saw* (1969) considers questions of authority, sexual identity and the role of psychoanalysis. Tragically, Orton's life was cut short when he was murdered at the age of 34 by his lover Kenneth Halliwell.

The trend towards angrier, rebellious theatre continued and later during the 1960s, at a time of Cold War and consumerism, many writers wrote dramas which showed the world as a cruel, oppressive, materialistic place. Theatre audiences were mainly middle-class and middle-aged, and radical playwrights sometimes wrote intentionally disturbing works to shock them. They wanted to make them aware of new social and political realities of the time, such as women's struggle for equality and the stupidity of war.

However, the content of dramatic works was still closely controlled by laws which limited what could be shown on stage. Until 1968 all public performances required a licence. These were obtained from the Lord Chamberlain, an official of the Royal Household, in an archaic practice originating in the sixteenth century when it was a used to control political content in drama. During the nineteenth century, licences were used as a form of moral censorship to prevent obscene and blasphemous plays. But in 1968 the law was changed and plays were subjected to the same tests as works of literature under the Obscene Publications Act of 1959. Prosecution depended on whether or not the book or play might be seen by someone who could be depraved or corrupted by it. Following the change in law, more provocative and daring works appeared on the British stage.

During the 1970s playwrights such as David Edgar, Edward Bond, Trevor Griffiths and Peter Schaffer wrote intentionally disturbing works. Many showed a fascination with the extreme forms of human behaviour. Fine descriptions of character and attention to dialogue were considered less important than visual 'shock tactics', with cold depictions of murder, torture, rape and cannibalism. One of the most disturbing was Peter Schaffer's *Equus* (1973). Its theme of spiritual and mental decline was developed by showing a young boy who expresses his affection for horses by blinding them. These were very difficult years for Britain and playwrights argued that deviant and violent behaviour was a natural consequence of life in a corrupt, decaying society. Many older members of the public stopped going to the theatre, but a younger, more liberal audience found such plays daring and attractive.

Howard Brenton and David Hare were both closely associated with radical drama at the beginning of their careers and since the 1970s they have both become major dramatists. Brenton had an early success with *Magnificence* (1973), an angry play about urban terrorism. His later play *Romans in Britain* (1980) featured the homosexual rape of a Druid priest by a Roman soldier. Many critics saw it as gratuitous sexual violence, a cynical attempt to gain publicity. But he defended it as an exploration of empire-building, a critique of colonialism and of the British military presence in Ireland. David Hare's approach has been less controversial than Brenton's. In *Slag* (1970), *Fanshen* (1975) and *Licking Hitler* (1978) he emphasised the way that individuals change as a consequence of their social environments. David Edgar's plays of the early 1970s were strongly socialist, but later during his prolific career he began a more thoughtful examination of politics and psychology, such as the delicate theme of South African politics. *The Jail Diary of Albie Sachs* (1978) gives a prisoner's view of the apartheid struggle in South Africa in the late 1970s.

These and other plays contributed to the political face of drama in the 1970s. It was a time when playwrights attempted to make statements in an impressive, dramatic style. But some writers considered that larger theatres were unsuitable places for the expression of radical views. Instead, smaller, more intimate environments were needed, where there were no commercial pressures on playwrights and artists. This led to a growing interest in 'alternative' drama.

New perspectives: alternative drama

The late 1960s saw an explosion of creativity across the arts. Alternative styles emerged in opposition to the large-scale commercial productions of the established theatres. New plays were frequently concerned with current issues and problems such as racial oppression and women's liberation. These were held in small, non-profit-making studios known as 'arts labs', where artists of all kinds could meet and work. Some theatre groups such as Hull Truck, Red Ladder and Cafe La Mama had no permanent base and toured continually, putting on shows in smaller studio theatres, schools and community buildings. Another movement known as 'poor theatre' did not use any elaborate scenery, costumes or lights. As with the equivalent art movement, *arte povera*, it was simple and basic. The only instruments of communication were the actors' bodies and voices.

One of the most vigorous and vocal of the new theatre groups was women's theatre. Around 1970, groups such as the Women's Theatre

67

Group, the Sadista Sisters, the Chuffinelles and Cunning Stunts toured schools and performed in the street. Their works dealt openly with questions of gender, sexuality and identity. They were often concerned with making audiences aware of the harsh realities of many women's everyday lives, for example by contrasting them with young women's fairy-tale expectations.

The pioneering nature of women's theatre, its new voices and identities gradually produced a gay theatre movement. The newspaper *Gay News* was used to recruit theatre staff and actors, and in 1976 a mixed-sex company Gay Sweatshop was formed. Women worked on plays which addressed issues such as lesbian parenting rights, while men worked on plays dealing with gay issues, such as lowering the age of homosexual consent. By 1978 the movement had been sufficiently confident and successful to produce a play with an openly homosexual theme. This was *Bent* by Martin Sherman, which dealt with the Nazi persecution of homosexuals in Berlin of 1934.

The platform created by alternative drama led to a greater representation of ethnic minorities. During the late 1960s and early 1970s, the only plays dealing with racial oppression had been presented by visiting actors and playwrights from the United States and South Africa, such as South African Athol Fugard's *Sizwe Bansi is Dead* (1972) and *The Island* (1974), which both publicised the injustices of the apartheid system. But new black playwrights gradually made their mark, such as Michael Abbensetts, whose *Alterations* (1978) presented an authentic West Indian view of black experience in Britain. However, by the end of the decade, theatre in Britain was still predominantly a white British male practice with an emphasis on the London stage and, as in other areas of the arts, black voices were still severely marginalised.

Furthermore, attendances were still falling and some theatres were faced with closure. Competition from popular music and television intensified the financial pressures. Although many plays were highly original and well written, the complex arguments and language of radical drama were sometimes difficult to appreciate. And because many plays could not be easily enjoyed by a non-specialised public, there was a feeling that drama was becoming too radical and specialised, and at the same time remote from society.

Musicals

During the mid-1960s in America, Galt MacDermot, Gerome Ragni and James Rado had created *Hair*, a successful musical. *Hair* used elements of rock music, circus and dance. It was cheeky, confident and impudent. It captured the mood of the times, announcing the imminent arrival of a new age – the 'age of Aquarius' – and its associated values of liberality and freedom.

In 1968 *Hair* opened in London and was an immediate success. It was also the first time that nudity had been seen in a theatrical production. Critics were circumspect, however. Some claimed the shows were blasphemous and pornographic, which generated even more publicity and interest. Others remarked that the nudity and swearing were carefully adjusted to shock nobody. The nudity of many performances in the late 1960s and early 1970s reflected the increased tolerance shown by the 1968 Theatres Act, which removed the need for licences for individual plays. The era of the 'permissive society' had arrived and 'anything goes' quickly became a cliché of the times.

Several other shows with nudity, song and dance appeared, such as *Oh! Calcutta!* (1969, Kenneth Tynan) and *Godspell* (1971, Steven Schwarz). Since then, the format has been successfully exploited in Britain by Tim Rice and Andrew Lloyd-Webber in musicals which have been popular around the world. Their *Jesus Christ Superstar* (1971) combined rock with religion to make a modern version of the story of Jesus. It built on the success of *Joseph and the Amazing Technicolour Dreamcoat* (1968), another biblical drama, and attracted huge audiences of young people. The duo had another big success with *Evita* (1978), which tells the story of the Argentinean 'first lady' Eva Peron.

The new musicals proved highly successful and many of those involved with them continued to exploit their success. In 1981 Lloyd-Webber went solo to make *Cats*, which celebrated poems from T.S. Eliot's *Old Possum's Book of Practical Cats*. Then came *Starlight Express* (1984), a train race on roller-skates, and *Phantom of the Opera* (1986), which tells the story of a disfigured composer who haunts an opera house and falls in love with a beautiful singer. The colourful, high-tech stage sets with accessible lyrics, lively music and energetic dancing guaranteed their popularity and made enormous profits. These and other shows quickly transferred to New York's Broadway and to theatres around the world where they have been successful for many years.

In the 1990s, these and other 'classic' musicals continued to draw the public. New ones such as Richard Eyre's *Guys and Dolls* (1982) and the Royal Shakespeare Company's production of *Les Misérables* (1985), directed by Trevor Nunn, attracted large audiences. More shows were imported from the United States, such as *Follies* by Steven Sondheim, which opened in London in 1987, and *A Walk in the Park with George* two years later.

In the 1990s almost half the total number of productions showing in the West End were musicals, a record number. Their combination of stories and songs, and the absence of political themes or difficult dialogue have proved popular with British audiences and overseas visitors. But despite their commercial success, many critics remain unenthusiastic. They refuse to take seriously a form of entertainment which mixes technology and pop songs, in which the actors could be changed without affecting the show.

Theatre and Thatcherism

In the 1980s the Conservative Government began to be much less generous towards the arts than any previous administration. Provoked by the oppositional nature of most productions, in 1982 the Secretary General of the Arts Council asked why artists should 'expect public money to advocate the overthrow, not of the particular party in power, but of the whole system of parliamentary democracy.' As a result, political dramas tended to become less shocking and more moderate.

Radical, alternative theatre groups such as 7:84 (7 per cent of the population hold 84 per cent of the wealth in Britain) and others, continued to write plays and tour. But they lost financial support from the Arts Council and many disappeared. As the government began to fully expose the theatre to market forces, the years of critical, state-subsidised theatre for the people appeared to be over.

One of the most highly praised writers of the time was David Hare. His career began in the late 1960s and, as he matured, his plays reflected his interests in social behaviour and political ideas. *A Map of the World* (1983) looks at issues of poverty and exploitation in the Third World. Between 1985 and 1991 he focussed on aspects of British society with four 'state of the nation' plays which took a close look at British institutions: the Church, the legal system, Parliament and the 'fourth estate' of the press.

The first of these was *Pravda: A Fleet Street Comedy* (1985), which was co-authored by Howard Brenton and deals with corruption of the mass media by their rich owners. The second was *Secret Rapture* (1988), which contrasts a female Conservative Member of Parliament with her unambitious, 'good' sister. In the third play, *Racing Demon* (1990), Hare examines the Church of England in a time of crisis. The fourth play, *Murmuring Judges* (1991), looks at the legal system and its weaknesses. It goes into the law courts and a busy South London police station, where the professionals are involved in their daily routine. Although these plays are not satires, they emphasise the comical aspects of public life in Britain. But they also discuss deeper questions, such as how one can do good in the world and how difficult it can be to do so. The plays were widely praised by the public and critics, and were among the most highly rated dramas of their time.

Other plays of the decade which were strongly critical of particular elements of the government's policies included David Edgar's *Maydays* (1983) and Howard Brenton's *The Genius* (1983). These took nuclear weapons as their theme and featured the Greenham Common nuclear base in Britain. Louise Page's *Falkland Sound* (1983) deals with the Falklands War and, following the crisis over the publishing of Salman Rushdie's *Satanic Verses*, Howard Brenton wrote *Iranian Nights* (1989) with Tariq Ali in support of the freedom of expression in literature.

The 'troubles' in Ireland continued without an obvious solution. In the past, Irish playwrights such as Brendan Behan had demanded radical action, but towards the end of the 1980s approaches were more tentative. The Irish playwright Brian Friel has written several plays dealing with the 'troubles'. *Freedom of the City* (1973) was an early work showing the situation in Northern Ireland of 1970, where British troops were stationed. But his later play *Translations* (1980) laments the process of anglicisation in his native country. It is set in the imaginary town of Baile Beag/Ballybeg, County Donegal, in 1833. British forces arrive to make a map of the area, anglicising the place names and defining it in ways which are foreign to the Irish-speaking natives. Its critical position shows the British as an occupying power which brutally robs Ireland of its Celtic identity, and suggests that the British and Irish will always be separated by cultural differences. His *Making History* (1988) explores how history is written and order is imposed on disordered themes and subjects, while the nostalgic play *Dancing at Lughnasa* (1990) looks back to his childhood in Catholic rural Ireland, as well as to the internal troubles in the North. In 1998 it was made into a successful film.

Building on their success in the 1970s, several promising young women playwrights began to emerge. One is Clare McIntyre, who writes humorous, observant feminist plays, such as *I've Been Waiting* (1986) which shows what she sees as the confusion, anxieties and obsessions of modern women. In contrast, Sarah Daniels' plays are more controversial. Like McIntyre, her plays depict women's issues, but her female characters are often strong, angry and complex. Men rarely appear in her plays, except when abusing a position of power. Her most critically acclaimed work is *Masterpieces* (1984) which deals with pornography, violence and lesbianism.

Caryl Churchill

Since she began her career in 1958, Caryl Churchill has had sustained success. Some of her most acclaimed works were performed in the 1980s and 1990s and included plays for radio, television and the stage. They introduce themes of importance to women and to women's consciousnes and combine her feminist interests with socialist politics. She is also respected for her intelligence, wit and skill in presenting plays. She experiments and re-invents with drama, but at the same time writes works which are popular with the general public and critics.

Vinegar Tom (1978) and *Light Shining in Buckinghamshire* (1978) are both feminist works which dealt with bodily abuse through alcohol, eating disorders and violence. *Cloud Nine* (1979) examines in role-plays how race and gender are socially constructed, and shocked the audience with its transvestite performers. But *Top Girls* (1982) is one of her best-known plays. Marlene, the protagonist, progresses from humble origins to become a successful career woman. She has left behind Angie, the child she had at the age of 17, and towards the end of the play, she returns to visit her articulate but poor, unambitious sister Joyce, who has taken on the role of Angie's mother. Its feminist message is that if women simply imitate men and male behaviour, then the women's movement will achieve nothing. Instead, women must find another, more original path. This is a theme common to several of her works in the 1980s and echoes the arguments of modern feminism.

The dynamic *Serious Money* (1987) shows the loss of liberal values in society, and an increasing public amorality and selfishness. It looks at the ways in which London money dealers become morally corrupt following deregulation of the stock market and became one of the most successful plays of the 1980s. But *Mad Forest: A Play from Rumania* (1990) has a quite different focus. It was written after a trip to Romania, weeks after the fall of the President Ceauşescu, and considers the new realities of life following the revolution there. The play was highly praised by drama critics and confirmed Caryl Churchill as Britain's leading female play-wright.

Comedy

During the 1970s and 1980s playwrights such as Alan Ayckbourn, Tom Stoppard, Neil Simon, Michael Frayn and Alan Bennett wrote some of the most highly praised comedies of the decade. Bennett has become known for his humorous use of language which often mixes provincial slang with the jargon of media and advertising. He established his reputation with plays such as *Habeus Corpus* (1973), a farce which includes traditional characters such as a henpecked husband, a frustrated wife, a sex-mad vicar and an everyday tea-lady. In *Enjoy* (1980) he wittily depicts the predicament of an elderly couple who occupy the last old terraced house in Leeds. A keen social observer, many of his works are inspired by his northern roots and frequently depict the traditional Yorkshire character and domestic life, such as the series *Talking Heads*, created for the stage and two television series in 1988 and 1998.

Alan Ayckbourn

Alan Ayckbourn became one of the most popular playwrights of the 1980s. His characters are often sad, pathetic individuals who are usually male. This has made Ayckbourn popular with feminists, but he does not declare his feminism openly; the same is true of his socialism. His sharp satirical portrayals of the manners, behaviour and language of the lower middle-classes were easily appreciated at a time when individualism and bourgeois values were strongly expressed in the politics of the Conservative Government. His humorous plays suggest a dislike of status-seekers and people who openly desire wealth. Some of the bleakest moments in his plays are reserved for these characters.

One of his best-known works is *Absurd Person Singular* (1972), which shows three married couples in three different kitchens on three different Christmas Eves. A woman attempts to kill herself, but visitors to her house do not realise and proceed to repair the gas oven and fix the electric light. *Joking Apart* (1978) is especially inventive, showing four scenes on four special occasions. Each one is four years apart and therefore, seen over twelve years, the protagonists pass from their 20s to their 30s. In contrast, *It Could Be One of Us* (1983) is a comedy thriller with five different endings.

During the 1980s, he wrote several highly-praised 'social' dramas, which contrasted with his familiar domestic comedies. The most admired of these was *A Small Family Business* (1987), in which a nation of shop-keepers becomes a nation of shoplifters in a family furniture firm of 'Ayres and Graces', whose members are implicated in drugs, murder and corruption.

Ayckbourn began his career at a provincial theatre in Scarborough on the north-east coast of England. Since then he has written over fifty plays which have been performed in London theatres, on television, in film and around the world. In the 1990s, Ayckbourn holds a privileged position as director and playwright at the Steven Joseph Theatre in Scarborough. But the local young, old and disabled also make plays for its stages, as Ayckbourn believes that the theatre should belong to the entire community, not only to a small middle-class community.

'Alternative' comedy

One of the more surprising developments of the early 1980s was the emergence of 'alternative' comedy. This has its origins in a small theatre (called the Comedy Store) in London's Soho, where members of the public were given the opportunity to tell jokes on stage until they were forced to leave by the jeers of a critical audience.

The new comedy was fresh and original. Both male and female comedians delivered commentaries, parodies and jokes which rejected conventional humour about sex, race and religion. Instead, they satirised traditional male behaviour and stereotyped attitudes towards social, racial and sexual matters. Comedians cultivated an individual style in presentations which were energetic, urgent and explicit. They quickly became popular and many comedy theatres and clubs opened around Britain.

The original Store also had a repertory company, known as Comic Strip. Members included actors and comedians such as Alexei Sayle, Rik Mayall, Robbie Coltrane, Ben Elton, Dawn French and Jennifer Saunders. Many had subsequent success writing and acting on television and in the cinema. Its popularity among young audiences led to the description 'the new rock'n'roll'. Others called it the new 'Alcoholics Anonymous' because it seemed to offer a secret forum where truths could be told confidentially. From the late 1980s it became an established form of entertainment, with frequent live shows on television and in small theatres around Britain.

Children's comedy: pantomime

One of the most traditional forms of entertainment for children around Britain is pantomime. It takes the form of a play which is performed during the Christmas period, and has a long history. The art originated in the eighteenth century with John Weaver, a dance master at the Drury Lane Theatre in London. He began to present ballet-like entertainments in which the meaning was conveyed by gestures instead of dialogue. It is based on *commedia dell'arte*, a style of comedy which flourished in Italy from the mid-sixteenth to the mid-eighteenth century.

In nineteenth-century England it began to acquire its present form, in which lively, colourful stories are told with music, singing and dancing. Fairy stories and Oriental tales are among the most common, and traditional titles include *Aladdin*, *Cinderella*, *Puss in Boots*, *Dick Whittington* and *Snow White*. They include irrelevant routines and topical jokes, which inspire children and their parents to loudly shout and cheer. The role of an older woman is traditionally played by a man who is known as a 'Dame'. The Dame is often the hero's mother, while the hero or 'Principal Boy' is played by a young woman. The roles are often taken by celebrities from television, sports or light entertainment, and plays are performed in theatres around the country.

Trends in theatre today

In Scotland the decade began with a frenzy of activity following the decision in 1987 to make Glasgow the 1990 European City of Culture. The city invested heavily in the arts in order to develop a modern, progressive image. Experimental productions were among the chief beneficiaries and some were staged in unusual venues, such as a former tram shed.

Plays were varied and eclectic. *Border Warfare* by John McGrath showed 2,000 years of Scottish history. Tom McGrath's *City* was a community play involving actors from all parts of Glasgow. Liz Lochhead's *Jock Tamson's Bairns*, a 'state of the nation' play, was constructed around the annual Burn's Night Supper. The *Ship* by Bill Bryden was staged in a shipyard and nostalgically remembered the construction of the *Queen Elizabeth II*, the last ocean liner built there. But in spite of the quality and novelty of many productions, there was no finance available for the continued support of the new theatre groups, and many disappeared.

But a short distance away in Edinburgh, the annual arts festival continued to be the biggest of its kind in Europe. Drama is its most important element and the festival 'fringe' offers a platform for alternative and more experimental types. These are characterised by surprise, excitement and originality. The venues are diverse – from church halls to playgrounds – and plays are watched by audiences ranging from two men and a dog to several thousand spectators. Festival productions are not limited to Scottish works and influences are drawn from all around Britain and the world.

With the economic recession at the beginning of the 1990s, there was a feeling of caution and conservatism which extended throughout the decade. Commercial theatres did not want to take risks with new productions, and preferred those that were established favourites. The trend continued and in 1996 45 per cent of West End shows were musicals. Several were established shows from the 1970s and 1980s: among them were *Guys and Dolls*, *Jesus Christ Superstar* and the rock musical *Tommy*. They were popular with tourists, for whom the music and spectacle may have been more important than the lyrics and themes. At the same time, plays were also being made of successful films and books, such as Irvine Welsh's *Trainspotting* and Nick Hornby's *Fever Pitch*. But only 10 per cent of shows were of modern drama and for the first time in forty years it was virtually impossible to find a play with a political message on a London stage.

Playwrights with Afro-Caribbean or Asian roots continued to write new plays. The themes of Caryl Phillips, Hanif Kureishi, Derek Walcott, Winsome Pinnock and Farrukh Dhondy reflected their experience of cultural change and racial identity. Many were adapted into successful television plays or screenplays for the cinema. But in 1998 there were only two London theatres which regularly staged black plays. Critics believed this was not because black perspectives were being ignored, but because cultural differences were becoming increasingly unclear; more black actors were appearing in classical productions and musicals, in roles traditionally played by white actors, and works by black writers were becoming more 'mainstream', addressing themes other than race and marginalisation.

One of the greatest influences on theatre of recent years has been growing financial pressure. This has created a tendency for writers to write plays for television more than the stage. At a time when the amount of theatre work was diminishing, the development of television as a business provided more creative possibilities and greater remuneration, and many actors preferred to work in television for the same reasons.

Today there are many writers still keen to create plays for the theatre, but new works are rarely profitable unless they are by well-known dramatists, such as Tom Stoppard or Alan Ayckbourn. They are usually on a very small scale and shown in small halls and studio theatres. This is partly to keep down production costs, particularly in London where the costs of

75

running a theatre have escalated greatly. It is also because the public have become unwilling to buy expensive tickets without an assurance that they will enjoy the production. This and the associated costs of details such as meals, drinks, car parking, the strict laws on drinking and driving, as well as the competition from television and other home entertainments, have all made the public more cost-conscious and only willing to pay high prices to see established works and fine acting.

But in spite of its difficulties, there continues to be generous coverage of new developments in the form of reviews and comment on new plays. Critical opinion towards the end of the 1990s looks back not with anger at the last forty years, but with positive feelings about drama's ability to capture the spirit of the times, and a realistic hope that it will continue to build on the strengths of its heritage.

Tom Stoppard

Tom Stoppard is one of the most consistently successful and critically acclaimed playwrights of recent years. He was born in Czechoslovakia, but settled and worked in Britain. He is an eclectic writer who does not limit himself to one subject matter or style, and his plays have little in common with each other.

Rosencrantz and Guildenstern are Dead (1967) is his best-known work and has become one of the most critically praised plays of this century. Its two protagonists are incidental characters from Shakespeare's play *Hamlet*. Stoppard brings them to the centre of the action where they talk in language similar to Beckett's characters in *Waiting for Godot*. The situation of the two men offers many dramatic and comic possibilities, as they only know what they are told and nothing else. The play is like a series of sketches between two stand-up comedians. It shows how people attempt to create a pattern in a chaotic world, and how this is difficult when truth is never singular and final, but always relative.

His plays mix frivolity with intellectual content and often express it in a literary way, playing tricks with the audience's perceptions. In 1968, *The Real Inspector Hound* featured theatre critics who become part of the play. In *The Real Thing* (1982) there is a play within a play. In *Jumpers* (1972), *Travesties* (1974) and *Arcadia* (1993), Stoppard mixes playful, cheeky verbal games with profound ideas.

Some of his best works show his outrage at violations of human rights. *Night and Day* (1978) considers the role of a free press and human rights in a totalitarian society. *Squaring the Circle* (1984) and *Professional Foul* (1984) deal with similar themes. *Dirty Linen* (1977) is a critique of corruption in Parliament, while *Arcadia* (1993) and *Indian Ink* (1995) use double time-schemes to consider life in English country houses and the days of the British rule in India.

As well as writing plays, he has also directed, and written extensively for film, radio and television. His many works are widely studied and presented, and in the 1990s he was critically praised as a dramatist of world renown.

Discussion topics and activities

1 Identify some of the main themes and influences expressed by British playwrights since the mid-1950s. Which period or style do you find the most interesting?
2 Summarise some of the main differences between theatre in your country and theatre in Britain. Try to consider issues such as themes, movements, the representation of women and minorities, censorship, finance and audiences.
3 Could some of the new movements such as gay theatre and alternative comedy be successful in your country? Give reasons why/why not.
4 Do you think plays should be written to shock, or should they be written to entertain?
5 Describe and give examples of the following: pantomime / musicals / radical drama / theatre of the absurd / kitchen sink drama.
6 Imagine a particular dramatic situation, perhaps one you have experienced. Write a short summary of it, then a description of the scene, the characters, and a short piece of dramatic dialogue.

Suggested further reading

Books

Aldgate, A. (1995) *Censorship and the Permissive Society* Oxford: Oxford University Press.
Berney, K.A. (ed.) (1994) *Contemporary British Dramatists* Andover: St James Press.
Beauman, S. (1982) *The Royal Shakespeare Company* Oxford: Oxford University Press.
Boose, L. and Burt, R. (eds) (1997) *Shakespeare, The Movie: Popularising the Plays on Film, Television and Video* London: Routledge.
Callow, S. (1995) *Being an Actor* London: Penguin.
Cameron, A. (ed.) (1990) *Scot-free: New Scottish Plays* London: Nick Hearn.
Churchill, C. (1990) *Shorts* (10 short plays) London: Nick Hearn.
De Jong, N. (1992) *Not in Front of the Audience: Homosexuality on Stage* London: Routledge.
Hanna, G. (ed.) (1991) *Monstrous Regiment: A Collective Celebration* (5 plays) London: Nick Hearn.
Lacey, S. (1995) *British Realist Theatre: The New Wave in its Context 1956–65* London: Routledge.

Morgan, F. (ed.) (1994) *The Years Between: Plays by Women on the London Stage 1900–1950* (5 plays) London: Virago.

Osment, P. (ed.) (1989) *The Gay Sweatshop: Four Plays and a Company* London: Methuen.

Shepherd, S. and Womack, P. (1996) *English Drama: A Cultural History* London: Blackwell.

Shank, T. (1994) *Contemporary British Theatre* Basingstoke: Macmillan.

Trussler, S. (1994) *The Cambridge Illustrated History of British Theatre* Cambridge: Cambridge University Press.

Wickham, G. (1994) *A History of the Theatre* Oxford: Phaidon Press.

There are also numerous anthologies of English literature which include chapters/sections on British theatre. A. Sanders' *The Short Oxford History of English Literature* (Oxford: Oxford University Press, 1994) contains a very clear and well-written account.

Journals

For comment on earlier works, see *Plays and Players*, especially for the period 1950–80, which carries extensive post-war British theatre criticism. For more recent works, see *The London Theatre Record* (1981–91), a leading journal of theatre criticism, which carries reviews of all major works of the period. In 1991 it became *The Theatre Record* (1991–).

5

Cinema

Introduction

Film-making has existed in Britain for over a century and in recent years it has become one of the most fashionable and creative areas of cultural life. Some of the best-loved and most highly-praised films are adaptations of classic novels, which have a reputation without equal for attention to details of dress, decor and setting. But the making of films in a simple, direct way about people's daily lives is perhaps its greatest strength. The 'documentary' style was developed in Britain and has influenced film-making around the world, while naturalistic films by directors such as Ken Loach and Mike Leigh are among the most highly praised.

In spite of its successes, the film industry has suffered from a lack of investment. Since the 1950s British film-makers have been unable to compete with the extravagant productions made by the wealthy Hollywood studios. The government does not invest large sums in film and for many years film-makers had to rely on the success of popular commercial genres, such as spy thrillers, horror and comedy. Consequently, some professionals have preferred to work in America, with the world presence of the major studios, plus the promise of big film budgets and earnings. The actor Charlie Chaplin and director Alfred Hitchcock were among the first to work in Hollywood, where their careers flourished.

Film-making in Britain is heavily centralised around the south-east of England, but its commercial heart is the central London district of Soho, where film production companies, publicity agencies and related trades have their offices. The majority of studios are based in outer London.

Pinewood and Shepperton are among the most established, and the new ones of Leavesden, Radlett and Three Mills are among the largest.

The majority of films are shown in cinema chains such as Warner, Virgin and Odeon, which are found all over Britain. They provide a total of approximately 2,200 screens and offer popular, well-publicised films to audiences of around 2.5 million per week. Productions of more limited interest are usually shown in 'art-house' or repertory cinemas, or on Channel 4 television. These screens offer more specialised programmes, such as short 'seasons' on a particular topic, as well as older films and films in foreign languages.

A growing number of courses in many colleges and universities offer training for careers in film and television. The National Film and Television School is one of the most respected institutions and is financed by the government, together with the film, video and television industries. A related organisation is the British Film Institute, which was founded in 1933 to encourage the arts of film and television. It has some thirty-five regional film theatres and incorporates film councils for Scotland, Ireland and Wales, as well as the National Film and Television Archive and the National Film Theatre (NFT).

All public cinemas are licensed by the local authorities. These have powers to prevent the showing of a picture if they believe it would be unsuitable. However, they generally follow the recommendations of the British Board of Film Classification (BBFC). This is a government body, established in 1912 to examine and classify material for public entertainment. It currently classifies more than 4,000 films per year and attempts to reflect public opinion by following a 'line' between the traditional moralists on the political right and progressive libertarians on the left. But critics complain that the British Board is among the strictest in Europe and demand that its secret reports be made available to the public.

The current system was introduced in 1982: 'U' films are open to everyone and 'Uc' films are especially suitable for children; those with 'PG' suggest parental guidance; '15' and '18' films are open respectively to those aged 15 and 18 years and over; R18 is a classification reserved for soft pornographic material and sex films, which can only be shown in special cinemas. The Video Recordings Act of 1984 subjects video material to the same requirements. Video rental is common in Britain, where some five million are hired each week.

In a major ceremony, the British Academy of Film and Television Arts (BAFTA) makes awards each year to films from around the world. Two other important events are the London Film Festival in November and the Edinburgh Film Festival in August. Both take place annually and show some 250 films which are often complemented with talks and interviews by international specialists. There are also several smaller annual events around the country, such as the Celtic film festival, which takes place in a different town each year.

Pioneers

Making movies in Britain began towards the end of the nineteenth century. At that time, there were no commercial cinemas and films were shown in fairgrounds, shops, theatres, schools and even in the open air. They were short, silent and often presented by the people who made them. Many were of humorous incidents, views or perhaps a brief record of some major event, such as a ship launch. But cinema of today has its origins in the mid-1920s when, after interruption during the First World War, a new generation of film-makers appeared. These included the directors Victor Saville and Alfred Hitchcock, producer Michael Balcon and stars such as Ivor Novello and Fay Compton. By the 1930s, the success of Hitchcock's thrillers had made him the most important director in Britain.

In 1929 Hitchcock directed the first British 'talkie', *Blackmail*. After the arrival of films with sound, cinema audiences grew fast and a small industry expanded to meet demand. But British productions were still relatively unknown abroad. This began to change with Alexander Korda's comedy *The Private Life of Henry VIII* (1933), which was a major success in America and became the first British picture to win an Oscar. Historical themes, together with adaptations of literary classics, soon became one of the most admired and respected styles of British film-making.

But the arrival of the Second World War interrupted progress. Most studios closed, while a few continued to make films for propaganda purposes. These aimed to encourage patriotic feeling and boost national morale. Several were documentaries, such as *London Can Take It* (Harry Watts, 1940) and *Listen to Britain* (Humphrey Jennings, 1941). Others were feature films, such as *In Which We Serve* (Noel Coward and David Lean, 1942), *Millions Like Us* (Frank Launder, 1943) and *The Shipbuilders* (John Baxter, 1944).

Early representations of Britain at war showed leading actors such as John Mills, Noel Coward and later Kenneth Moore demonstrating courage, strength and a stiff upper lip in adverse conditions. They provided influential role-models for the heroes of later war films, such as *The Cruel Sea* (Charles Frend, 1952), *The Dam Busters* (Michael Anderson, 1955) and *Reach for the Sky* (Lewis Gilbert, 1956). Such films reassured the post-war public: they gave moral justification to combat, romanticised war heroism and made audiences feel both proud and relieved. The immediate post-war period was a time of social tranquillity, as government and all sections of society worked together for the common good. There were few popular distractions and television was still an expensive novelty. The cinema became the main source of entertainment, in which the fantasy, romance and escapism of American films represented a post-war land of 'milk and honey.'

However, at Ealing Studios in West London, producer Michael Balcon preferred to ignore the influence of Hollywood and promote a more realist and characteristically British film industry. One of the best-known films to emerge from Ealing was the police drama *Blue Lamp* (Basil Dearden, 1950). It was a popular tribute to law, order and stability, which captured the mood of the era. It showed a paternal, protective police force and a calm, cohesive community, in which the chief character, P.C. George Dixon, was almost a sacred figure. The highly successful film led to its adaptation as a long-running television series, *Dixon of Dock Green*.

But Ealing Studios became better known for their distinctive comedy films. These have entered film history as nostalgic, detailed portraits of post-war Britain: a genteel country of friendly policemen, maiden aunts, village shopkeepers and numerous eccentrics who challenge conventional society and ridicule pomposity. Titles include *Kind Hearts and Coronets* (1949), a satire of upper-class manners, and *Passport to Pimlico* (1949), a humorous critique of British bureaucracy. *The Lavender Hill Mob* (Charles Crichton, 1951) is one of the most famous. It features a mild-mannered bank clerk who plans a gold-bullion robbery, eventually disguising the loot as Eiffel Tower paperweights. The Ealing style is especially noted for its fine 'character' performances, clever scripts and empathy for individuals who oppose big business and challenge the social order. It subsequently influenced numerous comedy films and television series, and is fondly remembered as a cosy celebration of English individuality.

Documentary film-making

One of the most characteristic types of British film is the documentary. This style of film-making began in the 1930s, when Scottish film-maker John Grierson (1898–1972) pioneered new techniques. Grierson wanted to make authentic records of everyday life and was the first to use the term 'documentary' to describe a style of film.

Grierson strongly believed that film-makers had a duty to reveal and describe society in order to understand and improve it. To achieve his aim, he worked with the government, making dignified, creative studies of different industries and workers in Britain and the British Empire. These included *Coal Face* (1935) and *Night Mail* (1936). Grierson's work quickly became influential, establishing objective, impartial techniques and the 'documentary' as a film genre. His later work demonstrated more social and environmental concern and included examinations of unemployment, pollution, education, health and housing. He also pioneered the use of interviews in film, using the camera to record the words of those directly involved.

Since the 1960s documentary techniques have become more common in television, where journalists and news reporters use them as essential investigative tools. In film, realism and authenticity evolved into free cinema, whose pioneers Lindsay Anderson and Karel Reisz explored authentic, natural aspects of British society. Among their first works were Anderson's *O Dreamland* (1953), about a day in the seaside town of Margate, and Reisz's *We are the Lambeth Boys* (1958), about an East London youth club. At first the public was bemused, but enjoyed seeing themselves and their lives represented in film.

Social realism

Interest in social life and its authentic representation was also present in theatre and literature. Between 1956 and 1959 the works of many new playwrights and authors such as John Osborne, Colin Wilson and John Braine attracted critical interest. Between 1959 and 1963 several of their novels and plays were adapted for the cinema which explored the reality of the British working class: their thoughts, language, living conditions and aspirations. Their works examined the changing nature of society: how increased affluence was leading to greater individuality, less idealism and a reduced sense of social responsibility.

The film adaptations were generally faithful to the novels, with films set in provincial, grey northern towns. They focussed on ordinary people in their natural surroundings, in small, sparsely furnished terraced houses, in the factories and the pubs. Actors forgot their drama-school RP accents and spoke in the regional vernacular to convey a sense of life, energy and authenticity. *Look Back in Anger* (Tony Richardson, 1959), *Room at the Top* (Jack Clayton, 1959), *Saturday Night, Sunday Morning* (Tony Richardson, 1961) and *A Kind of Loving* (John Schlesinger, 1962) were among the first and most highly praised of a body of work which became known as 'new cinema' or 'new wave'.

Richardson's *Saturday Night, Sunday Morning* was adapted from a novel by Alan Sillitoe and remains one of the most representative. It is set in a small Nottinghamshire town, where Arthur Seaton (played by Albert Finney), a hard-drinking, hard-fighting, virile young man, rebels against the tedium and restrictions of his marriage and his work. But, unlike many older members of his community, he has no political beliefs or ideology and is shown as alienated; detached from his own people and disinterested in political ideas.

The new wave introduced a new style of film-making. It was one without theory or glamour and therefore very different from the fantasy and escapism of Hollywood productions. Here were the first authentic representations of working-class life, depicting as a nightmare the reality of being trapped in the provinces with a wife and children. Films were usually in black and white, with little lighting. Modern jazz, pop music and silence were all employed to support the action.

The older generation of cinema-goers found the new films worrying and confusing, and many stopped going to the cinema. With declining audiences, competition from Hollywood and television, and little financial help from the government, the survival of the film industry depended on the profits from popular domestic genres which were made to attract the new teenage market.

The magnetism of youth

From the mid-1950s a new generation of teenagers and young single adults was emerging with its own fantasies and desires in film. The industry responded with films made specifically for young audiences: comedy, horror, sex, violence and the occasional literary adaptation were all common. Film-makers argued that their works reflected an increasingly liberal, permissive society. Increased affluence, the emergence of youth culture, the gradual emancipation of female sexuality and rising rates of crime and violence all supported their case.

Following its arrival in the mid-1950s, rock'n'roll music was also heavily exploited in film. The explosive rhythms in *Rock Around the Clock* (Fred Sears, 1956) led to riots in the cinemas. There were media reports of violence and hysteria among the teenage public and a delirium previously only generated by certain types of religious experience. American films featuring Elvis Presley were enormously popular with teenage audiences and British studios responded with musicals featuring English singers Cliff Richard and Tommy Steele, among others. These were undistinguished except in commercial terms. But their popularity ensured that films became important features in the career of many successful pop stars.

It was the Beatles who brought a measure of critical interest to the 'pop' musical. Their film *A Hard Day's Night* (Richard Lester, 1964) was an enormous commercial and critical success, on which *Help!* (Richard Lester, 1965) and the animated, surreal musical *Yellow Submarine* (George Dunning, 1968) subsequently built. These films helped to make popular music not just the 'property' of youth, but a kind of entertainment which was acceptable and accessible to all the family.

The mid-1960s was a turbulent time in which old certainties were challenged and became eroded. Traditional ideas about class, politics, drugs, sexuality and the place of women were all being interrogated in society and the arts. Some films were based on plays and novels which depicted the fashionable lifestyles of the young and beautiful. *Darling* (John Schlesinger, 1965), *Alfie* (Lewis Gilbert, 1966) and *Georgy Girl* (Silvio Narizzano, 1966), captured London's mood and the magic of a city in which a social revolution in attitudes and values seemed to be taking place.

One of the most unusual films to challenge conventional attitudes towards class and sexuality was *The Servant* (Joseph Losey, 1963), in which a Cockney manservant changes roles with his effeminate, aristocratic master. Although there is a suggestion of blackmail and repressed homosexuality, this tale by Harold Pinter (adapted from a novel by Robert

Maugham) does not deal with it openly, but uses broken dialogue, trivial conversation and silence to reflect the tension between the characters. Much angrier and more direct was Lindsay Anderson's *If …* (1968), which criticises the elitism, arrogance and cruelty of the public-school system. It is set in an exclusive but old-fashioned private school, where pupil Mick Travers (Malcolm MacDowell) leads a student rebellion with machine-guns and hand-grenades against the school authorities, in a film which often resembles the American *Rebel Without a Cause* (1955).

Women were also becoming more liberated and less confined by convention. An interrogation of women's traditional roles was depicted in a number of films which were set in a liberated, permissive, 'swinging' London. The new image could be seen in the leading roles played by Rita Tushingham in *A Taste of Honey* (Tony Richardson, 1962), Julie Christie in *Billy Liar* (John Schlesinger, 1963) and *Darling* (John Schlesinger, 1965), and later with Judy Geeson in *Here We Go Round the Mulberry Bush* (Clive Donner, 1968). Their roles ignored the traditional roles of marriage and childbearing, and instead emphasised freedom, innocence and sex appeal.

The speed and excitement of social change began to attract foreign film-makers, such as Michelangelo Antonioni, Jean-Luc Godard and François Truffaut. The public loved their extravagant, modish films which captured the mood of the moment. But the most successful were those already resident, such as Roman Polanski with *Repulsion* (1965) and *Cul-de-Sac* (1966), and Richard Lester with the Beatles films plus *The Knack … and How to Get It* (1965). Michelangelo Antonioni's *Blow Up* (1966) about a photographer involved in a London of drugs and parties, captured the atmosphere of the times and became a fashionable 'cult' film of the period.

The American director Stanley Kubrick has made numerous films in Britain. His works during the 1960s and 1970s were among the most stylish and critically praised, and included *Lolita* (1962) and *2001: A Space Odyssey* (1968). But his most notorious work was *A Clockwork Orange* (1971), in which violent, make-up wearing gangs enjoy a disturbing life of crime, sex, violence and Beethoven, which the state attempts to correct by brainwashing techniques and thought-control. Although it was adapted from Anthony Burgess's 1962 novel, which recalled allegedly true events of twenty years previously, the time of the action remains unclear. In the words of the protagonist Alex (Malcolm MacDowell) it is 'just as soon as you could imagine it, but not too far ahead – it's just not today, that's all.' But in the turbulent times of the early 1970s, it appeared to accurately document England's present. One of the most disturbing and controversial films ever shown in or about Britain, Kubrick withdrew it soon afterwards, following alleged copycat violence and demands that scenes be cut.

Popular genres

After the austerity of the post-war years, young audiences found the sex, style, excitement and escapism in many 1960s films novel and thrilling. When mixed with the themes of spying and Cold War tension, the result was the James Bond films. Many are adaptations of the thirteen thrillers written by Ian Fleming, which first appeared in 1952 with *Casino Royale*. In literary terms they were generally undistinguished, but the screen adaptations supplied a highly commercial combination of glamour, gadgets and exotic locations, in which the hero saved his exotic girlfriend and the world from evil despots with Eastern European accents.

The cocktail of ingredients was no more complicated than Bond's favourite Martini, and proved just as popular. Almost half of the world's population has seen a James Bond film, a series which began in 1962 with *Doctor No* (Terence Young), in which Sean Connery (a Scot) played the leading role. Since then the most famous secret agent in English fiction has been played by George Lazenby (Australian), Roger Moore (English), Timothy Dalton (Welsh) and Pierce Brosnan (Irish). But after some twenty-five years of the Bond formula, public interest began to decline. The disappearance of the Cold War, greater equality for women and popular

Figure 5.1 The classic Bond film *Goldfinger*, starring Sean Connery

tourism to exotic destinations left it looking tired and old-fashioned. However, in the mid-1990s public interest began to revive, as Bond was reborn as a modern, progressive, 'new man' in *GoldenEye* (1995) and *Tomorrow Never Dies* (1997), which led to renewed popularity.

Other popular genres of the 1960s included adaptations of well-known television comedy series, such as *The Likely Lads*, *Till Death Us Do Part* and *Monty Python*. They offered comical and often cynical satires of modern social attitudes, and reflected issues which the public found funny. Together with the *Carry On ...* films, they were among the most commercially profitable of the 1960s and 1970s.

The *Carry On ...* comedies began in 1958 with *Carry On Sergeant*. They appeared almost annually until 1980 and regularly found enthusiastic young audiences. Individual performances were usually caricatures: a fat, unattractive wife with a weak, mousy husband; a large-breasted young woman; an effeminate idiot; and a vigorous young bachelor. Early films were frequently set in familiar locations. State institutions were most common, such as a school, hospital or the army. Inside, infantile innuendo and *double entendres* were used to ridicule and subvert the official routine and its guardians.

Figure 5.2 Carry On Up the Khyber

The *Carry On ...* films are clear descendants of the Ealing tradition created under Michael Balcon, and became some of the most popular films in the history of British cinema. Although they were ignored by critics for many years, they have recently been the subject of new evaluation by a generation of public and critics who enjoy their irony and kitsch. These elements also attracted young fans to many horror films made by the Hammer production company. Many were directed by the hand of Terence Fisher and starred Peter Cushing and Christopher Lee, such as *The Horror of Dracula* (1958). Early pictures created an atmosphere with shadows and suspense, but in the 1960s they became more explicit, with vivid depictions of blood, sexuality and violence, such as *Frankenstein Must Be Destroyed* (1969). Plots were typically set on dark nights in elaborate Gothic castles. Common themes included a struggle between good and evil, the familiar and the unknown, or involved a scientific discovery over which man has lost control. But their repetitive and heavily commercial nature made them unpopular with critics, who described them with adjectives such as camp, kitsch and exploitative. However, as with the *Carry On ...* films, an enthusiastic teenage public was unworried about critical opinion and ensured their survival until the 1970s.

In spite of some isolated successes, the 1960s were difficult years for British cinema, which was seen as creatively inferior to big-budget American productions and stylish European 'art' films. Low levels of finance from central government meant a heavy dependence on commercial genres and, by the end of the decade, many critics considered it almost dead, sunk by the popularity of television and the glamour of Hollywood.

The 1970s: spectacle and show

Faced with difficult conditions at the beginning of the decade, and competition from video systems as well as television, the film industry continued to make numerous safe, commercial productions. Many were historical dramas, such as *Young Winston, Cromwell* and *Mary Queen of Scots*, which were always popular with audiences overseas. There was little attempt to critically engage with contemporary social issues or to challenge the public, but a notable exception was Alan Parker's *Midnight Express* (1978). Based on a true story of drug-smuggling and imprisonment in Turkey, it became one of the most highly regarded works of its time and won many international awards.

Advances in technology allowed the creation of dramatic new special effects. But these made film-making increasingly complex, specialised and expensive, so production was often shared among various companies. There were several British and American collaborations to make extravagant science-fiction works, such as *2001: A Space Odyssey, Superman II* and the *Star Wars* trilogy. In contrast, the turbulent years of the 1970s also witnessed unexpected adult enthusiasm for the simplicity and cosiness of children's films, such as *Bugsy Malone*, *The Railway Children*, *Watership Down* and *The Tales of Beatrix Potter*.

Although cinema attendances had declined, youth was still a major audience and was easily attracted by films starring famous singers and rock bands. These had previously been light and populist, but material gradually became more imaginative and substantial. The Who appeared in *Tommy* (Ken Russell, 1975), an adaptation of their 1969 album, and again in *Quadrophenia* (Franc Roddam, 1979), a colourful exploration of the life and times of a frustrated young Mod immersed in London's youth culture of 1964. With this film, popular culture began to discover its own history. Similarly, *That'll Be the Day* (Claude Whatham, 1974) was the first major British film to look back at the 1950s, and followed the successful American pop musical *American Graffiti*.

Some musicians began to appear in non-musical feature films. The Rolling Stone's singer Mick Jagger appeared in *Performance* (Nicolas Roeg, Donald Cammell, 1970), an exploration of sexual, social and narcotic practices in the London of the late 1960s. David Bowie appeared in *The Man Who Fell to Earth* (Nicholas Roeg, 1976), playing an alien who travels to Earth, looking for a way to save his dying planet. This was a highly praised film which raised questions about corporate imperialism, as well as Britain's decline as a world power.

Although audiences of the 1950s had been shocked by teenage attitudes and behaviour, by the early 1970s films about rebellious youth were part of the mainstream cinema. The new issues of racism, women's rights and the 'troubles' in Northern Ireland were considered provocative, dangerous, unprofitable topics, and, in the tough economic climate, film companies did not want to address them. Instead, it was the innovative and daring independent sector which explored them further.

Alternative voices, new directions

Until the mid-1960s there had been no significant social critique or creative experimentation in British cinema. But students in the art schools and colleges gradually became interested in the potential of film. Soon, a movement began to appear: film co-operatives and collectives were established and a network of independent cinemas grew up. These were known as 'art-house' cinemas and showed films of a less populist, more specialised nature.

By 1976 independent film-makers were becoming more numerous and formed an association – the IFA – to share their resources and ideas. Their freedom from commercial pressures was important: it allowed them to make political and artistic films, which larger organisations and production companies would not touch. Themes included the radical politics of the 'new left' which included an agenda of feminism and anti-racism.

Racial tension escalated in many British inner cities during the mid-

1970s, but it still had not been addressed by black directors in full-length features until *Pressure* (Horace Ove, 1975). This was an independent production by two Trinidadians: Horace Ove and Samuel Selvon. The story showed the reality of being young and black in London during the 1970s, and chronicles the attempts of Tony, an intelligent black school-leaver, to find a job. It is set against a background of a failing education system, police brutality and black power. It also explores the growing differences between the West Indians who came to Britain during the 1950s and 1960s, and their British-born children.

By 1980 pictures about black British people were becoming much more angry, explicit and partisan. *Burning an Illusion* (Menelik Shabazz, 1981) explores black love and consciousness, as seen through the eyes of Pat, a black woman. *Babylon* (Franco Rosso and Martin Stellman, 1980) features young, British-born Afro-Caribbeans in London's East End. The film is rich in Jamaican creole and portrays an exotic world in which the thoughts and culture of young Rastafarians are expressed within a cloud of cannabis smoke and through a thunderous avalanche of reggae music. *Rude Boy* (Jack Hazan and David Mingay, 1980) angrily depicts two Englands: one of prosperity protected by large, corrupt police forces; the other of youth with no future, who participate in race riots, support neo-Facists and collapse after cocktails of drink and drugs at punk concerts.

As well as racial issues, films also began to express the new politics of feminism in works such as *Maeve* (Patricia Murphy and John Davies, 1981) and *Doll's Eye* (Jan Worth, 1982). They examined issues such as rape, violence, pornography and the representation of women in the media. These and many others of the time sharply depicted feminist issues and politics in a way that no other commercial medium dared to do.

During his lifetime, Derek Jarman was one of the most stylish avant-garde film-makers. His film *Jubilee* (1978) used the punk phenomenon to express the nightmarish reality of life in Britain during 1977, the year of Queen Elizabeth's Silver Jubilee celebrations (commemorating a reign of twenty-five years). The characters, music and film sets together project a horrific collage of shocking metaphors, which include the murder of a rich pop star, the use of Buckingham Palace as a recording studio, an orgy in Westminster Cathedral and the castration of a police officer. The film ignores the politics of left and right, of feminism or racial equality. Instead, it promotes anarchy and nihilism, and subsequently became one of the most important documents of its time, depicting British institutions in crisis.

Although many independent productions were highly original and metaphorical, critics argued they were made by and for a predominantly educated, middle-class audience. They also argued that their stylistic diversity sometimes obscured the film-maker's message. However, their main achievement was to promote discussion and debate about issues which had once been considered minority and peripheral. It also gave new political issues an intellectual force and credibility, particularly those of gender and race, which helped them to later find expression in mainstream British cinema.

'The British are coming!': Film-making and Thatcherism

The early 1980s were times of rapid change and expansion within the film industry. The introduction of video, cable and satellite services promoted a growth of topics and allowed audiences more choice. Advances in technology also made it possible to make films and even set up a studio with relatively modest budgets. Many new production companies appeared and the worlds of advertising and pop music also began to use videos in product promotion.

The BBC began providing technical assistance and finance for a variety of projects. But the greatest impact was made by the new television company Channel 4, which between 1982 and 1997 became involved as producer or sponsor of over 200 intellectually adventurous, low-budget films which dealt with original and challenging themes. They were notable for their realism, their simplicity, their absence of special effects and their originality. C4 also provided a regular television slot, 'Film on Four', reserved for its own and other British productions. C4 films are known for their social awareness. High levels of unemployment, social unrest, riots and a war all provided inspiration for directors who portrayed a politically, socially and ethnically divided country.

Heritage and harmony

The beginning of the 1980s saw a strong demand for films showing a rose-tinted, nostalgic view of the past, of an orderly, exclusive, upper-class nation. These became known as 'heritage' films and one of the most representative was *Chariots of Fire* (Hugh Hudson, 1981). Based on a true story, the film deals with a Scot and a Jew running for England in the 1924 Olympics. It features several unconventional, rebellious characters who become proud and nationalistic in victory. The attention to period details and the film's morally satisfying ending, offered a rosy, comforting picture of British life and institutions at a time of increasing social hardship and unrest.

The arrival of *Chariots* was timed to perfection. Its nostalgic theme of British superiority coincided with the wedding of Prince Charles to Diana in 1981, victory over Argentina in the Falkland Islands (Las Malvinas) in 1982 and the victory of the ruling Conservative Party in the election soon afterwards. It became the film of the moment and won four Oscars. At the Academy Awards ceremony in America, scriptwriter Colin Welland famously declared 'The British are coming!' anticipating a revival in the fortunes of the British film industry. His prediction was correct and 'heritage' films, exploiting popular interest in an upper-class, imperialist Britain, were among the most commercially successful of the decade.

Some of the best-known productions were by the team of Merchant-Ivory. Ismael Merchant, James Ivory and Ruth Prawer Jhabvala worked as director, producer and scriptwriter to successfully romanticise historical films of upper-class living. Some of their finest were adaptations of novels by E.M. Forster, including *Room with a View* (1986), *Maurice* (1987) and *Howards End* (1992), while *Remains of the Day* (1993) was based on a Booker Prize-winning novel by Kazuo Ishiguro. Beautifully filmed, richly costumed and classically acted, they presented an idealised, romanticised picture of elegant, exclusive Britain and received numerous international awards.

These and other films, such as David Lean's *A Passage to India* (made in 1984, also from a novel by E.M. Forster), *Gandhi* (Richard Attenborough, 1982), *Another Country* (Marek Kanievska, 1984) and *Henry V* (Kenneth Branagh, 1989) were highly popular with audiences, and even tempted older members of the public back to the cinema. However, critics said they projected an elitist, exclusive version of a culturally homogeneous past, which was heavily romanticised and fundamentally false. At the same time, there was a loss of sensitivity and accuracy to their representations of British history. They argued that 'heritage' films were created for the pleasure of overseas audiences, where such imagery was in demand, and made quick, easy profits for the film-makers. But their popularity continued undiminished.

Peter Greenaway

One of the most stylish but unconventional of British film-makers to emerge in the 1980s was Peter Greenaway (b.1942). Allegorical stories, symbols, romanticism and games feature in his films. The visual scenes are elaborate and carefully constructed, often with large familiar paintings, which give his work a characteristic style which he mixes with wit and charm.

He began his career in 1966 and, like Derek Jarman, his early work was highly experimental, featuring surreal fantasy, playful narrative and absurdist titles such as *Goole by Numbers* and *Dear Phone*. But later in his career he began to make more conventional feature films. Several took a cynical look at the lives of the professional classes, such as cooks, architects and draughtsmen, which increased greatly in number during the 1980s. *The Draughtsman's Contract* (1983) is a humorous costume drama and one of his best-known films. Set in 1694, the comedy begins when an aristocratic Mrs Herbert contracts the services of a draughtsman to make drawings of the house to present as a gift to her husband.

Modern day Rome is the setting for *The Belly of an Architect* (1987), where Stourly Cracklite, a wealthy Chicago architect, supervises an exhibition of architecture with his young wife Louisa. But distracted by illness, he is unaware of a young Italian architect's jealousy of both his professional life and his wife.

A tale of greed and revenge, *The Cook, the Thief, his Wife and her Lover* (1989) is set in a smart restaurant. Sex, food and love are mixed together in a critique of vulgar consumerism during the Thatcher years. More playful was *Drowning by Numbers* (1988) which made Greenaway popular with feminists. It is set in a Suffolk seaside village, in the east of England, where three generations of women aged 19, 34 and 60, each named Cissie Colpitts, murder their three unsatisfactory husbands. But in a humorous twist, the local Coroner agrees to certify their deaths as natural in return for sexual favours.

More challenging and unconventional is *Prospero's Books* (1991), an interpretation of Shakespeare's final play, *The Tempest*. It is built around the twenty-four magic books which Prospero's friend Gonzalo gives him to take with him on his final voyage back to Italy. Amid much nudity, the 87-year-old Sir John Gielgud reads most of the dialogue, in a role he has played many times on stage. In Greenaway's more recent film, *The Pillow Book* (1996), a young Japanese girl grows up with a fetish for calligraphy, demanding that her lovers paint kanji on her flesh, as did her father. Its elaborate images, computer graphics and superimpositions made it one of the most individual films of its time. An art student, painter, writer and novelist, Greenaway remains one of the most enigmatic film-makers in Britain today.

Propaganda and caricature

The earlier initiatives of independent studios had done much to bring women's issues to the attention of mainstream, commercial cinema, which during the 1980s began to represent them in a more populist manner. Several films examined the feelings and frustrations of women unable to experience life outside the home, such as *Another Time, Another Place* (Michael Radford, 1983) a bleak exploration of domestic repression. Set on an isolated Scottish farm, during the Second World War, it focuses on a young woman's loveless marriage to a humourless Scot.

But there were also several lighter attempts to portray similar themes. The humorous *Educating Rita* (1983) was widely praised. Rita is a young, married hairdresser who begins adult-education classes. But gradually she becomes divided between her oppressive domestic life and the attractions of academe. The director was Lewis Gilbert and the writer Willy Russell. In 1989 the duo made *Shirley Valentine*, a humorous tale about a Liverpudlian housewife and mother who shares with her neighbour a holiday on a Greek island, where she finds happiness with local fisherman Costas Caldes.

As society's problems grew deeper in the early 1980s, Lindsay Anderson's *Britannia Hospital* (1982) offered a humorous tale of a hospital close to collapse, due to strikes, riots and terrorism. However, the lazy, incompetent staff and their disinterested, insensitive boss only begin to worry when preparations begin for a visit by the Queen Mother. The film is widely seen as a tragicomic allegory of Britain in chaos and is recognised as a bitter criticism of the Thatcher society of the early 1980s.

Later in the decade, government policy led to deregulation, expansion and competition in numerous professions. The effects on media and broadcasting were critically examined in playwright Richard Eyre's film *The Ploughman's Lunch* (1983). It focuses on the activities of a BBC journalist and presents a cynical view of news presentation and management of the 1956 Suez Crisis and the Falklands War, showing the hypocrisy and insincerity of the mass media. Lighter and funnier was *How to Get Ahead in Advertising* (Bruce Robinson, 1989), a sharp critique of the advertising world, which also questions its morality.

A major issue of the 1980s was the Cold War, the subject of *Defence of the Realm* (David Drury, 1985). A highly critical film, it analyses the stationing of nuclear weapons in Britain, the dubious activities of the security forces and the role of the media in supporting the government. But in Chris Bernard's *Letter to Brezhnev* (1986), the Cold War was given lighter, more humorous treatment. It presents two young women who meet two Russian sailors in a Liverpool discotheque. But unlike much of the British news media during the 1980s, the film avoids the stereotyping of Russians as evil and monstrous, and shows them as ordinary folk looking for a peaceful life.

The conspicuous consumption of food and drink became fashionable during the decade and the theme of food was used to make social comment in several films. Malcolm Mowbray's *A Private Function* (1984) is a humorous caricature of ambitious middle classes. It is set in a small Yorkshire town in 1947 and, during a time of post-war rationing, an unlicensed pig is being fattened for a civic dinner to celebrate the Royal Wedding of Queen Elizabeth II. More contemporary was *Eat the Rich* (Peter Richardson, 1987), a satire set in Bastards – a smart London restaurant. When Alex – a black waiter – is fired, he returns to kill the staff, changes the restaurant name to Eat the Rich and offers human flesh on the menu. Received by critics as cynical, bizarre and offensive, it was one of the most tasteless films of the decade.

Northern Ireland

Frictions in politics and social life were common during the 1980s, but nowhere were they more violently expressed than in Ireland. Following its election in 1979, the Conservative Party and the Labour opposition both expressed their wish to continue defending the six counties of Northern Ireland and the rights of the Protestant majority living there. In comparison with other issues, relatively few films dealt directly with Ireland's troubles. Their delicate nature, the difficulty of treating issues in a balanced and fair way, and their limited appeal to audiences outside the province, has deterred many film-makers. Early cinematic interest in Northern Irish politics developed during the 1930s with Brian Hurst's *Ourselves Alone* (1936), the title a translation of the Irish-Gaelic *Sinn Fein*, the Irish Republican Party.

Since then, the majority of films have been thrillers, with spying, conspiracy, violence, and murder, set amid guerrilla warfare and terrorism. The majority of films have been made by American or English directors, but in 1982 Irish film-maker Neil Jordan made his directorial debut with *Angel*, the first of several highly praised works. It examines how a quiet, passive civilian becomes involved in murderous terrorist activities following the death of his friend. In 1992 Jordan returned to exploit a similar theme with *The Crying Game*, which examined the formation of political and national feelings in Britain and Ireland, and *Michael Collins* (1995), the story of a man whose belief in guerrilla violence against the British forces is changed into a desire for peace after he witnesses the horrors of civil war.

Several films of the 1980s took a similar perspective on the role of the security forces. *Boy Soldier* (Karl Francis, 1986) argues against sending soldiers into the streets. But more explicit in its message is Ken Loach's *Hidden Agenda* (1990), which alleges conspiracy, corruption and 'dirty tricks' in Ulster.

The role of women within the Republican movement is explored in several films and short documentaries, such as *Maeve* (Patricia Murphy, 1981), while Pat O'Connor's *Cal* (1984) considers the life events which lead a peaceful young Catholic man to become involved with the struggle of the Irish Republican movement. But not all films about the tension in Ireland were sombre in their treatment. In the tragicomic *No Surrender* (Peter Smith, 1986) Protestants and Catholics in fancy dress, arguing punk rockers, a gay comedian and an incompetent magician, all meet in an energetic and occasionally farcical scenario, set in a Liverpool nightclub on New Year's Eve.

Ken Loach

Realistic films dealing with social problems and issues have become one of the main strengths of British cinema. One of its leading exponents is Ken Loach (b.1937), a critically admired director who has established a reputation for political awareness in his films. He was born in the English Midlands and went via Oxford University to the BBC During the 1960s he worked extensively in television, directing plays for the weekly drama series *The Wednesday Play*. These frequently dealt with some of the most controversial social problems of the period, such as drugs, teenage pregnancies and domestic violence. Their frank, realistic portrayals challenged the complacent, literary interpretations which were then common in television drama.

The struggle of the underprivileged against an uninterested society is a theme common to many of his works. These are lightened by humorous incidents, witty scripts and a message of optimism about people's ability to conquer their problems. His early film *Poor Cow* (1968) is a sensitive exploration of an impoverished single mother's search for a decent life, and since then his work has critically commented upon varied social issues. One of the most highly regarded of his works is *Kes* (1970). It is set among a coal-mining community in Yorkshire, and looks sensitively at how a baby kestrel gives a young boy's life a sense of meaning.

Since the 1980s his films have engaged more closely with politics and society. *Looks and Smiles* (1982) considers the desperate choices open to two young school-leavers at a time when employment opportunities are few. For greater authenticity the cast members were all amateurs, drawn from the South Yorkshire community of Sheffield, the setting for the film. *Raining Stones* (1994) is a tragicomic view of the effects of unemployment on a Catholic family in Manchester, while *Ladybird, Ladybird* (1993) looks at a single mother who is badly treated by men in general and by the social services in particular. In *Riff Raff* (1994) Loach humorously depicts the 'regional' personalities of a gang of labourers and their reactions when they are ordered to convert a much-needed hospital into a block of luxury flats.

But Loach has not restricted his work to films about England. *Hidden Agenda* (1990) considers the role of the British army in Northern Ireland and in *Land and Freedom* (1995) he focussed his attention on the Spanish Civil War. This intelligent and powerful film looks at contemporary social issues through the experiences of unemployed Liverpudlian David Carne, who goes to Barcelona to fight for 'land and freedom' in 1936. *Carla's Song* (1996) also dealt with political struggle. It is set in Nicaragua in the mid-1980s during the overthrow of the Sandinista government by the right-wing, US-supported Contras and tells the tragicomic tale of a Glaswegian bus driver and his Nicaraguan sweetheart. Loach's most recent film, *My Name is Joe* (1998), deals with the life of a recovering alcoholic – a widely admired work which brought him recognition as a major British director.

Black British film

During the 1970s and early 1980s the only films dealing with the experiences of ethnic minorities were made by relatively unknown film-makers with small budgets. Because their films did not have great commercial appeal, they could only be seen in small, independent repertory cinemas. But between 1985 and 1991 more finance became available and there was a renaissance in black film-making. This was thanks to grants to improve conditions which had been approved following the race riots of the 1970s and early 1980s. As a result, several black film co-operatives appeared, such as Sankofa, Black Audio and Ceddo.

One of the founders of Sankofa was Isaac Julien, who made several films expressing the anger and frustration felt by many black Britons. These include *Territories* (1984), *Remembrance* (1986) and *Looking for Langston* (1989), based on the black American poet Langston Hughes (1902–67). Another notable work dealing with the experience of black Britons is *Handsworth Songs* (John Akomfrah, 1986), a critical examination of racial conflict in modern Britain. It was filmed in Handsworth, Birmingham, during the riots of 1985.

But black film-makers were few in number and their themes gradually became incorporated into the commercial mainstream. One example is *Playing Away* (Horace Ove, 1986) a light, humorous observation of hypocrisy and prejudice in an English rural community, when a cricket team from Brixton visits a small country village for a friendly game as part of the village's 'Third World Week' celebrations, an encounter which has comical consequences both on and off the field.

In contrast, some of the most highly praised explorations of life in the inner cities came from a white British director, Steven Frears, in collaboration with Hanif Kureishi, a British-born Pakistani who has written several novels and film scripts. Frears' films brought to public attention the increasingly diverse nature of British society and the problems suffered by 'outsiders' and marginal groups. They offer a powerful critique of the Conservative Government's economic and social policies, but at the same time provide an optimistic message about people's ability to triumph over adversity in their lives.

His portraits of British life are set in suburban London. The entertaining, exotic *My Beautiful Launderette* (1985) deals with the adventures of Omar, the son of an Asian businessman. He opens a launderette in a tough area of the capital, together with Johnny, an old friend from school, who has now become a fascist punk. Both have their own problems, which intensify when they become lovers. The film explores themes of racial tension, youth, class and sex, in one of the most highly praised films about British Asian culture.

In 1987 Frears directed *Prick Up Your Ears*. Its theme is homosexuality in Britain during the 1950s and 1960s, when it was still a criminal offence, and tells the story of gay playwright Joe Orton, who was tragically murdered by his lover Kenneth Halliwell in 1967. It shows a repressed nation, divided by hypocrisy and a rigid class system, tensions which inspired Orton's angry plays and mirrored those of Britain in the 1980s. Frears and Kureishi again collaborated on *Sammy and Rosie Get Laid* (1987), which presented a satirical interrogation of British Asian society. Sammy and Rosie are a mixed-race couple who live a bohemian lifestyle in a marginal area of London. Theirs is a happy, 'open' marriage in which both have lovers, but when Sammy's father, a Pakistani gangster appears, there is mutual disapproval of each other's lifestyle, politics, class and culture.

Film-making in the centenary decade

Historical films, realist films dealing with contemporary issues and films with a strongly regional flavour were among the most successful of a period when, one hundred years after the first movies were shown, British film-making began to discover a new sense of its own abilities and achievements.

But the beginning of the 1990s saw Britain deep in economic recession. At the same time there was a loss of public confidence in the institutions of government, church and monarchy, which appeared weak, indecisive, uncaring and out of touch. This period was marked by the continuing popularity of Merchant-Ivory 'heritage' films and others produced in a similar style, such as Richard Attenborough's *Shadowlands* (1993) and Mike Newell's *Enchanted April* (1992). But with the exception of his highly successful *Four Weddings and a Funeral* (1994), a romantic comedy about the affairs of the upper-middle classes, interest in refined, aristocratic living declined.

The influence of literary sources continued to be strong, but instead of idealised 'heritage' films, creative directing produced fresh, imaginative, simplified versions of classic novels. This approach was developed in the United States, where Franco Zeffirelli directed *Hamlet* (1990) and later *Jane Eyre* (1996). Inventive and energetic productions of *Romeo and Juliet* (Baz Luhrmann, 1996) and a modern reworking of *Great Expectations* (Alfonso Curon, 1996) set in 1970s Florida and 1980s New York respectively, were also received enthusiastically by British audiences.

The creative, modern interpreting of classic novels was soon exploited by British directors. *Carrington* (Chris Hampton, 1995) focussed on the Bloomsbury Group, a literary and artistic circle prominent during the 1930s. But instead of portraying Virginia Woolf, its most prominent member, his subject was Dora Carrington, an obscure painter. The same year, Taiwanese director Ang Lee made a modern version of Jane Austen's novel *Sense and Sensibility*, in which three recently impoverished sisters show no concern for personal happiness in their search for suitable husbands.

One of the most highly praised films was Michael Winterbottom's *Jude* (1996), adapted from Thomas Hardy's controversial novel *Jude the Obscure*. It tells a sad but exciting tale of two young lovers in Victorian England who are both unhappily married, but not to each other. Unable to marry, they cohabit and start a family, and later Jude wishes to go to university to study Classics. For a young couple of modest means, such ambitions were unthinkable in Victorian times. Jude is not a genteel, nostalgic 'heritage' film, but reflects in a fresh, energetic way a modern predicament known to many young families.

Several other notable films were inspired by true historical events and reflected contemporary demands for constitutional change, first with a planned devolution of political power to Scotland and later due to the unpopularity of the monarchy. Cinematic interest in Scotland was reflected in *Braveheart* (Mel Gibson, 1995), in which William Wallace fights to liberate the Scots from the tyranny of rule by the English during the thirteenth century. Its emotional approach to devolution was shared by *Rob Roy* (Michael Caton-Jones, 1995), the story of Rob Roy MacGregor. Set in Scotland during the early 1700s, beautiful scenery and tough action distinguish a film about a man who refuses to sacrifice his integrity to save himself or his family. The issue of the British monarchy in crisis was delicately explored in two films: *The Madness of King George* (Nicolas Hytner, 1995), set in 1788, and *Mrs Brown* (John Madden, 1997), set in Victorian England. Both were highly praised and used a historical perspective to examine the unpopularity of the monarch of the period: in the former George III and in the latter Queen Victoria.

Born into an Italian family living in Britain, Anthony Minghella has directed one of the most outstanding films of the 1990s. *The English Patient* (1997) is based on a Booker Prize-winning novel by Michael Ondaatje, a Canadian writer. It tells the story of the Hungarian explorer Lazlo Almasy and his affair with the beautiful Catherine Clifton in pre-war Cairo, through to 1945 and the last weeks of his life, when he is a patient in an abandoned Italian monastery. Made with a modest budget of only £2 million pounds, it was nominated for Oscars in twelve categories and won nine, becoming the most highly regarded British picture for many years.

New realism

The political ground was changing, and new pictures appeared which reflected current concerns. Many were made in a style known as 'naturalism' or 'new realism'. This kind of film-making was less overtly political and attempted to naturally represent ordinary people's proud battles in difficult circumstances.

Studied individual portraits are one of the main characteristics of the films of Mike Leigh (b.1943), who became one of the most highly regarded directors of the 1990s. He began working in London's fringe theatres during the 1960s, where he earned a reputation for sharply observed social commentary. Since making his first major film *Bleak Moments* in 1971, he has worked extensively in theatre and television, for which *Abigail's Party*, an early 1970s comedy of social manners among the lower-middle class, was among his best-known works. In 1988 he made the highly praised *High Hopes*. It considers the tensions between families of different social backgrounds in London during the mid-1980s. The film is both serious and funny, and sharply criticises the growing inequality, greed and selfishness into which society appeared to be descending. This was followed by the touching *Life is Sweet* (1991) and the tragicomic *Naked* (1993).

His films are revealing studies of class and manners which rely more on detailed characterisation than on plot and action. They are distinguished by convincing performances and by the natural style of acting, which Leigh encourages by creating scripts only after extensive improvisations by the actors. But his films are lightened by humorous incidents and perceptive remarks, which are well demonstrated in the acclaimed *Secrets and Lies* (1996). His ability to accurately and sympathetically chronicle the manners and lifestyle of Britain's lower classes have encouraged critical comparisons with Charles Dickens.

British screenwriter/director Alan Parker has directed numerous pictures for British and American companies, several of which were highly regarded musicals: *Bugsy Malone* (1976), *Fame* (1980), *Pink Floyd – The Wall* (1982) and *Evita* (1997). In 1991 he made *The Commitments*, based on Roddy Doyle's novel about a group of friends who form a soul band to sing their way out of a depressed Catholic area of Dublin. The style was typical of many popular films of the 1990s, which were accompanied by a lively pop soundtracks and showed their youthful protagonists dancing defiantly through the continuing economic recession.

The Full Monty (Peter Cattaneo, 1996) epitomised the trend towards 'new realism' in film-making, and became the most successful film of the mid-1990s. Set in the industrial city of Sheffield in West Yorkshire, it tells the story of a group of unemployed steelworkers who learn to do striptease to earn a living. Funny and highly metaphorical, this low-budget film was also successful in America, where it was described as the 'ultimate feel-good movie' and rivalled *Titanic* for many Academy Awards. Also from Yorkshire was Mark Herman's tragicomic *Brassed Off* (1996). Although it did not enjoy the commercial success of *The Full Monty*, it was critically praised for its humorous but sensitive depiction of Grimley, a declining mining community, and the passion of the musicians in the colliery band. The Irish community in Liverpool was the subject of *Hear My Song* (Peter Chelsom, 1991) which takes a light-hearted look at their dreams and desires, while Ken Loach's *Riff Raff* (1991) is a comedy of Irish, black and Geordie dreamers and activists – proud people who fight back instead of allowing themselves to be crushed by an uncaring political system.

Two of the most successful 'realist' pictures of the mid-1990s were set in Scotland. Director Danny Boyle worked with producer Andrew Macdonald and writer John Hodge on the dark thriller *Shallow Grave* (1994), before the same team made *Trainspotting* (1995). Initially a best-selling novel and then a play, the story succeeds in creating humour from the unlikely ingredients of heroin addiction, AIDS and poverty. Unlike many films and plays, these represent the point of view of a drug addict, and are set in the poverty and squalor of the 'other' Edinburgh, a side rarely seen by visitors to Scotland's capital.

Several other films were notable for their portrayal of contemporary issues. In 1997 John Boorman made *The General*, set in Northern Ireland and about the 'troubles' there. Unlike many films about the province, it does not take sides. Instead, it illuminates the situation as seen through the eyes of Martin Cahill, a violent but humorous armed robber who hates the IRA, the Protestant Loyalists and all forms of authority.

Another depiction of life 'from the inside looking out' is found in *Nil by Mouth* (1997). It marked the debut for actor Gary Oldman as a writer-director. His film is part autobiographical, with an honest depiction of Ray, a violent, unemployed man who spends his time drinking and indulging in petty crime. *To Die For* (Peter Mackensie, 1994) is a rare film which explores the sensitive issue of AIDS, while *Damage* (Louis Malle, 1992) is set at a time when the affairs of MPs, both financial and romantic, were coming under increased public scrutiny, and shows how a love affair wrecks the career of Dr Stephen Fleming, a British Member of Parliament.

Compared to the previous decade, film-making in the 1990s paid relatively little attention to the situation of British Asians and Afro-Caribbeans. Funding for projects about ethnic issues became increasingly difficult to obtain from the Arts Council. Some critics argued that, as with women's issues, these had gradually became incorporated into mainstream film-making, where their situation, experiences and problems were shown as similar to those of society in general. But others claimed their views were simply being ignored.

On of the few notable films was *Bhaji on the Beach* (Gurinder Chadha, 1994), a charming story of three generations of Punjabi women, from serious old aunties to coquettish teenagers, all on a day trip to Blackpool from their home town of Birmingham. When it was first shown, Asian communities protested at their humorous depiction by the director, a British Asian woman. The experiences of a black British woman were also the theme for *Babymother* (Julian Henriques, 1998), a musical drama set in the monotonous London suburb of Harlesden. It focuses on Anita, a young 'babymother' who is bringing up two children while trying to become a professional dancer. But a more critical exploration is offered by Hanif Kureishi in his warm, reflective and humorous film *My Son the Fanatic* (1998), about a dissolute Indian taxi-driver whose son becomes a fundamentalist Muslim, in a picture which examines immigration, prostitution and adultery, as well as the growth of Islam in Britain.

Towards the end of its centenary decade, the future of British film-making looked bright. In 1997 cinema box offices took 23 per cent of their income from admissions to British films, the highest for many years.

101

Cinema attendances increased, film production increased and British talent was regularly recognised in film festivals around the world. The industry also began to receive the benefits of greater institutional support. A new government department, the Department of National Heritage, was created in 1992 with the responsibility for government policy on films and film funding, and this together with money from the National Lottery appeared to substantially improve prospects. Channel 4 set up a new studio, 'Film Four', to integrate into a single company the production, distribution and sales of films, which further heightened the industry's expectations.

Enthusiasm was undoubtedly related to a new patriotism and cultural confidence which followed the social changes and renewal of 1997. But criticisms that were common twenty years earlier could still be heard: there were not enough women directors in British cinema. Their perspectives were missing, as were those of black directors. Similarly, the open discussion of gay and lesbian issues did not occupy the cultural centrality which it had in the United States, and it needed to be amplified. Furthermore, directors were criticised for refusing to offer solutions to the difficult problems raised in their films, whether about drugs, AIDS or racism.

But overall there was an air of optimism in British cinema which had not been seen for several decades. During perhaps its most successful period ever, it played to its strengths and found a new self-confidence and identity. This provided an intelligent and critical view of society, one which extended outside national politics and boundaries, and engaged with human life and experience.

Discussion topics and activities

1 What do you consider to be most distinctive characteristics of the British cinema since 1945? Which style do you prefer and why?
2 Refer to the text and other sources to explain the following: documentary film-making / social realism in film / Ealing comedies / heritage films.
3 Should the state give funds to encourage the making of certain types of films to create a national cinema, or should the film industry be left to sink or swim in the free market, like any other industry?
4 If you were a film censor, what would you prohibit and why?
5 Choose one of the films mentioned in the chapter. After watching it, write a review for a 'quality' newspaper, saying what you liked about it and why. Alternatively, write a script of the review and read it on video camera to an imaginary television audience.
6 Imagine you are a film-maker. Decide what type of film you would like to make (e.g. crime, historical drama, thriller) and when and where it would be set. Then write a brief synopsis of the story and decide which actors you would like in the main roles.

Suggested further reading

Books

Aitken, I. (1990) *Film and Reform: John Grierson and the Documentary Film Movement* London: Routledge.

Barr, C. (ed.) (1986) *All Our Yesterdays. 90 Years of British Cinema* London: BFI.

Boose, L. and Burt, R. (eds) *Shakespeare, The Movie: Popularising the Plays on Film, Television and Video* London: Routledge.

Curran, J. and Porter, V. (eds) (1983) *British Cinema History* London: Weidenfeld & Nicholson.

Dickenson, M. and Street, S. (1985) *Cinema and State: The Film Industry and the British Government 1927–84* London: BFI.

Dewe-Mathews, T. (1998) *Censored: The Story of Film Censorship in Britain* London: Chatto & Windus.

Friedman, L. (ed.) (1996) *British Cinema and Thatcherism* London: UCL Press.

Higson, A. (1995) *Waving the Flag: Constructing a National Cinema in Britain* Oxford: Oxford University Press.

International Dictionary of Films and Film-makers (1997) Detroit: St James's Press.

Landy, M. (1991) *British Genres: Cinema and Society 1930–1960* Princeton: Princeton University Press.

Murphy, R. (1997) *The British Cinema Book* London: BFI.

Park, J. (1990) *British Cinema* London: Batsford.

Robertson, J.C. (1993) *The Hidden Cinema: British Film Censorship in Action 1913–1975* London: Routledge.

Warren, P. (1993) *British Cinema in Pictures: The British Film Collection* London: Batsford.

Walker, A. (1985) *National Heroes: British Cinema in the 1970s and 1980s* London: Harrap.

Young, L. (1996) *Fear of the Dark: Race, Gender and Sexuality in the Cinema* London: Routledge.

There are also numerous guides to film and video which contain details and synopses: *Halliwell's*, *The Time Out Film Guide* and the *Virgin Film Guide* are among the most comprehensive and appear updated every year. In addition, the British Film Institute publishes the *British National Film and Video Catalogue* (annually since 1963, with video citations since 1984). A useful yearbook is also published annually by the BFI.

Journals

All the major newspapers and many monthly fashion magazines include regular articles on film. *Empire* is a monthly magazine which is less academic and more general than some of those mentioned below.

The *Journal of Popular British Cinema* appears four times each year, and began in 1996. Its articles reflect upon a new area of interest within film studies: that of popular genres.

Monthly Film Bulletin was published every month by the British Film Institute between 1934 and 1991, giving a synopsis and a critical review of every feature film released in Britain during that time. In 1991 it merged with *Sight and Sound*.

Sight and Sound (quarterly, 1932–91; monthly, 1991–).

Screen has been the major journal of film theory since 1971. It first appeared in 1959 and is available quarterly.

Films

Many of the films mentioned in this chapter can be bought at some of the more specialised record and video stores in Britain. In addition, the BFI has an extensive public library of books, films and film scripts, and organisations such as The British Council frequently make films available to the public.

The National Film and Television Archive has over 300,000 titles from 1895, and provides detailed information and a viewing service for students and researchers.

6

Television and radio

Introduction

Everyone born in Britain since 1940 is part of a generation which grew up with television. In the UK the average television set is switched on for between five and six hours a day, and the average British adult watches for approximately three hours. Recent research has shown that the average child born in the mid-1990s, when 18 years of age, will have spent more time watching television than any other activity except sleep.

Although there are many satellite and cable stations, the most established are the five national terrestrial channels. Two of these are provided by the British Broadcasting Corporation (BBC), and three are provided by independent broadcasters.

The BBC

BBC1 shows programmes which have a broad appeal, while those of BBC2 are often more specialised. These include leisure, lifestyle and documentary programmes, as well as the Open University broadcasts (which allow home study for university degrees) and other education programmes for schools and colleges.

The BBC also has five national radio stations. Radio 1 broadcasts current pop music, live concerts and news. Radio 2 plays a wider range of popular music, which includes light classics. Radio 3 broadcasts almost exclusively classical music and occasionally jazz. Radio 4 offers news and current affairs, together with arts programmes, religion and cricket commentary. Radio 5 broadcasts mainly live news and sports programmes, which are orientated towards younger listeners. The national stations are complemented by thirty-nine regional and local BBC radio stations. These are mostly speech-based and increasingly broadcast in the languages of the local communities: Radio Cymru broadcasts in Welsh, Radio Nan Gaidheal broadcasts in Gaelic and several others broadcast in Asian languages.

A distinctive characteristic of the BBC is that, unlike most other broadcasters, it does not broadcast advertisements. It is funded by annual licence fees, paid by over 21 million households (99 per cent of the country) that own a television set. The absence of commercial pressures allows programme planners to be in direct contact with the needs and expectations of the general public. Programmes have traditionally been created not with a need to attract viewers for commercial publicity, but with a sense of responsibility towards the community. Its documentaries, plays and current affairs series critically engage with society and, in this way, television has come to occupy a cultural centrality which is unique to Britain.

But in recent years the BBC has had to adapt to new technology and competition. In 1991 it began international television broadcasts with World Service Television. BBC World shows news and current affairs programmes to some 43 million homes worldwide, and BBC Prime shows a programme of light entertainment and drama to an audience of around 4 million in Europe. These do not receive any income from television licences or from government. Instead they generate income through voluntary subscription.

The BBC also broadcasts international radio. The World Service broadcasts in English and forty-three other languages, and is funded by the Foreign and Commonwealth Office. It has a programme of current affairs, business, sport and the arts, and is regularly listened to by around 140 million worldwide.

Independent television

The commercial broadcasters try to emulate the high standards of quality and service set by the BBC. There are numerous commercial satellite stations, but only three commercial terrestrial channels. These are Channels 3, 4 and 5, which all rely on income generated by advertising. Channel 3 (ITV) is independent and makes a broad range of popular programmes. It comprises fifteen independent companies which broadcast to fourteen regions, with two – Carlton and London Weekend – for southeast England.

Channel 4 is an independent national service which began broadcasting in 1982. It encourages innovation and the making of distinctive programmes for minority interests and audiences, and also sponsors many distinctive low-budget films. In Wales, the service is known as Sianel Pedwar Cymru (S4C), which transmits many programmes in the Welsh language. The newest terrestrial station is Channel 5 which began in 1997. It makes and shows popular programmes to a wide audience around the country. The majority of programmes shown on all channels are made in Britain, America, Australia, New Zealand and Canada; foreign-language films and programmes are rare.

Independent local radio began in 1973 and in recent years the number of stations has expanded greatly. There are currently around 200 that make their money from the sale of advertising time. Many serve local ethnic minorities and broadcast in the language of the community. They offer a general programme of entertainment, news, sport, consumer information and phone-ins. Although local radio is well established, national independent stations are still a novelty in Britain. There are only three: the first was the classical music station Classic FM which opened in 1992.

Broadcasting content is strictly controlled by the Independent Television Commission's code of practice on violence, taste and decency, especially before 9 PM when young children may be watching. All tobacco advertising is prohibited on television and cigarette advertising on the radio. Political advertising is also banned, but each major party is allowed a number of broadcasts every year.

Journalism, communications and broadcasting are growth areas and there is no shortage of interest in careers. Training for posts in independent television or the BBC has become increasingly possible thanks to a growing number of courses in many colleges and universities. The National Film and Television School is one of the most respected training institutions. It is financed by the government, together with contributions from the film, video and television industries. Outstanding work in television is recognised each year by the National Television Awards at a prestigious ceremony in London.

The formative years

The British Broadcasting Corporation was founded in 1922 by a group of companies making radio equipment. In November 1936 it transmitted the first television pictures. But for many years radio was considered the senior service. It was older, more established and offered a better choice of programmes. Transmissions came from Broadcasting House in London, an impressive building built for the BBC which opened in 1932. Above its entrance the sculptor Eric Gill used a theme from Shakespeare's play *The Tempest* to symbolise radio: Prospero sending the spirit Ariel into the world. The classical theme continued with its motto 'Nation Shall Speak Peace Unto Nation', adapted from a line in the Old Testament 'Nation Shall Not Lift Up A Sword Against Nation' (Micah 4:3).

Life inside the BBC was formal, old-fashioned and badly paid. When appearing on camera, announcers had to wear traditional evening dress and spoke with a formal RP accent. But newsreaders were not televised, as it was believed that a change of facial expression could threaten impartiality.

During the war the BBC established a reputation for reporting the truth and afterwards it occupied a role of cultural importance and authority. Under its first Director-General, Lord Reith, there was a strong ethic of public service. The BBC aimed to educate, inform and entertain. Television programmes carried an air of self-improvement and there were regular series on gardening, cooking, classical music and drama. In 1949 a regular weather forecast began for farmers and, no doubt, in recognition of the traditional British interest in the weather.

On both radio and television there are still several programmes which survive from the early years. *The Archers* (1950–) is a radio soap opera which was originally created to transmit useful information to the agricultural community. It is set on the imaginary Brookfield Farm in Ambridge, and has become the world's longest-running radio drama series. *Desert*

Figure 6.1 Sir Winston Churchill during an epic speech relayed to the world by the BBC, 14 July 1941

Island Discs (1942–) mixes music with talk. A well-known 'personality' is interviewed and invited to choose eight records they would take to a desert island, together with one book (apart from the Bible and Shakespeare which are already there) and one luxury. These continue to be among the most popular programmes on radio.

Between 1945 and 1955 the BBC strengthened its reputation for patrician values in broadcasting: that it knew best what was in the nation's interests. It broadcast only in the evenings, with a break between 6 and 7 PM to allow children to be put to bed. It saw itself as the guardian of the nation's morals and the official provider of culture to the community. Its role as an unofficial nanny to the nation earned it the nickname 'Auntie'.

The Coronation of Elizabeth II in 1953 led to increased demand for television sets. With more viewers, there was greater interest in offering an independent, commercial channel. In September 1955 Independent Television (ITV) began. News bulletins were read by men and women on camera. Regional accents began to be heard and the diversity of material helped to break down class and regional prejudice. The public were also attracted by a range of openly populist programmes. These included westerns, crime dramas, variety shows and American sitcoms, such as *I Love Lucy*. The BBC believed that it was vulgar to be popular and lost many viewers.

Realism in television (1955–70)

During the decade after the introduction of commercial television, factual programmes of both channels began to examine life in the provincial towns and cities. The currents of realism across the arts were expressed in new styles of programme-making. News reporting and documentaries became more intimate, immediate and involved with everyday life, as ordinary people described their experiences and problems on camera. At the same time, television drama began to closely reflect everyday situations, in plays, police series and soap operas.

The social and political changes of the 1950s created a demand for documentary programmes which could describe and explain them clearly to the public. In 1953 the BBC created *Panorama*, a documentary programme dealing with current affairs. Since then, it has investigated and reported on a variety of social and political events. Its reports from war zones such as Suez, the Falklands, Libya and the Gulf were often impartial and did not support the government. This led to Parliamentary criticism that it was the propaganda work of traitors and Communists. But in the late 1990s it continues to be the most respected, authoritative and independent programme of its kind. It sets the standard for documentary journalism, in which the BBC has become a world leader.

The impartiality of the BBC was further emphasised with the creation of controversial programmes such as *What the Papers Say* (1956–). This

109

Figure 6.2 A British family views one of the first experimental transmissions of colour television

irreverent, anarchic bulletin is still presented each week by a different jour-nalist, who indicates the bias and sometimes hypocrisy shown in a variety of national newspapers. Its satirical tone has often been criticised by government and Margaret Thatcher once tried to ban it.

Dramatisations of everyday life first became established during the mid-1950s, when theatre playwrights such as Harold Pinter, Dennis Potter and

Alan Bennett, and film directors such as Ken Loach and Tony Garnett made challenging, memorable dramas for *Armchair Theatre* (ITV, 1956–) and *The Wednesday Play* (BBC1, 1964–70). Sensitive and even taboo subjects such as wife-beating, alcoholism, sex and drugs were represented on television for the first time. Jeremy Sandford's *Cathy Come Home* (1966) dealt with homelessness and Nell Dunn's *Up the Junction* (1965) revealed the horrors of illegal abortion. The content of these dramas shocked people, but they also contributed to greater public understanding of serious social problems. They even led to Parliamentary debate and action in the areas of care for pregnant women and the provision of social housing.

But the most controversial depiction was Peter Watkins' *The War Game* (BBC, 1965), which showed the possible effects of a nuclear attack on Britain. The BBC Director-General Sir Hugh Greene decided not to show the shocking programme because it was too realistic and could influence public attitudes against the government's pro-nuclear policy. Instead, the film could only be seen in selected cinemas and was not broadcast until twenty years later.

Police drama is one of the most popular genres on British television. At different times in their history, police and crime series have reflected different images of British society. During the 1950s police series presented a conservative, consensual image. The most popular was *Dixon of Dock Green* (BBC, 1955–76), set in the imaginary police station of Dock Green in East London. Each episode resembled a moral tale, paternally delivered by the nation's best-known policeman, PC George Dixon. The series showed an idealised 'little England' in which everyone knew their place in society. For many years it reflected the post-war political consensus. Everyone respected the police and worked together in the common interest and crime was seen as a temporary difficulty caused by the disruption of war.

But more realistic depictions of society gradually appeared in crime series and even soap operas. Unlike the earlier *Dixon of Dock Green*, viewers often found Troy Kennedy-Martin's police drama *Z Cars* (BBC, 1962–78) uncomfortable to watch. It was set in the imaginary location of Newtown, a modern urban 'jungle' close to Liverpool. It showed policemen who looked, talked and behaved in a realistic way. They drank heavily, gambled and were sometimes violent. It began to show crime as a threat to society and a social problem which needed to be firmly dealt with. The series was a critical and popular success, and established a new style of writing and directing television drama series.

The popularity of television began to affect other communications media. Radio audiences fell, in spite of a strong drama and comedy content, with plays by Samuel Beckett, Harold Pinter and Dylan Thomas, whose *Under Milk Wood* (1953) was acclaimed as one of the finest dramas ever broadcast. *The Goons, Hancock's Half Hour* and *Round the*

Figure 6.3 'Evening all ... ': *Dixon of Dock Green*

Horne were mad, outrageously funny radio comedy shows of the late 1950s, but listeners still left radio for television. Later, cinema and theatre audiences also began to fall, and demand even dropped for evening news-papers, forcing many to disappear.

Coronation Street

The enthusiasm for social realism on television led to the creation of *Coronation Street* (ITV, 1960–), ITV's most successful series ever. It is a serial drama or 'soap opera' (the term was imported from America where such programmes were sponsored by detergent manufacturers) and was created by Tony Warren, when he was only 23. It deals with the daily lives of working-class folk and 'petty' bourgeoisie in a short, grey, narrow street in the imaginary northern town of Weatherfield, close to Manchester.

When it first appeared, a programme featuring the daily lives of ordinary folk had never been seen on television before and some critics doubted it would be successful. Earlier series such as *The Grove Family* featured middle-class southerners with RP accents, and at first the public were shocked by the northerners' rough speech and manners. Early episodes resembled the dramatic realism of *Armchair Theatre* and *The Wednesday Play*, but they have gradually evolved into a lively series with moments of humour, tragedy, surprise and farce.

Although Ken Barlow (played by Bill Roache) is the only remaining member of the original cast, the characters have changed relatively little over the years. The dominant personalities tend to be female and stories are told with humour, pace and the occasional moral lesson. The programme has a wide range of fans. Since the mid-1960s each episode has been regularly seen by an audience of 15–20+ million of all ages in all parts of the country. In the late 1990s it continues to be the most popular programme on British television, watched and referred to by almost everyone.

Adventure and imagination: fantasy dramas (1960–70)

Detection and spying were popular themes in many television programmes of the period. The escalating tension in the Cold War and the success of the James Bond films inspired many elaborate espionage series. Fashionable clothes, fast cars, exotic locations and memorable theme music were common features of several exciting and original dramas. For many fans and critics it was a 'golden age' of creative television.

One of the most popular and enduring was *The Saint* (ITV, 1962–9, 1978–9, 1989–90), based on the stories of Leslie Charteris, who had been writing crime adventures since the 1920s. The protagonist was Simon Templar, a suave, sophisticated crime fighter, originally played by Roger Moore. Fights, flirtations and exotic locations provided a highly popular mixture in this relatively conventional series, which established Moore's reputation on the small screen.

Much more imaginative was *The Avengers* (ITV 1961–9, 1976–7). Early stories in the series were conventional, but they soon became more absurd and surreal, making it one of the most original ever shown on television. It featured two private detectives; the lead was played by Patrick MacNee as John Steed, who had a variety of female assistants during the life of the series. The most popular was Diana Rigg as Emma Peel. Chic, upper-class and independent, she symbolised modern progressive attitudes and values opposite Steed's restrained conservatism. Wittier and brighter than her co-star, the elegant, attractive Peel regularly threw villains around

113

with graceful, balletic ease, in performances which were clearly feminist in pre-feminist times. Her tight-fitting, provocative outfits even offended some viewers, who wanted to have the series banned. Surrealism was also an element of *Randall and Hopkirk (deceased)* (ITV, 1969–70), in which 'Marty' Hopkirk was the deceased partner in a firm of detectives, who returned as a white-suited 'ghost' invisible to everyone except Randall, his crime-fighting partner. As with *The Avengers*, distinctive period settings and imaginative plots contributed to the appeal of this short-lived but memorable detection drama.

Exotic locations had strong appeal for a generation of Britons who had begun to experience foreign holidays and continental fashions for the first time, and several other series had a more international flavour. *The Champions* (ITV, 1969–71) were three agents with fantastic abilities who worked for the secret Geneva-based organisation 'NEMESIS', combating crime around the world. More realist was *Department S* (ITV, 1969) which featured three Interpol agents. But one of the most stylish and flamboyant was Jason King, who later appeared in his own series *Jason King* (ITV, 1971–2), in the role of a playboy author-adventurer.

The most long-lived of the fantasy dramas was *Dr Who* (BBC, 1963–90), which featured the adventures of a 'Time Lord', known only as 'The Doctor', an eccentric, anti-authoritarian loner. His home was the 'Tardis', which outside resembles a police call-box, but inside is an enormous craft, capable of travelling backwards and forwards through time and space. The Doctor and his crew had numerous enemies: the most famous were the Daleks. These were motorised one-eyed robots who did not kill, but famously 'exterminated' the opposition, while a young generation of viewers at home watched from behind the sofa in terrified amazement. After seven different doctors and assorted adventures in time and space, the series finished. Fans were outraged, but in 1996 the BBC made a successful Dr Who film for television and there was talk of another series. It won a BBC award for the best television drama of all time in the same year.

Fantasy and escapism were features of many popular and original programmes, not only with adults' series, but also with children's such as *Supercar, Fireball XL5, Stingray, Thunderbirds, Captain Scarlet* and *Joe 90*, which were first shown consecutively between 1961 and 1969 on ITV. Created by Gerry Anderson, they featured different teams of futuristic, international 'policemen' based in space, on land or at sea. With the exception of Joe 90 (a myopic 9-year-old) the main protagonist was a square-jawed, fair-skinned male with a mid-Atlantic accent. In a thinly disguised Cold War scenario, each episode saw the Americanised hero and his team save the world from an enemy force. Although the puppet series were intended for juvenile audiences, they were also enjoyed by many adults and successfully captured the imagination of a generation with sci-fi plots, distinctive theme tunes and an exotic mixture of characters.

The Prisoner

The Prisoner (ITV, 1967–8) is regarded by many critics as the most distinctive and original fantasy drama ever written. It was created and written by Patrick McGoohan, who also played the leading role of 'Number Six'. Its stories and themes have become the subject of numerous debates and discussions, and of much academic writing.

Each episode opens with a sports car racing through the streets of London, whose driver – a secret agent – resigns from his post in a Whitehall office. But when he returns home he is kidnapped by government forces. They send him to a beautiful, Italian-style village, which seems like paradise. But in reality it is a prison inhabited by superficial, passive citizens who are afraid to think for themselves.

In the village, no one has a name, only a number. McGoohan becomes prisoner Number Six. He is interrogated about his professional past, but refuses to give any information. He insists that his life is his own and that he is not a number, but a free man. He demands to know who is in charge of the village, the identity of Number One.

Each of the seventeen episodes deals with psychological attempts break him and his own attempts to escape. These all fail, but the last episode of this enigmatic series suggests that Number Six is the real Number One: that he holds the key to his own sense of freedom. The series is thus the story of a man attempting to escape from himself.

Like many of its contemporaries, *The Prisoner* was surreal, stylish and entertaining. But unlike them it also raised many important political questions about totalitarian societies, democracy and liberty. Each year, its fan club meets to discuss themes and re-enact scenes in the original village of Portmeirion, a mediterranean-style village on the coast of North Wales.

The golden age of popular television (1965–75)

By the mid-1960s, the BBC was beginning to recover the viewers it had lost to ITV ten years earlier. But radio was still losing listeners. In spite of a growing variety of popular music, BBC radio offered little more than the Top Twenty. Only Radio Luxembourg, a European commercial radio station, provided occasional relief. Many young people wanted to hear a wider choice of music and in 1964 a new station, Radio Caroline, began broadcasting from a ship in the North Sea. Its owner, Ronan O'Rahilly, had no official permission, but because the station was outside the territorial waters of the United Kingdom, the authorities were powerless to stop him.

In its maritime isolation, Caroline played a mixture of popular and progressive music, and broadcast 'alternative' news about underground culture, drugs, politics and sexuality. It was an immediate success and other illegal stations soon appeared, such as Radio London in the estuary of the River Thames. They became known as 'pirate' stations and after only one year they had an estimated audience of 15–20 million listeners. Records were not limited to the Top Twenty and distinctive programmes, such as John Peel's *The Perfumed Garden*, provided an exotic mix of poetry, classical and folk music.

But in 1967 the government introduced the Marine Broadcasting Act, which forced many stations to close down. At the same time, there was a major reorganisation of radio into several regional stations and four national ones. Radio 1 began broadcasting pop music and needed experienced DJs, and soon afterwards former 'pirates' Dave Lee Travis, Kenny Everett, John Peel and Tony Blackburn joined the station, where they went on to long and successful careers.

The massive interest in 'pirate' radio indicated the potential size of the audience if the right programmes could be found. But the major broadcasters were old-fashioned and out of touch. In 1946 the BBC had begun to make programmes for children with *Andy Pandy* and *The Flowerpot Men*. But a decade later there were still no programmes for older children, until ITV created the music shows *Cool for Cats* (ITV, 1956–61) and *Six-Five Special* (ITV, 1957–8). The most successful was *Ready, Steady, Go!* (ITV, 1963–6), which offered live music to a studio audience dressed in the latest 'mod' fashions, dancing the latest dances and speaking the latest slang, all within studio adorned in the pop art style. Audience participation was part of the show and televising the 'party' helped to spread not only music, but also popular culture to audiences around Britain.

In 1964 the BBC launched *Top of the Pops* to compete with *RSG*. The first show was broadcast from a converted church hall in Manchester. It gave special emphasis to the Top Twenty, a list of the bestselling records in the UK the previous week, compiled from record sales in a number of record shops throughout the country. The songs played on the show were usually those moving up the chart and it quickly became a magnet for young viewers. Groups and singers appeared in a studio decorated like a coffee bar, with a dancefloor for the studio audience, which was an integral part of the spectacle. It was an immediate success and appearances rapidly became essential for any groups with a single to promote. In the artists' absence, a dance troupe known as Pan's People performed to the music. Their exposed flesh and sexually provocative choreography caused offence among the 'Clean Up Television Campaign', a puritanical pressure group organised by Mrs Mary Whitehouse.

Sitcoms

In a decade when popular television was becoming established, some of the most popular and successful programmes were situation comedies, or 'sitcoms', which each week featured regular characters in some familiar setting. Many of the protagonists are anti-social monsters, fools or people who simply can't cope with daily life. Together with crime series and soap operas, they are regarded by many critics as one of the richest forms of modern cultural expression, and are regularly among the most watched and analysed of popular programmes.

The late 1960s and early 1970s is often regarded by fans and critics as a 'golden age' of sitcom. Many reflected social changes of the time and some of the most highly praised exploited the tensions between those who were enthusiastic about the bright new world of freedom, opportunity and consumerism, and those who were cynical about it. For example, *The Likely Lads* (BBC, 1964–6) and *Whatever Happened to ...* (BBC, 1973–4) depicted Bob and Terry, two young men from the north of England, one slow, introverted and aspirational, the other knowing, extroverted and cynical. The successful comedy series *Steptoe and Son* (BBC, 1962–5, 1970, 1972, 1974) exploited similar tensions between an aspirational, optimistic middle-aged son and his traditional, pessimistic, elderly father who together sold second-hand objects from their East London yard.

Till Death Us Do Part (BBC 1966–8, 1972, 1974–5) is one of the most controversial sitcoms ever shown on television. Its direct involvement with the society and politics of the time caused public concern about its negative social influence. Written by Johnny Speight and regularly watched by a large audience of some 15 million, it was set in London's East End. The leading character was family-man Alf Garnett, a working-class Tory bigot, who rejected entirely the liberalism, tolerance and progressive social attitudes of the time. Alf was the epitome of political incorrectness and regularly delivered abusive, hypocritical tirades against blacks, Jews, Communists, gays and feminists. Many viewers could not understand why the BBC showed the series. But Speight argued that Alf exposed many common hypocrisies and prejudices of people in the pubs, factories and boardrooms of Britain, and in this way he could ridicule them.

Nostalgia was not fashionable in many programmes of the period, but a popular exception was *Dad's Army* (BBC, 1968–77). This was a sitcom set during wartime Britain, in the fictitious, genteel south-coast village of Walmington-on-Sea. It featured the local Home Guard (a unit of part-time, semi-retired soldiers based in their home towns and villages) and their preparations against a possible invasion by the German forces in 1940. Many episodes showed comical attempts by the traditional authoritarian figure of Captain Mainwearing to impose his will on the rebels and eccentrics in his unit, and their subtle forms of resistance and disobedience. Its gentle critique of institutional power and attempts by individuals to subvert it exploited a tradition of British comedy famously pioneered by Ealing Studios in their films of the late 1940s. The repeats of *Dad's Army* were among the most popular programmes of the late 1990s.

Some of the most highly regarded sitcoms of the 1960s were provocative and challenging, and their characters were often rebels, misfits and eccentrics. But later in the 1970s sitcoms became increasingly cosy, comforting and bland. The 1970s was a difficult decade for many people in Britain and audiences looked for reassurance and comfort in light entertainment. However, this often involved crude stereotyping: in spite of their progress in the legal and cultural sphere, young working women were still frequently shown as sex objects and blacks as figures of fun. Portrayals of harmonious, happy families and an idealised version of domestic life were abundant. Suburban southern England was the preferred location and representations of life in the north or other regions were rare.

Bless this House (ITV, 1971–6) showed a cheerful suburban couple and the escapades of their teenage children. *Man about the House* (ITV, 1973–6) and *Robin's Nest* (ITV, 1977–81) similarly showed the humorous, cosy side of a suburban flatshare, in which a young man shares a flat with two young girls. These and other series humorously exploited the differences between the generations known as the 'generation gap'. Other sitcoms also attempted to divert and reassure their audiences with satires of those in more difficult circumstances. At a time of housing shortages and high unemployment, *Rising Damp* (ITV, 1974–8) created genteel humour from the tension between Rigsby, a tyrannical, nosy, exploitative landlord, and his impoverished tenants. Even institutional life was shown as cosy and comical in *Porridge* (BBC, 1974–7), which depicted the antics of a couple of prison inmates. Radical, alternative left-wing ideas were ridiculed and rubbished in the satirical *Citizen Smith* (BBC, 1977–80). But strong individual performances and humorous scripts made all these series among the most popular of their time and many were regularly watched by audiences of over 12 million viewers.

Fawlty Towers (BBC, 1975–9) is among the most successful and enduring of 1970s comedy series. Created by John Cleese of the *Monty Python* team, it featured Basil Fawlty, the neurotic and politically incorrect owner of a southern English seaside hotel. Basil is the typical 'little Englander': a middle-class, middle-aged male who is philistine, banal, socially awkward, self-satisfied. He fears his wife, but regularly insults and humiliates his staff and guests. But since its creation, the series has become one of the most popular and critically praised comedy series ever made and the subject of frequent nostalgic repeats.

Broadcasting: consolidation and conservatism (1970–90)

During the 1970s there was a clear trend towards more conservative and less adventurous programme-making, in which tradition, continuity and nostalgia were the dominant themes of many genres. The televising of popular events such as the wedding of Princess Anne at Westminster Abbey in November 1974 and a selection of programmes about Queen Elizabeth's Silver Jubilee in June 1977 were two of the decade's biggest televisual events, watched by record numbers of viewers. In a time of

Figure 6.4 Basil Fawlty 'explains' to his Spanish waiter Manuel in an episode of
Fawlty Towers

uncertainty and change, the monarchy was still respected as Britain's most
prestigious institution.

But it was also a time of economic turbulence and industrial unrest,
and, while the Sex Pistols grimly sang of 'anarchy in the UK', programme-
making reflected little of the public demands for political and social
change. With the media's incapacity to recognise or represent Britain's
problems, social commentators began to talk of the country's inability to
face change.

Historical series had been largely neglected since the 1950s. But during
the 1970s many new ones appeared which romanticised the lives and times
of past monarchs, such as *The Six Wives of Henry the Eighth* (BBC,
1970), *Elizabeth R.* (BBC, 1971) and *Edward VII* (ITV, 1975). These and
other series, such as *Upstairs Downstairs* (ITV, 1971–5), about an upper-
class Edwardian household and their servants, offered cosy, nostalgic
evocations of past greatness and reminded viewers of the order and
stability of a great nation. Historical interest also extended to several new
series about the Second World War, with their traditional theme of
strength and solidarity in the face of adversity. *Colditz* (BBC, 1972–4) was
a drama series set in a German prison camp, which at times resembled an

austere English public school. *Secret Army* (BBC, 1977–9) and *Manhunt* (ITV, 1970) depicted the heroic efforts of the resistance movement in occupied Europe, and *Enemy at the Door* (ITV, 1978–80) showed tense relationships between Germans and the local people of the Channel Islands, the only British territory occupied during the war. Their traditional theme of strength and solidarity in the face of adversity was a familiar and reassuring one to many people during the difficult years of the 1970s.

Historical and traditional influences continued to be in vogue throughout the 1980s and intensified following the Royal Wedding of Prince Charles in 1981, which had an estimated worldwide audience of 500 million, a record at the time. Several major drama series were adapted from classic novels to recreate the atmosphere and settings of an age of elegance. They provided an encyclopedia of period-style which captured audiences both in Britain and abroad. Among the most successful was *Brideshead Revisited* (ITV, 1981), dramatised by John Mortimer from Evelyn Waugh's novel and starring Jeremy Irons, John Gielgud and Laurence Olivier.

However, the popular interest in royalty, history and tradition was offset by the appearance of several new soap operas which, unlike others of the time, attempted to more accurately represent life in contemporary Britain. *Brookside* (C4, 1982–) is a modern street in a Liverpool suburb. The series regularly features the Grants, a numerous Catholic family. It was also the first to deal with major social issues of unemployment, crime, homosexuality and AIDS. The series was created by Phil Redmond, who earlier created the soap opera *Grange Hill* (BBC, 1978–), which is set in an imaginary school in the south of England. Another major arrival was the soap opera *EastEnders* (BBC, 1985–). It was created by Tony Holland and Julia Smith, and continues to be enormously successful for the BBC. It is set in Albert Square, in the fictitious London borough of Walford. The Beale and Fowler families regularly feature in this realistic series, which emphasises the humour and solidarity of the East End working class. Like *Brookside*, the programme deals with more controversial topics, such as AIDS, crime, racism and homosexuality. The series has become highly popular and often rivals *Coronation Street* in the ratings.

In a further trend towards realism in television, non-whites were increasingly represented in a number of specially written soap operas and sitcoms. *Empire Road* (BBC, 1978–9) was one of the few to receive critical praise. It was a soap opera written by West Indian playwright Michael Abbensetts for a black cast, but it failed to reach a wider audience and was cancelled after only one year. Since then, depictions of non-whites in all types of series have generally been heavily criticised as unrepresentative and stereotyped, such as in sitcoms like *The Fosters* (ITV, 1976–7) and also in crime series.

Moreover, only bland shows could attract audiences large enough to justify investment in them. *Mind Your Language* (ITV, 1977–9) was set in a language school and crudely caricatured the students in terms of national stereotypes. *It Ain't Half Hot Mum* (BBC, 1974–81) comically portrayed the British Army cheerfully oppressing the Indian natives during the last days of the Empire. *Love Thy Neighbour* (ITV, 1972–6) depicted a white, racially prejudiced proletarian couple and their easy-going West Indian neighbours. But despite its crudity and racially stereotyped humour, for four years it was among the most popular comedies of its time.

During the 1980s the attempts to write for a black cast continued. Several were by Farrukh Dhondy, who was born in Poona, India, and later studied at Cambridge University. He has also written children's books about young blacks and Asians in London, the cultural differences they encounter and the misunderstandings. In 1983 he wrote *No Problem* (C4 and LWT, 1983–5) with Mustapha Matura, a West Indian writer, which depicted a London household in which the parents had returned to Jamaica, leaving their five children in charge. However, like many other earlier series and the later *Tandoori Nights* (C4, 1984, 1987), with its 'star' Jimmy Sharma (a British Asian curry-house owner), it was strongly criticised for producing stereotypes and for its failure to represent any of the contemporary problems faced by black British youth. However, other critics argued that sitcoms could not and should not do this, as their purpose was simply to offer light entertainment.

Crime series (1975–90)

While many dramas and light entertainment programmes were cosy and reassuring, crime series began to show an increasingly aggressive and confrontational society. *The Professionals* (ITV, 1977–83) and *The Sweeney* (ITV, 1975–6, 1978) showed hard detectives with a cynical attitude towards rules and authority. This reflected the changing focus of British policing, which began using rough, tough methods in an attempt to stop the anarchy, into which, for several years in the mid-1970s, Britain appeared to be descending. In the dramatisation of the novel by John Le Carré, *Tinker, Tailor, Soldier, Spy* (BBC, 1979), even spying was shown as a much less desirable activity than in the glamorous fantasies of James Bond films.

During the 1980s crime series of all types grew in popularity. Some commentators argued it was because Britain is more penally minded than many other countries, a place where crime and punishment are more integral aspects of everyday life. Others pointed out that the Conservatives had initiated a public debate on law and order and that crime series were beginning to reflect this, showing it as a major social problem to which public, not personal solutions were needed. High levels of unemployment, drug addiction and racial discrimination sometimes forced people into marginal situations where the law was broken through necessity.

121

This scenario began to be reflected in several realist crime series of the time, such as *The Bill* (ITV, 1984–), set in the imaginary area of Sun Hill in London's East End. It is a realistic series which takes a less judgmental attitude to criminal behaviour. Although it was initially criticised for sometimes showing policemen as liars, cheats and bullies, it also received praise for its realistic representation of contemporary crime and police procedure.

As ethnic groups became more established in society, their presence was reflected in several drama series and detectives were increasingly played by non-whites. *Gangsters* (BBC, 1976, 1978) was a realistic crime series whose hero was Khan, a Pakistani undercover agent, and Britain's first ethnic leading man. But many were not shown as integrated members of either the white or black communities. Instead, they were isolated, lone individuals, such as *Wolcott* (ITV, 1981) and *The Chinese Detective* (BBC1, 1981–2). Some critics welcomed the originality of the portrayals, but as with the representation of non-whites in sitcoms and soaps, many critics said they were unrealistic and unrepresentative.

One of the most significant changes in the evolution of realist crime series was in the portrayal of women detectives and police officers. Here were feminine, disciplined ladies with a social conscience, playing major roles in the maintenance of law and order. *Juliet Bravo* (BBC, 1980–5) depicted female police inspector Jean Darblay, in charge of a provincial police station. Her fight was not only against crime, but also against the personal and professional pressures of being a woman in a macho, male-dominated profession. Similar themes were also explored in *The Gentle Touch* (ITV, 1980–4), in which a widowed policewoman has to cope with her children and career, while in the series *C.A.T.S. Eyes* (ITV, 1984–7) a policewoman is put in charge of a special intelligence section. The series were praised for their representations of women, which seemed to reflect the problems experienced not just in the police, but in many other fields of employment.

To maintain interest in the popular genre of crime series, new types were created. These were often quite diverse and combined romance with intrigue. Several presented detectives as intelligent, liberal, progressive 'new men' with colourful lifestyles in attractive locations. The wealthy Channel Island tax haven of Jersey was the setting for *Bergerac* (BBC, 1981–91), while historic Oxford and its countryside was home to the opera-going real ale lover *Inspector Morse* (ITV, 1987–97), a character adapted from Colin Dexter's Morse detective novels.

Another style is the historical adaptation. *The Adventures of Sherlock Holmes* (ITV, 1984–5, 1986–8) was said to be the most accurate portrayal ever made of Sir Arthur Conan Doyle's detective hero. The details were carefully recorded from stories which appeared in the *Strand* magazine of the 1890s and coincided with the popularity of Victorian and Edwardian houses, interiors and fashion in Britain of the 1980s. Occasional adaptations of Agatha Christie's traditional crime stories were also popular and won critical admiration. *Miss Marple* (BBC, 1984–) featured Christie's spinster detective Miss Jane Marple, the heroine of some thirty short stories published between 1930 and 1976. *Ruth Rendell Mysteries* (ITV, 1987–92) and *Poirot* (ITV, 1989–) were all popular series with a similar historical appeal.

The growth of public interest in all types of crime series led to the creation of several documentaries and 'reality' programmes. Some were popularly known as 'fly-on-the-wall' series or 'factual entertainment', in which filming took place discreetly in order not to influence events. *Police* (BBC1, 1982) recorded daily life in a Thames Valley police station and was one of several programmes on the police directed by Roger Graef. *Living in Styal* (ITV, 1982) recorded daily life in a Cheshire prison for women. But *Crimewatch* (BBC, 1984–) is a different type of series which continues to report unsolved real crimes and includes reconstructions, video films and phone-ins. These and other programmes helped to open the debate about policing, crime and punishment to a wider audience, and also made the public more aware of the problems of policing.

Politics and television

For many people the early 1980s were difficult years. The traditional industries of coal mining, steel and manufacturing were destroyed, together with their local communities. Unemployment rose to record levels. There were riots in the streets of many cities and there was a war with Argentina. Attitudes and events were mirrored in several highly praised dramas of the time.

The social costs of Conservative policies were sharply reflected in Alan Bleasdale's *Boys from the Blackstuff* (BBC, 1982). The series was set in Liverpool and showed the loss of the dignity of work in a tragicomic style – with strong performances by local characters – and typical Liverpudlian wit, in a drama which was among the most critically admired of the decade. However, even if a Labour Government was returned with a massive Parliamentary majority, it would be powerless against the right-wing forces of the civil service and press. This was the theme of *A Very British Coup* (1988), a drama series adapted from the novel by Labour MP Chris Mullin.

The Government's secrecy over nuclear defence were themes explored in Troy Kennedy-Martin's short series *Edge of Darkness* (1985). The story dealt with a police detective who investigates the murder of his daughter, a Green Party activist. But this well directed drama also addressed wider issues connected with environmental exploitation and the dangers of nuclear weapons, issues which had become of increasing public concern during the early years of the decade.

Throughout the 1980s there were numerous documentaries which were critical of the government's policies on major public issues, such as the Falklands War, rioting in the cities and unemployment. The programmes, such as *Panorama*, were made mostly by the BBC and emphasised its objectivity and impartiality in programme-making. This was frequently a problem for the Conservatives who expected more patriotism and support from national broadcasting media. In 1987 the journalist Duncan Campbell made an investigative series *Secret Society* (BBC, 1987) about political and military secrecy, but two of the six programmes were initially withdrawn due to political pressure from the government: one relating to a secret military satellite named Zircon, the other to allegations of 'dirty tricks' and illegal practices by the government during an election. This provoked a public controversy, as the government had no legal right to ban programmes in this way. However, one of the programmes was finally shown at a later date.

Two series which almost legitimised 'cheating' and malpractice in government were *Yes, Minister* (BBC, 1980–2) and later *Yes, Prime Minister* (BBC, 1986–8). They were popular political satires, which showed government officials' comical attempts to manipulate the democratic process to gain power and prestige in Westminster and Whitehall. But during the 1980s they often seemed like authentic accounts of official practice.

In 1987 political satire was allowed on television in the pre-election period for the first time since 1964. In spite of the cruel mimicry of the grotesquely funny, animated puppets of *Spitting Image* (ITV, 1984–92) and the new 'alternative' comedy which had emerged in the theatre, the 'establishment' had successfully absorbed its critics and the Conservatives won the election comfortably.

Broadcasting in the 1990s

During the 1990s a revolution in broadcasting began. In 1989 two new satellite stations merged to form BSkyB, offering a range of new channels. The British government did not have the legal powers to regulate the new satellite stations, but it recognised that a global communications network would soon be a reality and that British terrestrial television had to be prepared for greater competition. Digital, twenty-four-hour and heavily sponsored television would soon be present in many British homes, with access to 200 channels predicted by 2008. To this effect, the Conservative Government introduced the 1991 Broadcasting Act, which reorganised broadcasting, exposing it more fully to market forces.

The Act introduced a number of important changes. Fifteen broadcasting licences were given to those regional companies who, having reached certain standards of quality, could make the highest financial offer to the government. Also, the BBC and ITV were required to commission 25 per cent of their programmes from independent programme-makers, instead of relying exclusively on those made 'in house'. This provided more diverse points of view and input, but it also led to job losses. The Corporation began to rely on programmes from private companies, which were often cheaper. But critics argued that if costs became the chief consideration, it would lead to a loss of impartiality, integrity and quality in its programme-making.

A third requirement was the legal obligation on each private broadcaster to present programmes made in and about its region. A Gaelic broadcasting committee was appointed by the Independent Television Commission (ITC) to ensure that a broad selection of television and radio programmes is broadcast in Gaelic for reception in Scotland. Gaelic television began broadcasting in 1993 and other local stations were encouraged to serve ethnic minorities.

In March 1997, a new, privately owned channel, known simply as Channel 5, began broadcasting. It is subject to the same programme requirements as ITV and offers a complete service of news, sport and light entertainment. This was followed in October 1998 by the introduction of digital television, providing access to many more channels. Some critics said that more television would inevitably mean a lowering of standards in the struggle to win audiences, while others said it would offer more choice.

This is my life: television today

Authenticity, realism and an interest in other people's lives were prominent characteristics of many series of the 1990s. 'Factual entertainment' is a term which described new styles of programmes made in the mid-1990s. Some were consumer-based 'lifestyle' programmes, often with themes such as food, cars, homes or decorating. Others were about travel and tourism, particularly for young people. They reflected a need, which many had, to escape from a country deep in recession.

Another type of factual entertainment is the 'docusoap', which mixes documentary with drama. Discreet 'fly-on-the-wall' techniques were used to make programmes about daily routines in a hospital, a customs and excise department, a large hotel, Heathrow airport, a driving school, a cruise ship and an animal hospital, among many others. They provided simple, honest insights into the social lives and experiences of communities and individuals, and were cheap and easy to make. They also found large audiences and made temporary celebrities of many of the people who appeared in them. But critics said there was no creativity or analysis in such programmes. They complained that methods were sometimes not as authentic as they appeared and that they reduced the importance of serious documentaries about current affairs.

In *Video Nation Shorts* (BBC, 1995–), the public can even become stars of their own piece. Viewers submit their own two-minute videos, in which they talk to the camera on matters of topical importance. Some critics complained there was too much voyeurism in television and not enough serious analysis or quality programme-making. This could not be said of *Secret Lives* (C4, 1997–), a documentary series which scrutinised the lives of famous individuals from society and the arts, and whose well researched programmes frequently exposed a much darker side to their subjects' carefully constructed public image. Gay issues slowly began to find expression. *Out* (BBC, 1996) was a weekly information and news programme for gay men and women, but was slow to gain acceptance, and two years later the first gay series *Queer as Folk* (C4, 1999–) arrived to a critical reception.

Television increasingly became a public forum for the debate of topical matters. In 1994 the future of the monarchy was discussed in detail during a two-and-a-half hour BBC profile of Prince Charles called *Charles: The Private Man, the Public Role*, in which he spoke at length about his life and future expectations. This was followed in 1995 by a special *Panorama* interview in which the Princess of Wales talked frankly about her marriage to Charles and life within the royal circle. The programme captured the interest of the nation and was watched by 22.8 million viewers. These initiated many programmes dedicated to frank and open discussion of royal affairs, which reached fever pitch following the death of the Princess in August 1997.

Drama

The 1990s were not noted for the quantity of serious drama. As in previous years, the most critically praised were romantic interpretations of the past and were based on novels of the same name, such as Jane Austen's *Pride and Prejudice*, George Eliot's *Middlemarch* and D.H. Lawrence's *Lady Chatterley's Lover* (BBC, 1993). Among the more imaginative adaptations was Jeanette Winterson's *Oranges Are Not the Only Fruit* (BBC, 1990), which was critically received as one of the finest of recent times. The part-autobiographical work features a woman evangelist, who adopts a daughter and raises her to be a missionary, before discovering her lesbian tendencies.

Family tensions and personal struggle were also the themes of *The Buddha of Suburbia* (BBC, 1993), a humorous insight into the life of a young Indian boy caught between his family's strict Indian culture and liberal Western ways of suburban Britain in the 1970s. The story was adapted from a novel by Hanif Kureishi. This was in sharp contrast to the nostalgia and rural pleasures of *Darling Buds of May* (ITV, 1991–3), based on H.E. Bates' stories of the Larkin family. One of the most popular dramas of its time, it deals with an unmarried couple and their numerous, attractive and in many ways ideal family, set on a farm in rural Kent during the 1950s.

In recent years soap opera had been a particularly successful television genre, but *Eldorado* (BBC, 1992–3) was a spectacular failure. An ambitious, international production from the creators of *EastEnders*, it focused on the lives of an expatriate community on the Costa del Sol in southern Spain. A multinational cast promised the attractions of sun, sand and sangria. But after negative reactions in the press and an audience of only five million, the sun set on the series after only twelve months.

Crime series continued to be diverse and original, and provided some of the most highly praised and popular drama on television. Violence and car chases, two characteristic elements of so many earlier series, were now unfashionable and rarely seen in police dramas. Even one of the more traditional detectives, *Spender* (BBC1, 1991), set in the tough urban area of Newcastle and featuring Jimmy Nail as Jedd, focused on his moody, melancholic nature more than on catching villains. Women continued to take more prominent roles as detectives and police officers. In *Prime Suspect* (ITV, 1991, 1992), Helen Mirren was highly praised as Jane Tennison, the tenacious, intelligent detective who leads an investigation into the murder of a Soho transsexual, but also has to deal with an arrogant, sexist and corrupt police force.

Black and Asian characters were occasionally cast in central roles, for example in *Thief Takers* (ITV, 1997–), a successful drama with a well-written script and realistic plot. Other crime series included *Sam Saturday* (ITV, 1992–4), with the unorthodox character of Detective Inspector Sam Stones, a young, Jewish, divorced policeman who lived alone and looked after his mother, while *Pie in the Sky* (BBC, 1996–) featured a semi-retired detective looking after a country restaurant. The countryside was also the setting for *Heartbeat* (ITV, 1992–). Based on the books of retired policeman Nicholas Rhea and set in the late 1960s, the nostalgic series showed the humorous side of policing in the rural northern area of the Yorkshire Dales.

Comedy

Humour and sitcoms continued to offer some of the most lively and original material on television, as modern relationships became the subject of several successful comedy series. *Men Behaving Badly* (ITV, 1992; BBC, 1994–8) resembled the earlier *Likely Lads*, depicting the escapades of two young men in a South London flatshare, while the comical *Absolutely Fabulous* (BBC, 1992–5) provided a comical portrait of two 1960s generation colleagues from a fashion magazine. *One Foot in the Grave* (BBC, 1990–) provided a rather different but nevertheless humorous commentary on the challenges and opportunities of old age.

A more cynical and subversive commentary on life is offered by *Rab C. Nesbitt* (BBC, 1990–). It is set in Glasgow and features the sublime adventures of Rab, his family and friends. In the classic Glaswegian style, Rab is a cheeky, subversive character. To comic effect, he dresses like a tramp, in a string vest and a blood-stained bandage. His opinions are direct but always good-natured and are delivered in a thick monologue of Glaswegian slang on such varied topics as drugs, marriage, justice, the family, God, sex and war. *Rab C. Nesbitt* is a singular series and one of the most unusual and original ever made.

Repeats of popular 'classic' series from the 1960s and 1970s, such as *Dad's Army*, *The Likely Lads*, *Monty Python*, *Steptoe and Son* and *Porridge* continued to attract large audiences, but one outstanding new success was *I'm Alan Partridge* (BBC1, 1997–), a comic portrayal of a failed television presenter, which won a BAFTA award for best comedy and was said by many critics to be the best comedy series since *Fawlty Towers*.

Political satire appeared to be in decline, but one of the most successful comedy shows was *Have I Got News for You* (BBC, 1990–), in which Ian Hislop (the editor of the satirical magazine *Private Eye*) and comedian Paul Merton fearlessly satirise the week's news in politics and society. *Drop the Dead Donkey* (C4, 1990–) similarly deals with elements of the week's news, in a topical sitcom set in the newsroom of a commercial television company.

The last four decades, have seen increasing competition for viewers' attention. It became more intense as the public continued to watch approximately the same amount of television as ten years previously. However, a small number (1 per cent of the population) do not have or want television in their homes. Many of them read the journal *White Dot* for mutual support and encouragement. But at the end of the decade it is the viewers who have their finger on the button. Unlike in previous decades, decisions about what to watch now rest not with the television companies, but with the viewer.

Discussion topics and activities

1   What do you consider to be the most distinctive characteristics of British television since the 1970s?
2   What are the advantages and disadvantages of having a state-run monopoly of television, funded by a television licence? Would you like to see it in your country?
3   Use the text and other sources to explain the following: pirate radio / the ITC / fantasy and realism / soap opera / crime series.
4   In what ways does television affect your life?
5   Think about the representation of women and minority groups in television dramas and soap operas in your country. Is their depiction realistic, is it stereotyped, or does it depend on the type of programmes?
6   Take an example of a soap opera or crime series with which you are familiar. Describe its main characteristics and say what you like or

dislike about it. Write a review of a recent episode for the television section of a 'quality' newspaper.

Suggested further reading

Books

Alvarado, M. and Stewart, J. (1985) *Made for Television: Euston Films Limited* London: BFI Publishing.

BBC Annual Report and Accounts (1997–8) London: BBC Publications.

Brandt, G. (ed.) (1981) *British Television Drama* Cambridge: Cambridge University Press.

Briggs, A. (1995) *History of Broadcasting in the UK, 1922–75* Oxford: Oxford University Press.

Bryant, S. (1989) *The Television Heritage* London: BFI Publishing.

Cain, J. (1992) *The BBC: Seventy Years of Broadcasting* London: BBC Publications.

Chapman, G., Cleese, J., Jones, T., Gilliam, T. and Palin, M. (1989) *Monty Python's Flying Circus: Just the Words, Vols 1 and 2* London: Methuen.

Cornell, P. and Day, M. (1993) *The Guinness Book of Classic British Television* Enfield: Guinness Publishing.

Daniels, T. (ed.) (1989) *The Colour Black: Black Images in British Television* London: BFI Publishing.

Fulton, R. (1990) *The Encyclopaedia of TV Science Fiction* London: Boxtree.

Halliwell, L. and Purser, P. (1996) *Halliwell's Television Companion* London: Collins.

Harbord, J. and Wright, J. (1995) *Forty Years of British Television* London: Boxtree.

Hunter, A. (ed.) (1991) *Chambers Film and TV Handbook* London: Chambers.

Kingsley, H. (1988) *The Papermac Guide to Soap Opera* London: Papermac.

Selby, K. and Cowdray, R. (1995) *How to Study Television* Basingstoke: Macmillan.

Taylor, R. (1994) *The Guinness Book of Sitcoms* Enfield: Guinness Publishing.

Tibballs, G. (1991) *The Golden Age of Children's Television* London: Titan.

Vahimagi, T. (1994) *British Television: An Illustrated Guide* London: BFI Publishing.

Journals

Listener (Listener Publications Limited, 1929–91)

Radio Times (BBC Magazines, 1923–)

Spectator (Spectator Ltd, 1828–)

Television – The Journal of the Royal Television Society (Royal Television Society, 1927–)

TV Times (Independent Television Publications, 1955–)

Information on television and radio programmes can be found in all the national daily newspapers, which often comment on those of the previous day. The quality Sunday newspapers also carry reviews of the previous week's terrestrial television programmes and a preview of the next.

Many television series from the 1960s, 1970s and 1980s are broadcast on the satellite channel UK Gold, while the BBC's Learning Zone programmes often examine the treatment of issues such as racism and political correctness on television.

7

Popular music and fashion

Introduction

For many young people in Britain, music is an important element of youth culture. It is part of a world of fashion, image and style, which together express identity and individuality. But it is also one of Britain's most valuable creative industries, currently worth over 4 billion dollars to the UK economy.

Music also forms part of a communal experience and can be heard 'live' in a variety of settings, from small pubs to large fields and football stadiums. During the summer months, festivals of all types of music are held. Some take place over several days, such as Glastonbury in south-west England, while in London the Notting Hill Carnival is Britain's biggest street party. It is held by the Caribbean community each year and features exotic types of dance music, from Caribbean steel bands to reggae and rap.

Music broadcasting is well established in the mass media. BBC Radio 1 and 2, together with numerous independent radio stations, broadcast hundreds of hours each week. Jazz and classical music are widely appreciated. Jazz can be heard on specialist radio and television programmes, as well as on Jazz FM in London and the north-west, while BBC Radio 3 and the independent station Classic FM broadcast classical music around Britain. As well as music on radio and television, there are numerous newspapers, style magazines, fanzines and a flourishing specialised music press which all carry regular columns of information, gossip and comment on music of all kinds.

Many musicians begin without any formal training. Others learn at school and complete their studies at one of the prestigious London centres, such as the Royal College of Music, the Guildhall School of Music and Drama and Trinity College of Music. Outside London, the main centres are the Royal Scottish Academy of Music and Drama (in Glasgow), and the Welsh College of Music and Drama (in Cardiff). Many other colleges and universities also offer degrees and diplomas in musical study.

For many years, jazz, classical and pop music were seen as very different types of music. But as popular music has become more diverse, this has begun to change. In recent years pop musicians have increasingly recorded jazz, classical and classical-influenced music. At the same time, jazz and classically trained players have recorded popular songs. Classical pieces are regularly used in advertising, film soundtracks and television films, while singers such as Pavarotti have entered the British music charts with their recordings.

However, interest in more traditional recordings of classical music has declined. In 1996 the sales of classical music accounted for only 6.4 per cent of music compact discs. Full-length symphonies and operas did not sell easily and new recordings appeared which featured only selected extracts of classical works.

Early popular music

Before the nineteenth century, folk music was the most common musical form in Britain. Stories and information were communicated in folk songs, which often reflected the region and occupation of the author. But during the early nineteenth century the folk tradition declined in England, as people moved from the countryside to the towns and cities. There, music was made and heard in the park, the street and the public house. In the industrial areas of the north, brass bands were numerous and there were choral societies in many areas. Music-making was also a popular practice in the home, where for many years the piano and the voice were the principal sources of entertainment.

As the Victorian cities grew in size, public entertainments became more extensive and varied. Larger public houses and theatres known as 'music halls' were built for 'variety' shows of singing and comedy. Soon afterwards, chains of music halls opened in cities around the country. Local and regional influences began to disappear as London became the centre of musical activity for agents, songwriters, musicians and performers.

One of the most profitable activities was professional songwriting. Songwriters and music publishers got an agreed sum or 'royalty' from their published songs or 'sheet music'. These were frequently improved by the common but illegal practice of bribing famous singers to adopt their material. By the end of the nineteenth century, popular entertainments and music-making were established commercial practices. The entertainments world was popularly known as 'Tin Pan Alley' and London's Denmark Street was its commercial heart.

During the early 1920s, traditional jazz and 'ragtime' music began to arrive from the United States. The dances which accompanied the music were more informal and easier to learn than the complicated European ones and dancing became popular and fashionable. British hotels and restaurants began to provide ballrooms and dancefloors in imitation of the fashionable New York establishments. The BBC broadcast concerts from exclusive London hotels, such as the Savoy, the Dorchester and the Grosvenor House, while couples at home rolled up the carpet and danced to the music. Its popularity grew and soon afterwards dancehalls opened around Britain.

The arrival of American musicals such as *Porgy and Bess* and *Oklahoma* during the 1930s brought the smoother, more sophisticated music of Cole Porter and George Gershwin to British ears. Their songs were relaxed and assured, glamorous and seductive, just like the singers who performed them. This popular style of singing was known as 'crooning', which involved the intimate expression of private emotions to the audience in songs sung slowly and sentimentally. In Britain, many women singers became successful, such as Gracie Fields and 'the Forces' sweetheart' Vera Lynn. The liberated sound of modern jazz, or 'bebop', had also begun to arrive from America. But its anarchic, ironic, rebellious nature required concentration and dedication, and its popularity was largely confined to intellectual audiences.

After the Second World War, popular music consisted of slowly and sentimentally sung ballads, usually telling stories of unrequited love. These were sung by Italian-Americans, such as Frank Sinatra, Perry Como, Mario Lanza and Dean Martin. British 'crooners' included Frankie Vaughn, Dickie Valentine and Ronnie Hilton. Theirs was relaxed and rhythmical music, created for refined, elegant dancing.

A gramophone and records were still expensive items and popular music was a mainly adult pastime. But with new technology, production costs soon fell. Radios became smaller and, with the invention of the transistor radio by Sony in 1955, the number of listeners quickly grew. In America, new radio stations appeared everywhere. They offered lively music shows to capture and seduce a generation of affluent young Americans. Advertising was an important source of income and to create more airtime for publicity, stations demanded shorter songs of under three minutes. Commercial musicians began to write short, lively songs to capture the listeners' attention.

In 1955 a list of the twenty top-selling singles was published in the British music journal *Record Mirror*. It was compiled from the previous week's record sales at a number of shops around the country. Initially it was used by the industry to provide information about the most popular kind of music, but it was soon used for publicity and encouraged young fans to buy the most popular kinds of music. The 'Hit Parade' or 'Top Twenty' had arrived.

Rock'n'roll: the coming

By 1955 in America, the dream of a free, prosperous, consumer culture appeared to be coming true. There was full employment and businesses were beginning to market their products to affluent teenagers. This newly found independence was often expressed in the kind of clothes they wore, the kind of music they listened to and the heroes they idolised.

But many felt a sense of dissatisfaction. In spite of their material success, America was almost at war with Russia and the political situation was tense and confused. Many young men felt contemptuous of the world their parents had created and initially found rebellious new heroes in the cinema. American stars such as Marlon Brando and James Dean were playing angry, anti-authoritarian roles in films such as *The Wild One* (1953) and *Rebel Without a Cause* (1955). However, it was during 1955, the year of Dean's death, that rebellion found sonorial expression in the soundtrack to *Blackboard Jungle*, a film about a group of aggressive young students. It was considered a turbulent and shocking movie, but its musical significance lies in the moment the unknown band of Bill Haley and the Comets assault the audience with the movie's theme-song, 'Rock Around the Clock'. This was rock'n'roll music: vibrant, spirited and anarchic.

When the film came to Britain, its effect was electrifying. The youthful audience rose from their cinema seats to jump and dance. The theme-song was released as a single and for five months it was the most popular record in Britain. When a quickly made movie of the same name was released in 1956, it led to vandalism and riots in many cinemas. Some municipal authorities banned it, while its effects on youth were discussed in Parliament, police stations, pulpits and the press. It was as if a Martian spaceship had crashed in London.

The term 'rock'n'roll' was first used by the American DJ Alan Freed to describe a cocktail of country music, blues, jazz and religious music known as gospel. This was largely exploited by black musicians such as Chuck Berry. Its name was derived from the frequent mention of 'rock' and 'roll' in the song titles and lyrics, which in black American-English meant 'have sex' or 'make love', but its significance was lost on the innocence of the British public.

As rock'n'roll grew in popularity, white American musicians copied the sound. The alien music was often spoken in tongues and animal cries: A Wop Bop A Lu Bop, Be Bop A Lula, Oooooeeeee uh-uh oooooh yeah! Few could understand the lyrics and the critics had no language with which to discuss it. There were no previous points of reference, nothing with which to compare it. But for white British youth it was a cry of liberation and sexual freedom. In the words of Prime Minister Harold Macmillan, they had never had it so good.

The arrival of rock'n'roll had a great effect on British youth culture. Among the early fans were 'New Edwardians', better-known as 'Teddy Boys' or 'Teds'. Their long, elaborate jackets with velvet on the collar and pockets revived a style cultivated by young male aristocrats during the time of King Edward VII (1901–10). The jacket was worn with American country-style clothing: 'bootlace' ties, narrow 'drainpipe' trousers, brightly coloured socks, heavy suede shoes with thick rubber soles and hair swept up and back, heavily greased with Brylcream. Their appearance was a florid sight in the coffee bars and cinemas of 1950s Britain.

The Teds disliked conformity, austerity and authority, and sometimes there were fights and acts of vandalism. The media began to associate them with rebelliousness and a threat to society. Their differences in style, in tastes and opinions, and more visibly in music, clothes and behaviour began to mark what journalists described as the 'generation gap'.

While many people were excited and enthusiastic about the changes taking place in British society, others felt their authority was in danger, and that the traditional social order was breaking down. The BBC did nothing to promote the new music and at first the music press were almost as hostile as Parliament and the Church. In the early 1950s the *Melody Maker*, a leading music weekly, openly criticised rock'n'roll and defined jazz as quality popular music.

After Haley there were other Americans who gained enormous fame in Britain and sold millions of records, such as Elvis Presley, Buddy Holly, Eddie Cochran and Jerry Lee Lewis. Few British singers could match their popularity. The most notable, such as Tommy Steele, Marty Wilde, and later Cliff Richard and Adam Faith, were not native speakers of this new musical language. They had little knowledge of the origins of rhythm and blues, country music and gospel. They had little understanding of how the cries and shouts were derived from communion with the Lord. Instead, the demands of British show-business softened their song. They removed its heat and punch, making it more restrained and commercially acceptable. But by 1962 rock'n'roll was in decline and many critics wondered if popular music had a future.

Skiffle

Although the explosive, driving rhythms of rock'n'roll were easy to compose, they were difficult to imitate, as electric instruments and amplification were still scarce in Britain. But around 1953 an acoustic type of music known as 'skiffle' had emerged in and around the clubs of London's Soho. It was fast and rhythmical, and required a minimum of musical expertise. The instruments were few: a 'washboard' (a type of percussion instrument), two acoustic guitars and an acoustic bass, with the option of a kazoo, a banjo or a piano. Music was played with few keys and few chords, but the vigorous rhythmic support for the vocals made it distinctive and infectious.

Like rock'n'roll, its origins were black and American, and almost anyone could do it. A D-I-Y musical revolution began, as youths without any musical knowledge or training picked up an instrument and taught themselves to play. Stars emerged, such as Lonnie Donegan and Ken Colyer. Donegan's *Rock Island Line* (1956) was the first British record which sold well in America, reaching number 6 in the US charts. The music was popular with people of all ages and between 1956 and 1958 there was a 'boom', with up to 40,000 small groups in Britain. Skiffle was free of commercial pressures and could be played by virtually anyone. It was popular with young, left-wing intellectuals in the art schools. They found its elemental, authentic sound an attractive, democratic one.

Its popular influence spread. The BBC's Religious Department authorised a Twentieth-Century Folk Mass which included skiffle music. The Salvation Army had the Hallelujah Skiffle Group and the breakfast cereal *Rice Krispies* offered a free 'skiffle whistle'. But proposing the washboard as a new route to the future of rock'n'roll was never taken seriously and by 1958 the acoustic music began to disappear in favour of a more exciting amplified sound.

As popular music began to be exploited by the industry, numerous venues opened around Britain where bands could be seen and heard. Newcastle, Manchester and Birmingham offered a range of clubs and dancehalls, but it was the cosmopolitan seaport of Liverpool which provided the focus for an international revolution in pop. Its clubs, coffee bars and dancehalls were already venues for poetry and jazz, and there was even a local pop paper, *Mersey Beat*. Between 1962 and 1964 hundreds of local groups began competing for attention, playing a mixture of black-influenced pop songs with faster, more aggressive rock'n'roll – a sound which became known as 'Mersey Beat'. Few bands survived or progressed, but one became the most famous in the world: the Beatles.

The Beatles

The history of the Beatles begins with a little-known Liverpool skiffle band – the Quarrymen – which comprised four working-class Liverpudlians who would later compose and play the most successful music in the history of pop: John Lennon (1940–80), Paul McCartney (b.1942), George Harrison (b.1943) and by 1962 Ringo Starr (b. Richard Starkey, 1940).

The group earlier played under different names with different personnel, but inspired by their new manager Brian Epstein their fortunes changed. 'Love Me Do' (1962) was highly successful and over the next two years the Beatles had numerous fresh, exciting singles which reached

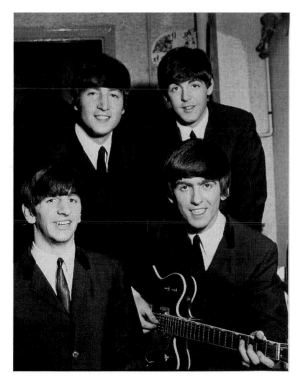

Figure 7.1 The Beatles *c.* 1964: (clockwise from top left) John, Paul, George and Ringo

number 1 in the British music charts, such as 'She Loves You', 'I Want To Hold Your Hand' and 'Can't Buy Me Love'.

With their distinctive long hair, white shirts, narrow ties and dark suits, they mixed charm with cheek. Because they looked and spoke like their fans, many people identified with them and they quickly became popular around Britain. They sang short, attractive songs about everyday life and used popular slang in the lyrics. Many were sentimental and expressed a nostalgia for the past. Before the Beatles, most pop groups copied well-known American hits, or used the material of a professional songwriter. However, most Beatles' hits were written by Lennon and McCartney, with the main contributor on each song providing the lead vocals.

In 1963 they were described in *The Sunday Times* newspaper as 'the greatest composers since Beethoven' and in 1965 they were awarded the MBE by Harold Wilson, the Labour Prime Minister. Their intense popularity became known as 'Beatlemania', which in the United States was even more fanatical than in Britain. But in 1966 the intense hysteria which accompanied their appearances everywhere led the Beatles to stop touring.

137

As the group matured their music became more eclectic. It embraced a variety of styles, from the soulful 'Got to Get You into My Life' to the music-hall humour of 'When I'm Sixty Four'. In 1967 the group released *Sergeant Pepper's Lonely Hearts Club Band*, a radical departure from their earlier material, but also a highly accomplished and varied recording. In a pioneering style which influenced the recording and packaging of subsequent popular music, one song flowed into the next and the lyrics appeared in print on the record sleeve, which was designed by the pop artist Peter Blake. But the music also indicated the band's interest in drugs and mysticism, and they lost many of their former fans. However, the album's sophistication also found them a new, more intellectual audience, and marked the arrival of pop music as an object of serious comment.

The band were still popular and famous, but they were also under pressure. They began to look for more independence, both creatively and personally. When their manager died in 1967 the band members began to work more independently, but financial and musical problems started to have a greater importance. By 1970 all members of the group had made solo albums and in the same year the group officially broke up, after fifteen US and thirteen UK number 1 albums, and twenty-one US and seventeen UK number 1 singles. During their eight years together they created the best-loved body of songwriting and music in the whole of post-war pop.

British rhythm and blues

Many British musicians were attracted to black American music: the emotion of black soul singers such as James Brown; the rhythmic, soul-blues of Ray Charles, and the harder, more energetic urban blues of Muddy Waters, John Lee Hooker and Howlin' Wolf. Several composers began to incorporate different elements of the black musicians' work into their own musical repertoires, mixing them with other influences to produce a new kind of music.

The principal British exponent was Alexis Korner and his band Blues Incorporated. His was the world's first noted white blues group. Between 1962 and 1967 they influenced many other emerging British bands, such as the Animals, the Yardbirds (with Eric Clapton and Jeff Beck), the Spencer Davies Group (with Steve Winwood), Fleetwood Mac and the Rolling Stones. Their style became known as British rhythm and blues (r'n'b). At first they were seen as exotic musical acts playing a strange kind of music, but they soon found enthusiastic audiences. To publicise it, a network of new clubs appeared around the country, the most famous being the Marquee in London's Wardour Street, and in 1964 an open air National Jazz and Blues Festival was organised at Reading in Berkshire.

The Rolling Stones

The most successful and long-lived of the early British r'n'b groups is the Rolling Stones. They were formed in 1962 by Mick Jagger (b.1943), who abandoned his studies at the London School of Economics to focus on a more colourful career in music. Keith Richard (later Richards, b.1943), Brian Jones (1942–69), Bill Wyman (b. William Perks, 1936) and Charlie Watts (b.1941) joined soon after, replacing other musicians. They began making regular appearances at clubs in West London, in and around the suburb of Richmond. Andrew Loog Oldham began to manage them and, in contrast to the more conservative image of the Beatles and other groups of the time, developed their image as wild, sexy and bohemian. They had long hair and wore strange exotic clothes, at a time when most people wore short hair and dressed modestly.

Pop groups were desperate for good publicity, but the Stones made no attempt to be polite to journalists. Although they desired commercial success, they conspicuously rejected the traditional means to achieve it, such as hard work and personal sacrifice. Many of the older generation were shocked by their appearance and behaviour, which ensured their appeal to a younger audience.

Their musical influences are various, but have been largely based around rhythm and blues, supplied from Richards' guitar and Jagger's blues-inspired vocals. Their early material consisted of cover versions of well-known blues and rock'n'roll songs, and were immediately popular. Their first two albums – both entitled *The Rolling Stones* – went to the top of the music charts.

To compete with the Beatles they began writing their own songs, with Jagger usually composing the lyrics and Richards the music. The rhythms and themes of their early songs (notably on the album *Aftermath* in 1996) provided an explosive combination. In 1965, their first number 1 single in both the UK and America was '(I Can't Get No) Satisfaction', a success which was repeated with 'Jumpin' Jack Flash' in 1968. Both showed the power and energy of the group at their best and established them as an exotic, potent, musical force.

In 1969 Brian Jones left the group, and shortly afterwards was found dead in his swimming pool. Mick Taylor joined the band, but left in 1975 to be replaced by Ron Wood. In 1993 Bill Wyman left, and was replaced by Darryl Jones. No other group has had more British or American album hits, and thirty years after their formation their live shows continue to break box office records around the world.

Since the late 1970s spectacular concerts in huge sports stadiums around the world have become a central part of their career. But they have continued to release a steady succession of singles and albums in addition to their own solo projects. Their most critically praised albums were those of the late 1960s and *Exile on Main Street* (1972), although *Emotional*

Rescue (1980) and *Voodoo Lounge* (1993) were also widely admired. Public interest in the band has also been sustained by the colourful private lives of its members, with Jagger's first marriage to the Nicaraguan model Bianca Perez-Mora and subsequently to the American model Jerry Hall, while Richards' problems with drugs and the police have become the stuff of legend.

Mods!

While the Beatles and the Stones were seducing British audiences with their shows, soul (especially from the Tamla Motown label) and Jamaican ska (or 'bluebeat') were the main musical styles of black America and the Caribbean. They had a strong regular beat and were good records for dancing. In the affluence and excitement of London in the early 1960s, their popularity grew in parallel with pop. Few bands could play live dance music, so clubs offered recorded music or 'discs' and became 'discotheques', one of the first being La Discotheque which opened in 1964 on London's Wardour Street.

Dance music was also heavily promoted on the television programme *Ready, Steady, Go!* (ITV, 1963–6). A 'club' atmosphere was created in the studio, in which the audience was part of the show. New dances such as the Bunny Hop, the Locomotion and the Twist were performed by fashionably dressed fans. The programme transmitted visual messages around the country about music, dance and fashion in the metropolis. In London during this time, the fashion was minimal and modernist.

For some years a clearly defined, sartorial style had been developing among some young fashion-conscious Londoners known as 'mods'. The male interpretation typically included a lightweight, continental suit with a three-button, two-vent jacket, narrow trousers, button-collar shirt, narrow tie, zip boots and short hair, with long green anoraks known as 'parkas' to protect their clothes. The female style of mini-skirt, thick, bright make-up, thick mascara and short, straight hair imitated a 'look' made popular by leading models such as Twiggy, Jean Shrimpton and Mary Quant.

Consumerism was a central element of mod style and one of its most conspicuous features was the Vespa or Lambretta scooter, usually festooned with many lights and mirrors. By 1964 it provided many London mods with a way to reach Brighton, a popular coastal resort which became the location for confrontations with groups of 'rockers'. The 'rockers' were a more traditional manifestation of working-class culture. Central elements were motorcycles, leather jackets, denim jeans and long hair, in imitation of the American motorcycle gangs of the early 1950s, as seen in the American films *The Wild One* (1953) and *Rebel Without a Cause* (1955). But mod style was more influential and spread to rock music through the influence of The Who and the Small Faces.

The Who had their first hit with 'I Can't Explain' (1965). Roger Daltrey's powerful vocals, Pete Townshend's chopped guitar chords, John Entwhistle's jet-engine bass and Keith Moon's manic drumming supplied the energy and aggression in their music. They had a reputation as arrogant, angry and unpredictable, and – to the delight of their fans – the band spectacularly smashed their instruments at the end of their shows. 'My Generation' (1965) was one of their most famous songs, a violent musical declaration about the inability of a younger generation to communicate with an older one.

Although several male mod bands became highly successful, there were still few women singers in British pop. Those who managed to develop a career, such as Lulu, Dusty Springfield and Cilla Black, sang sentimental songs in the jazz and cabaret style, before working elsewhere in show business where their talents were more appreciated.

Soul and reggae

During the late 1960s black dance music from Jamaica and the USA continued to grow in popularity. The light, crude, highly rhythmical ska became briefly fashionable, made popular by artists such as Prince Buster and Judge Dread. Ska preceded the slower, smoother, more hypnotic reggae music of Bob Marley, Peter Tosh and others.

Marley was born in Jamaica and became the first international star from a developing country. His songs, such as 'Get Up, Stand Up' (1973), were often influenced by his Rastafarian beliefs, and gave support to the poor and underprivileged. Before his death in 1981, his music had become some of the most distinctive and admired in modern pop.

Paradoxically, ska and reggae also became fashionable among a minor but violent subculture known as 'skinheads' who were known for their racism and violence. This made them easy recruits for an ultra-right wing organisation, the National Front. They quickly earned a reputation for attacking blacks and Asians, as well as other minority groups such as hippies and gays. Wearing a characteristic 'uniform' of button-collar shirts, tight, short Levi jeans, heavy boots (ideally twenty-seven-hole Dr Martens) or 'loafer' shoes, and shaven heads, their display of stylised aggression in the football stadiums of Britain marked the start of soccer hooliganism.

Skinheads gradually disappeared from both the terraces and streets until the early 1980s when a brief revival saw 'neo-skinhead' bands such as the 4 Skins, Cock Sparrer and Sham 69 playing punk-inspired rock music. This was part of the 'Oi' movement, an anti-authoritarian alliance of far-right groups in Britain and abroad. But their crude political message of racism, hooliganism and street violence was much louder than its artistic one and, as a musical force, it quickly disappeared.

'Northern soul' was another important point of access for fans of black dance music. During the late 1960s fans began to meet in the clubs of towns in the north of England to collect and dance to black American soul music. However, fans did not want to hear the latest records, but those by obscure artists from the earlier in the decade. Many were made before major record companies signed the artists and changed their style to make them more commercially acceptable, therefore records were often extremely rare. They were not produced in large quantities, but sometimes reached Britain in the belongings of American servicemen and students, or could sometimes be found in specialist record shops. Fans believed these recordings were more original and authentically expressive than later, more commercial material.

Some soul clubs founded their own record labels to reissue records. Special all-night sessions were organised in which distinctive, acrobatic dancing in stylish baggy clothing was standard. In 1970 the term 'northern soul' was first heard to describe this scene of DJs, collectors and dance fans, which reflected its origins in northern towns such as Wolverhampton, Stoke, Leeds and Nottingham. Wigan Casino became the best-known club, its name synonymous with the music of obscure artists such as the Pioneers and the Prophets.

During the 1970s 'northern soul' remained highly popular in the Midlands and north. However, its records were old and rare so there was no major investment by the record industry. Consequently it has remained isolated and uninfluential, even though an enthusiastic group of fans continue to 'keep the faith' and maintain the tradition.

Progressive music

During the mid-1960s popular music began to change and diversify. Some musicians decided they did not want to write short, popular songs for the radio and the charts. They wanted the freedom to write longer songs, to experiment with musical sounds and to demonstrate their musical virtuosity. The Beatles had already begun to play with lyrics, sound and song-length in progressive albums such as *Rubber Soul* (1965), *Revolver* (1966) and *Sergeant Pepper* (1967). Following their example, many other musicians began rejecting the limitations of the traditional three-minute pop song, writing longer pieces for LPs. Album sales increased and a chart of the most popular LPs (long playing records) began in 1964.

Pink Floyd and Soft Machine were some of the earliest innovators and were later followed by Yes, Genesis (later with Phil Collins) and Emerson Lake and Palmer. They found a keen and loyal following among the largely middle-class public in colleges, art schools and universities. By 1970, some groups had begun writing a series of songs based around a particular theme – these were known as concept albums. Although their aims were still commercial, progressive musicians now wanted to achieve them using different methods to those working elsewhere in pop. During the 1970s progressive bands went on to become highly successful in

Britain and America, with their characteristic extended solos, pompous lyrics, grand orchestration and extravagant costumes. For some years they influenced many other groups in Europe and America who copied their style.

Meanwhile, other musicians who had started playing r'n'b progressed into blues and rock music. Eric Clapton, hailed at the time as the most talented guitarist in Britain, had left the Yardbirds and formed Cream in 1966. Groups such as Led Zeppelin, Deep Purple and Black Sabbath, founded a related style of 'heavy' rock music. Its elements of fantasy, repetitive guitar 'riffs', screaming vocals and thunderous bass and drums quickly proved influential. They were popular with 'hippies': young Americans who conspicuously rejected conventional ideas and lifestyles, and instead experimented with alternative ways of living based on peace and love. By 1967 this had spread to London, where a hippy dress-style involved exotic, Asian clothing, often mixed nostalgically with items of clothing from the nineteenth century. Long hair, sandals and faded jeans were also common elements of a unisex 'look' which many older people found decadent and provocative.

For some hippies, the simplicity and purity of folk music represented an attractive alternative to the commercial nature of modern rock. In Britain, folk had gained a reputation as an earnest musical form, which during the 1950s and 1960s became popular among left-wing students, bohemians and Irish expatriates. In the United States Joan Baez, Bob Dylan and others combined its simplicity with lyrics of radical protest to widen its appeal. They were idolised in Britain, where Donovan and others sang a mixture of folk and rock. Later in the 1970s, folk rock became established with the success of British groups such as Fairport Convention, Steeleye Span and the Albion Country Band. They played numerous small festivals and events held quietly and discreetly, outside the commercial mainstream. But they rarely appealed to a mass audience and, for many of their fans, this helped to maintain their attraction.

All that glitters ...

By 1970 a musical 'third way' had been proposed. This involved combining elements of folk music and electric pop. Some of the earliest exponents were Marc Bolan and David Bowie. In 1971 Bolan formed the rock group T. Rex and began wearing glitter and make-up. This was considered daring and provocative, but ensured maximum publicity for the band. Between 1971 and 1973 they had a succession of hit singles, such as 'Ride a White Swan', 'Get it On', 'Jeepster' and 'Hot Love'. They mixed dreamy poetic vocals with an exciting electric sound, in celebrations of hedonism and sexuality.

The popularity of T. Rex and David Bowie influenced many others to adopt a similar stage image. The Sweet, Mud and the Bay City Rollers

143

were among the first to cultivate a theatrical, sexually androgynous 'look'. Many fans began to imitate their heroes, wearing make-up, glitter, velvet and ludicrously high platform shoes, and concerts began to look like fashion shows. The glamorous, theatrical style became known as 'glam' rock. However, there was little musical unity among its exponents. The strong, rhythmic beat and 'sing-along' choruses of Gary Glitter and Slade, the lyrical simplicity of Elton John, the heavy metal pop of Queen and the avant-garde pop-rock experimentalism of Roxy Music were all received enthusiastically by millions of fans.

Although Queen later became one of the most successful bands of their time, Roxy Music were immediately respected and influential. They were led by Brian Ferry, who had been taught by the pop artist Richard Hamilton. Ferry brought wit, intelligence and pop art style into their music, into their theatrical stage act and into their album sleeves of statuesque models. In their five albums, released between 1972 and 1975, the music was innovative, wild and distinctive, and was consistently admired. For both groups and fans, style was becoming as important as musical ability. But many music critics were less enthusiastic. They saw the new trends as vulgar, ostentatious, highly commercial and a victory of artifice over art.

David Bowie

One of the most enduring and influential performers to emerge from the early 1970s is David Bowie (b. David Jones, 1947), a singer, songwriter and guitarist who has become one of the most successful, controversial and influential of British singers. He came into music from dance and drama, and, after leading several modest rock bands, he began as a solo artist. In 1969 he had his first major success with the single and album *Space Oddity*, a dreamy, folk-inspired mixture of singer-songwriting based on the views of an alien visitor to Earth. It also marked the projection of his songs through different stage characters, beginning with the astronaut Major Tom.

Bowie became interested in the music of American singers Lou Reed and Iggy Pop, and at the same time began to introduce more shocking and theatrical elements into his own performances. In 1971 he changed to a heavier rock sound for the album *Man Who Sold the World*. To publicise it he wore glitter, make-up and even a dress, which at the time was considered taboo. Shortly afterwards he made *The Rise and Fall of Ziggy Stardust and the Spiders from Mars* (1972), a sequence of songs about a mythical pop star. Ironically, it was the record which made Bowie famous. It was critically received as the first post-modern record in popular music and marked the first of many high points in his career.

His performances were also significant for their incorporation of theatre and costume. In 1973–4 his controversial stage shows were the most elaborate ever seen, with the artist appearing in concert with a painted face, florid, provocative costumes, and publicly admitting his bisexuality. This was followed by *Aladdin Sane* (1974), an album which suggested imminent nuclear war. Soon after came *Diamond Dogs* (1975), a dark album about an Orwellian nightmare future, released at a time of high unemployment, strikes and inflation.

Since the mid-1970s Bowie has worked with numerous different bands and backing musicians, and has consistently made stylish and highly varied albums. He later became involved with soul, funk and New Romantic bands. He also began a career as an actor, playing the leading role of John Merrick in the Broadway play *The Elephant Man* (1980) and making several films, among the most acclaimed being Nicolas Roeg's *The Man Who Fell to Earth* (1974). In the late 1990s Bowie was critically respected as original and influential performer who, during the past thirty years, changed the style of British pop.

The roots of rebellion

During the mid-1970s all the major bands in the world were British. Pink Floyd, Led Zeppelin, Genesis, Yes, Emerson Lake and Palmer, the Moody Blues and the Rolling Stones had all become wealthy and successful, but rarely visited Britain. Although their performances had become larger and more spectacular, their financial interests frequently eliminated any subversive behaviour or risk-taking. But recent lengthy 'concept' albums and experiments with classical music were seen by many fans as pompous, excessive and extravagant. Lawyers, accountants, agents and publicists ensured that their business was as safe, organised, predictable and profitable as any other. The result was increasingly conservative pop and rock music.

Writing about popular music became serious and deferential, and few journalists dared to criticise the pop and rock 'establishment'. Articles appearing in the music press such as *Sounds*, the *New Musical Express*, *Melody Maker*, *Time Out* and the American *Rolling Stone* began to resemble sycophantic literary reviews and there was boredom with the elevation of popular music into a 'high' art form.

In response, some British musicians began to revive the honest simplicity of styles from the 1950s and 1960s. They played short, direct three-minute songs in a mixture of r'n'b, rock'n'roll and American country music styles. This fundamentalist revival began in the south of England, in small pubs and clubs such as London's Hope and Anchor and Greyhound. The public liked the simple, home-made but professional sound of these groups, and many established a strong local following. Fans and business people often combined to begin their own independent recording companies, such as Stiff and Chiswick, and recorded the music of artists they liked. These initiatives encouraged many others to start bands, and soon there was a D-I-Y movement of young groups such as the Stranglers and Eddie and the Hot Rods. Their enthusiasm, energy and attitude made many established groups appear even more tired and decadent.

Ian Dury's Kilburn and the High Roads and Brinsley Schwarz were two respected and influential bands, but the most successful and long-lived was Dr Feelgood. Wearing sharp 'mod' suits from the 1960s, they played a mixture of blues, r'n'b and rock'n'roll. Their music was elemental and electrifying, with Lee Brilleaux connecting with the audience and the manic Wilko Johnson supplying the current. *Down by the Jetty* (1975) was the first of many albums in a catalogue extending into the 1990s.

But reinterpretations of songs from the 1950s and 1960s were not enough to satisfy many fans. There was a deepening social and economic crisis, high youth unemployment and many young people felt that society had ignored them. There was anger at the complacency of an older genera-tion in government as well as in pop. This frustration was about to be expressed in a defiant, primitive musical language.

In 1975 a British businessman, Malcolm McLaren, had returned to Britain after working in America, where he had briefly managed American bands such as the New York Dolls. They seemed not to care about the music, but were more interested in shocking their audiences. His idea was to create a band not with talent, but with a potential to shock and disgust. In this way, they would become so notorious that people would pay to see them. Soon he was managing the Sex Pistols.

The Sex Pistols

There were four founder members: Johnny Rotten (b. John Lydon, 1956) on vocals, Steve Jones (b.1955) on guitar, Glen Matlock (b.1956) on bass and Paul Cook (b.1956) on drums. The band was created to attract atten-tion on stage and off stage, everywhere they went. Dressed in leather jackets, torn clothing, safety pins, swastikas, zips, clips, studs and chains, with spiked, brightly dyed hair, the 'look' was unique and provocative, simultaneously suggesting eccentricity and perversion. It was quickly adopted as a unisex fashion by fans around the country.

The Sex Pistols' first recording contract was with EMI, one of Britain's oldest and most conservative record labels, and the band soon released their debut single: 'Anarchy in the UK'. Their music was loud, primal and hostile. It consisted of simple guitar solos, repeated chords, a heavily distorted sound and defiant, abrupt endings. Songs were sung with energy and fire, in a Cockney accent infused with insults and rejections, all volcanically delivered in a tone of bored sarcasm.

The band soon became notorious and stories of their confrontational behaviour began appearing in the tabloid press. Then, following a televi-sion appearance in which the band swore and abused the presenter, they were sacked by EMI. A tour followed, but many municipal authorities cancelled concerts to 'protect' local people. A new bass player, Sid Vicious (b. John Ritchie, 1957), arrived to replace Matlock. Vicious was a disturbed youth whose anti-social behaviour of vomiting, drug taking and assaults were encouraged to gain publicity.

The group found a new recording contract with A&M Records and planned a new single, 'God Save the Queen', a satire on the Silver Jubilee celebrations of Queen Elizabeth II in 1977. To ensure maximum attention, the group signed for the company outside Buckingham Palace and publicity depicted an image of the Queen with a safety pin through her nose. But soon afterwards the group became involved in more anti-social behaviour and assaults, and they were sacked once again.

'God Save the Queen' reached number 2 in the music charts. This was followed by 'Holidays in the Sun', 'Pretty Vacant' and an album *Never Mind the Bollocks, Here's the Sex Pistols*, which went to number 1 in the album charts. This was a major achievement after the BBC and London's Capital Radio had banned every single except 'Pretty Vacant', and the negative media attention following an unsuccessful prosecution for the use of the word 'bollocks' on their LP cover.

With the advances from EMI and A&M, plus record sales from singles, the group made a substantial sum from their notoriety. Next was a tour of the United States, but internal problems saw Rotten and Vicious leave the group. This was followed by tragedy, when Sid Vicious died following a heroin overdose while on bail for the alleged murder of his American girl-friend, Nancy Spungen. The group was finished and never recorded again.

McLaren subsequently organised a biographical feature film *The Great Rock'n'Roll Swindle* (Julian Temple, 1980) which featured the infamous Ronnie Biggs, who had earlier escaped from prison. Rotten went on to a new musical career with the band Public Image Limited (PiL), while the others disappeared from the music scene.

During their brief period of fame they only recorded some twenty-five songs which appeared on just five singles and one album in the United Kingdom. But their infamy led to the appearance of around fifty illegal recordings on various albums. During their time the Sex Pistols illuminated the face of white British pop, and their influence has been enduring.

Pop music: just do it (yourself)

The arrival of punk led to an increase in amateur music-making, as groups around Britain began to form and play. Many musicians invented comic, self-deprecating stage names, such as Captain Sensible and Johnny Moped. At concerts fans did not dance, but jumped up and down in a style known as 'pogoing', and in an inverted gesture of appreciation, enthusiastically spat on the bands. As with the arrival of rock'n'roll, there was nothing to compare it with, no previous points of reference. The signs and symbols of punk did not speak a familiar language. But to many bored, unemployed teenagers leading dull, suburban lives, it was a call to battle. The world outside watched with a horrified fascination.

During 1976 the Damned, the Clash, the Jam, the Stranglers, the Buzzcocks and others, played with speed, energy and a raw, untutored sound. Most groups were all male, but several had female singers, such as Siouxsie and the Banshees and X-Ray Spex. There was also one all-girl band: the Slits. Although they were not openly feminist, their music was not aggressive, macho punk, but was more complex in sound and rhythm. Their intimidating stage presence changed the conventional roles of female pop singers and challenged the traditional role of women in pop as background vocalists.

Meanwhile, a new, alternative pop culture began to emerge, consisting of small independent record companies and distributors, graphics companies, magazines, fanzines, fashion designers and journalists. All supported the kinds of music which the commercial mainstream would not consider. However, the major record companies soon began to take an interest, signing punk bands, softening their style, to make them acceptable to a wider public.

Marketing became more sophisticated, with coloured vinyl, picture discs, extra tracks and limited, numbered editions. Moreover, the arrival of the music video channel (MTV) early in the 1980s, meant that videos became an important element in the promotion of any band.

The commercial demands all combined to weaken the communal ethos of punk and by the early 1980s many of the 'new wave' bands had lost their originality. The repetitive nature of their sound, their negative posture and the commercial pressures from record companies made many appear dull and bland.

But as interest in punk declined, reggae music grew in popularity. Like earlier punk, it expressed a symbolic challenge to the politics of the Conservative Government and a rejection of the right-wing racism of the National Front. Several bands, including the Clash, the Police (led by Sting), PiL and the Gang of Four, all recorded reggae songs, and Bob Marley acknowledged their shared interests in his song 'Punky Reggae Party'. Several mixed-race bands formed to play the popular mixture of pop and reggae, known as ska. This became known as the Two-Tone movement, a political pop music whose principal message was one of anti-racism.

Between 1979 and 1982, mixed-race bands such as the Selecter, the Specials, the Beat and UB40 expressed a defiant, anti-Thatcher manifesto and gave their support to the Rock Against Racism movement, appearing in numerous free public carnivals. This demonstration of left-wing populism embraced black and white musicians and subcultures, and helped different forms of black music to become established in Britain.

It was not the first time music had been used in this way. In 1976 Rock Against Racism was organised with the Socialist Workers' Party to fight racism and make the public more aware of the tactics of the National Front, a fascist organisation. Their activities featured many concerts in which well-known artists played without payment. Similar concerts were subsequently held for Africa, such as the Live Aid shows of July 1985, held simultaneously in London and Philadelphia in the United States. They were organised by the singer Bob Geldof to raise funds for famine relief.

As pop and rock music indicated their exhaustion, the public looked for new musical forms to fill the vacuum. The integrity and authenticity of folk music once again began to attract new fans. An Irish band, the Pogues, brought a mixture of Irish folk and punk to new audiences in open air festivals, clubs and concerts. British audiences began to discover New Age music, which was arriving from the United States. Clannad fused Irish folk with New Age music to create a new musical form. New Age music's repetitive and relaxing rhythms found appreciative audiences at the World Of Music And Dance (WOMAD) Festival, started in 1982 by the rock musician Peter Gabriel to promote Anglo-Celtic and 'world' music. During the 1980s and 1990s this grew in size and importance, as world music – embracing such diverse forms as Gregorian chants, African drums and Mayan humming – began to represent authentic, non-commercial alternatives to dance and pop.

Club and street mix

In Britain's discotheques of the mid-1970s, some of the most popular dance music was by the Bee Gees, a British group who worked in America. They had phenomenal success with the soundtrack to the American film Saturday Night Fever (1977). The film featured John Travolta as Tony Manero, a young man with a monotonous job in a paint shop by day, who becomes the 'king of the dancefloor' by night. With sales of over 30 million, it became the biggest selling film soundtrack of all time.

Meanwhile, the traditional soul-based American dance music was beginning to sound increasingly uniform and anonymous, as record companies tried to market bands to larger audiences. But the latest technology began to provide a fresh stimulus. New methods of recording, mixing and reproducing music were employed to create clean, hard, repetitive drumbeats, which were ideal rhythms for dance. Innovative record producers became more influential. Around 1977 the German producer Giorgio Moroder popularised an infectious, rhythmical, electronic dance music (later known as 'Euro disco') through the music of the American vocalist Donna Summer. The creation of larger, twelve-inch singles also allowed longer recordings, which were better for disco dancing than the shorter, three-minute ones which were more suitable for radio stations. A new electronic keyboard instrument, the synthesiser, also offered a wide spectrum of electronic sounds.

These trends were assimilated within British pop, and the late 1970s and early 1980s saw bands such as Gary Numan, Heaven 17, Spandau Ballet, Human League, Visage, OMD, Depeche Mode and others, using synthesisers and tapes to make restrained, refined, futuristic pop and dance music. The bands and their fans became known as New Romantics, for whom affluence, club-going and cool, detached posing were central elements of their style. Between 1979 and 1983, many new synthesiser bands came and went. But although they were short-lived, their impact on popular music was highly influential. They created a link between the music and fashions of disco, pop and rock, which would change the character of British popular music during the 1980s.

Although dance music was once seen as aspirational, conformist and repetitive, new technology allowed the creation of original and challenging new forms. In America, the energetic new sounds of 'rap' (a form of public poetry/oratory) came up from the streets of New York and Chicago. This involved the performers shouting lyrics over music which had often been taken from another record. Later, a technique known as 'scratching' was incorporated, with DJs manually turning the vinyl disc to and fro to create amplified noises. These sounds were then recorded to make new musical mixes.

In America, dance music continued to diversify, as rap and 'scratching' were soon followed by 'sampling'. This involved the use of a sampler machine to record and mix musical extracts from different records. They were cheap to buy and were soon used for the creation of sophisticated sonic collages. It marked the beginnings of a popular musical revolution, in which musicians and songwriters were becoming marginalised. The new innovators were those with the technical knowledge to mix and manipulate diverse musical sounds and sources. Some critics called them 'sonic outlaws' who stole and copied other people's music, while others defended their right to make 'fair use' of existing material.

Dancing into the future

The new creative techniques were further exploited with house music, which became established in Britain during the mid–late 1980s. This mixed 1970s disco-funk with gospel-style vocals, heavy bass and drums. They were then remixed using computer-assisted techniques and synthesisers. It was loud, minimalist and functional, perfectly suited for wild, high-energy dancing. 'House' took its name from the Warehouse, a Chicago gay club, popularly believed to be its place of origin. But its wild bohemian sound was quickly adopted in clubs of all types, particularly in Liverpool and Manchester, which rapidly became the new centres of British dance culture.

Since the 1960s the Spanish island of Ibiza in the Mediterranean Sea has been a popular destination for British tourists. But in the summer of 1988 its fine historic buildings and sandy beaches were not the principal attractions for young hedonists who descended there. Instead, large improvised parties were the main tourist attraction, which featured ecstatic, non-stop dancing *en masse*. It became popularly known as the 'Summer of Love', as thousands attended the open-air parties. The events marked the beginning of the so-called 'Acid House' movement, created after the coming together of 'House' music and the drug Ecstasy, a type of amphetamine commonly known as 'acid' (not LSD). For many fans they were central elements in an emergent subculture of hedonism, dance and communality, not seen since the late 1960s.

Traditional, formal clothing had been the preferred dress style of many clubs and discotheques around Britain. However, it was gradually rejected by revellers in favour of baggy clothes, dungarees and informal beach wear, which was often adorned with a 'smiley' motif. The music was equally eclectic, and included dub, rap, rock and house music, together with electronic influences from diverse parts of Europe. The techno-anthems of Cabaret Voltaire, Kraftwerk and Tangerine Dream, Adamski and 2-Unlimited were enjoyed in a dancing frenzy of apolitical hedonism.

The new electronic possibilities produced varied sub-genres. One of the most common styles was 'techno'. Intense, hypnotic and ear-splitting, it was the 'punk rock' of dance, whose hard, repetitive, electronic sounds featured futuristic electronic 'bleeps' and an industrial-strength bass. The mix involved sampling, hip hop, rap and other styles, but the most distinctive feature was its rhythm, supplied at a breakneck 124–35 beats per minute, compared to the usual 120 bpm or less for 'house' and other kinds of dance music.

During the late 1980s, the new sounds and styles began to be imported and developed in Britain by amateur producers and DJs who wanted to recreate the atmosphere of Ibiza parties. In 1991 the Ministry of Sound, a south London club, became involved in promotions. But official permission was impossible to obtain for such large, informal gatherings. Instead, illegal events were held in huge venues such as empty warehouses and other buildings, often near London's M25 orbital road. They were known as 'warehouse parties' or 'raves', where crowds danced for several days and nights until they were stopped by the police. But in 1994 the Conservatives prohibited raves with legislation known as the Criminal Justice Act. The new laws united thousands of young people against the government, as alternative lifestyles of all kinds came under legal attack and dancing became a political act.

In spite of the opposition, and perhaps because of it, dance music continued to dominate the early 1990s. Styles included the speed and darkness of 'hardcore', the emphatic drums and bass of 'jungle', the dreamy, New Age spiritual sound of 'Goa trance' and the soulful sensuality of 'garage'. Even the American 'easy listening' music was rediscovered, as the mellow, relaxed sounds of Burt Bacharach, Dionne Warwick and others threatened to become fashionable again, as an antidote to the aggression of 'house' and its many varieties.

151

There was also growing interest in Asian dance music. This had begun to develop in the late 1970s when traditional folk music from the Punjab region of India began to be played with electronic instruments. A decade later, Asians in Britain had incorporated new musical forms, such as the bass of Western hip hop, reggae and 'techno' music. The mixture was popularly known as 'bhangra', and seemed to reflect the dual identity felt by British Asians, many of whom have grown up within two cultures. But it also found an audience among white British, who were attracted by its exotic nature and mystical appeal. A decade later, bhangra, like 'house' before it, had begun to fragment into several different styles with its own specialist labels (such as Outcaste and Nation) and established artists, such as Apache Indian and Cornershop.

In the mid-1990s British dance music continued to fragment and mutate. New forms were regularly produced using 'remixology' to produce exciting new racial and musical mixes. But critics argued it removed expression, passion and personality from the music, generating hybrids with no musical pedigree. It also removed politics from music and, in spite of the political, social, economic and legal problems, there was still little explicitly political pop. The exceptions were the punk-inspired bands such as Crass and the Levellers, who continued to loudly express their opposition to authority in general and the Conservative Party in particular, while Billy Bragg and Paul Weller publicised and supported numerous socialist causes with 'benefit' concerts and fund-raising projects.

BritPop

During the late 1980s and early 1990s there was renewed interest in white British and American pop of the mid-1960s. Primal Scream, the Jesus and Mary Chain, and the Smiths were some of the most distinctive bands who recreated the classic sound, often combining it with an introspection and pessimism. Guitar bands offered an alternative to electronic dance music, but at first there was little enthusiasm. Later, groups such as Oasis, Blur, Pulp, The Verve, the Stone Roses and Radiohead, among others, emerged with the characteristic sound of British pop in the late 1990s. A 'wave' of new British music dominated the international music scene which became popularly known as BritPop, even though most of the prominent bands were English, from either London or Manchester.

Critical opinion was divided about the new music. Some remarked that at its best BritPop sounded like all the greatest British rock music produced during the past forty years. But others were less generous, criticising the 'nostalgic reworkings' of earlier bands as shameless imitations. They also described it as it conservative, insular, parochial and self-consciously proletarian – the province of white working-class males.

On the other hand, dance music by bands such as Tricky, Massive Attack and Portishead continued to evolve and diversify. Many tracks were highly original and sounded unlike anything heard in Britain before. But the fashionable 'look' of the 1990s, both in BritPop and in the dance clubs, was a familiar one. It took inspiration from the 1960s with slim-fitting suits, Beatle-style haircuts, hippy Indian clothes, together with the surfing 'chic' of anoraks, loose-fitting sweatshirts, flared jeans and dark glasses.

One of the most astonishing commercial events of the decade was the appearance of the Spice Girls, an all-female singing quintet. Scary, Sporty, Baby, Posh and Ginger were selected after mass auditions. They were given an extensive course of singing and dancing tuition to create a group which both young boys and girls would like. Their most intensely hysterical fans were aged 8–12 years and there were few young families without a minia-ture 'Scary' or 'Baby' doing a perfect rendition of 'Wannabe', one of their biggest hits. Their first album *Spice* sold 16 million copies. From 1996 they had two-and-a-half years of success not matched since the Beatles. Some critics said they proposed a new ethos of equality with provocative sexuality, or 'girl power', although their lyrics still spoke of safe sex and loving one's mother. Many others believed their success was not built on substance or ability and predicted a swift decline in their fortunes.

BritPop and dance were Britain's dominant mood in the late 1990s. The US had ceased to be a significant influence and Britain stood proud in splendid isolation musically, creatively and culturally.

Discussion topics and activities

1   Which performers and movements do you consider the most inter-esting in British pop since the 1960s, and why?
2   Refer to the text and other sources to describe and explain the following: Teds / Mods / skinheads / hippies / punks / raves.
3   In Britain, fashion and music are often closely related. Is it the same in your country?
4   'Rhythm crazed teenagers terrorised a city last night.' This was an authentic newspaper headline following a rock'n'roll concert. Imagine you were in the audience. Write an article describing the experience either for a traditional right-wing newspaper which does not approve, or for a lively music magazine with an enthusiastic young readership.
5   Choose either a concert or a record with which you are familiar. Write a review of it for a music magazine read by teenagers.
6   Could music without lyrics ever be considered political?

Figure 7.2 The Spice Girls *c.* 1997: (from left to right) Sporty, Baby, Ginger, Posh and Scary

Suggested further reading

Books

Barnes, R. (1979) *Mods!* London: Eel Pie.

Burchill, J. (1978) *The Boy Looked at Johnny: The Obituary of Rock'n'Roll* London: Pluto.

Chambers, I. (1985) *Urban Rhythms* London: Macmillan.

Chapman, R. (1991) *Selling the Sixties: The Pirates and Pop Music Radio* London: Routledge.

Clarke, D. (1995) *The Rise and Fall of Popular Music* Harmondsworth: Penguin.

Coon, C. (1982) *The New Wave Punk Rock Explosion* London: Omnibus.

Dewe, M. (1998) *The Skiffle Craze* London: Planet.

Gambaccini, P., Rice, T. and Rice, J. *The Guinness Book of British Hit Albums* Enfield: Guinness Publishing.

Gambaccini, P., Rice, T. and Rice, J. *The Guinness Book of British Hit Singles* Enfield: Guinness Publishing.

Garratt, S. (1998) *Adventures in Wonderland: A Decade of Club Culture* London: Headline.

Hebdige, D. (1979) *Subculture: The Meaning of Style* London: Methuen.

Jasper, T. (1991) *The Top Twenty Book* London: Blandford Press.

Knight, N. (1982) *Skinhead* London: Omnibus.

Kureishi, H. and Savage, J. (1995) *The Faber Book of Pop* London: Faber & Faber.

MacRobbie, A. (ed.) (1989) *Zoot Suits and Second Hand Dresses* London: Macmillan.

Polhemus, T. (1994) *Streetstyle* London: Thames & Hudson.

Savage, J. (1991) *England's Dreaming* London: Faber & Faber.

Savage, J. (1996) *Time Travel* London: Chatto & Windus.

Stuart, J. (1987) *Rockers!* London: Plexus.

Yorke, P. (1980) *Style Wars* London: Sidgewick & Jackson.

Encyclopaedias of different popular musical genres e.g. rock, reggae etc. are also available from Virgin Books.

Journals

The weekly music press, in particular the *NME*, *Melody Maker* and *Sounds*, provide a valuable source of information and commentary on the changing music scene, record reviews, concerts, interviews and so on. Their advertising section also gives interesting details about fashions of the period. Press archives can usually be consulted with a prior appointment.

Recordings

The National Sound Archive of the British Library in London holds most British musical recordings and has facilities for their inspection.

Art and sculpture

8

Introduction

The British have always had an uneasy relationship with modern art. It is sometimes said they are by nature more literary than visual and respond more to language than appearances. Certainly, contemporary art has never enjoyed the same esteem as literature, drama or music, and public taste has frequently favoured conventional art more than innovative and avant-garde works. There has been little comprehensible discussion of art in the media and new movements are often received with scepticism and controversy. Consequently, it has never been easy for artists to become established in Britain and many have chosen to work abroad, where the public is frequently more appreciative.

However, Britain is home to several fine collections. The principal one is held at the National Gallery, which opened in 1824 and currently holds over 2,000 works of Western painting from the thirteenth to the nineteenth century. Modern art and sculpture is held at the Tate Gallery, which opened in 1897. Portraits and photographs of distinguished figures from British history can be seen at the National Portrait Gallery, opened in 1856. All the galleries are located in central London, but numerous regional collections are held in towns and cities around the country.

In Scotland, the National Gallery of Modern Art, the National Portrait Gallery and the National Gallery of Scotland hold the three main collections, and all are situated in Edinburgh. Scottish art is not a separate school, although certain styles such as Expressionism have consistently recurred throughout its history.

157

Within Britain, London is the most vital and active city for the artistic avant-garde and home of the most innovative and influential schools. The Royal College of Art (RCA), the Institute of Contemporary Arts (ICA), the Slade, St Martin's College, the Central School, the Euston Road School and Goldsmiths' College, among others, have helped to develop and encourage the work of almost all the significant and influential British artists.

Until the 1960s there were no special entry conditions to art school, which often attracted bright but rebellious, unacademic students. This promoted an eclectic social composition and each school had its own distinctive style. But the individuality of the schools was lost in the 1980s when many merged to form the London Institute. With over 20,000 students, it has become Europe's largest centre for education in art and design. A modern, progressive environment offers multi-cultural influences and technology is frequently used to create new work.

Exhibitions of more progressive and avant-garde art are often held at the Institute of Contemporary Arts (ICA) in London, while the Royal Academy has a reputation as a more traditional centre. It was founded in 1768 and is the oldest art academy in Britain. Its well-known summer exhibition is held between May and August each year and comprises works submitted by members of the public, both professional and amateur.

The London location of the principal schools, together with opportunities to make contacts, show and sell work, all mean that students from the regions generally feel the need to move there to study art and develop their careers. This promotes the highly centralised nature of the British art scene and the absence of almost any significant regional movements.

Influences and movements

Support and sponsorship have always been important for artistic development and they have often influenced the kinds of work created and shown. In earlier times art had an instructive role and Church, government and wealthy patrons strongly favoured works which carried a moral message. This was reflected in the work of eighteenth- and nineteenth-century landscape artists, such as Joseph Turner (1775–1851) and John Constable (1776–1837). The theme of the countryside as a repository of spiritual and moral truths was an influential one and is also found in the literature and poetry of the time. Landscapes became one of the most traditional styles of painting, as well as Britain's major contribution to Western European art.

Faced with the horrors of industrialisation and increasing social disorder of the mid-nineteenth century, there was a return to the old certainties offered by religion. This is amply reflected in the work of the Pre-Raphaelite Brotherhood. William Holman Hunt (1827–1910) and others painted biblical and literary scenes, which offered spiritual comfort and moral guidance. But sentimental portraits of families and their animals

158

were also popular and are commonly found in the work of Sir Edwin Landseer (1802–73).

A characteristic shared by many traditional works is their figurative, representational nature, in which the subjects are clearly identifiable. But in the twentieth century, artists began to represent how and what they saw in a much more liberated and individual way. Movements taking place in Paris and later New York strongly influenced British artists in the latter half of the century.

The origins of the New York School lay in the 1930s and 1940s, when numerous leading artists and intellectuals fled to New York from Europe, leaving behind a continent in turbulence and war. After the end of the Second World War, many settled in America and began to teach. In Paris, painters who had absorbed the influences of Modernism and Surrealism in art, such as Marc Chagall, Max Ernst, André Breton and Piet Mondrian were attracted by the new possibilities in America and left the ruins of Europe to establish the New York School of Painting and Architecture. They incorporated ideas in their work from figures such as Joseph Albers, Hans Hoffman, Walter Gropius and Mies Van der Rohe, who had all been members of a German design school known as the Bauhaus. This demanded functionality, simplicity and purity in the design, and rejected any decoration or adornment.

Abstract Expressionism

When the ideas and influences of the New York School were expressed in painting, the result was quite unlike anything seen before. The presentation of people or things was excluded. The work had no subject, apart from its own elements. For example, a hard block of pure colour or simply the brush marks on the canvas were the 'theme'. The painting had no meaning apart from its own existence. It was an object which mirrored the actions which had produced it – an 'action painting', created by making gestures with the paint: throwing it, dripping or smearing it on the canvas. It became known as Abstract Expressionism and its leading exponent was Jackson Pollock. The following decade, it spread to influence a generation of artists around the world. By the 1970s, the creation of abstract pictures was even considered to be educational and therapeutic.

While an avant-garde was becoming established in New York, the centre for bohemian and artistic activity in post-war Britain was the small fishing village of St Ives in south-west England. Its local community of artists was known as the St Ives School, whose constituents (such as Patrick Heron, Peter Lanyon, Roger Hilton and William Gear) regularly contributed work to the prestigious exhibitions held at the Royal Academy. The group were influenced by the powerful cultural waves coming out of America and began representing the village and its land-scapes in the new Abstract Expressionist forms. But their technique was

159

less dramatic and expressive. It consisted of a laborious application of greens, greys and other dark tones. These were considered honest and authentic colours, necessary for making faithful representations of the natural environment.

William Gear adopted a style known as tachisme. Instead of using brush strokes to paint, he created abstract compositions using shapeless marks or blotches. At the exhibition *60 paintings for '51* at the Festival of Britain, there was a strong representation from St Ives and Gear's painting *Autumn* won a prize of £500. But the public were shocked that a painting with an unrecognisable image could win so much money and questions were asked about it in Parliament. There was little understanding or appreciation of his abstract work and it was not the last time that public anger over a work of art would be expressed in the House of Commons.

Meanwhile, a London-based movement, the Constructivists, aimed to 'construct' abstract images. The most notable exponent of was Victor Passmore, who had earlier become established as a romantic, figurative painter. His technique used controlled, horizontal and vertical shapes in a balanced, attractive way. The works were often not flat or smooth, but had contours. They appeared solid and composed, cool and restrained. In consonance with the mood of the mid-1950s, they reflected an orderly optimism.

Social realism

In sharp contrast to the self-referential, subjective influences of American art were the communal themes and the realist style favoured by other British artists of the mid-1950s. These were closely associated with the rebellious, anti-aesthetic ideas of the 'new wave' in writing. Like many musical and literary tendencies in the 1950s and 1960s, it was focussed outside London in the industrial areas of northern England.

The aim was to reveal society and ordinary people – to frankly represent them and not deceive with fantasy and abstraction. The subject matter often featured domestic environments. This was usually bed-sitting room accommodation, with all the furniture in the same room, and naturally included a bed, table, stove and sink. In 1954 the art critic David Sylvester described the new genre as 'kitchen sink school', a type of social realism which was subsequently used to describe works in the cinema, theatre and on television. It received strong support from the political left, including the critic and author John Berger, who organised exhibitions to promote it.

The best-known of the Social Realists was John Bratby. His work was intentionally shocking, unsubtle and anti-intellectual, and became notorious for its 'inartistic' subject-matter. He created compositions of dirty breakfast tables with old cereal packets, cigarette ash and beer bottles. The pictures were composed using thick, dirty-looking paint, which looked liked toothpaste. They seemed to satirise the fine, delicate still-life paintings of artists such as Matisse. The public were shocked by such works, as they were by the realism in many novels and plays of the time. But, like the earlier pictures by the St Ives School, they could still be understood and commented on by non-experts. The same could not be said of later abstract painting and subsequent movements, which would gradually alienate a general, non-specialised public.

Francis Bacon

Abstract painting and Social Realism were significant and contrasting tendencies in British art of the 1950s. But two artists who would make highly significant, original contributions to British art were associated with neither.

Francis Bacon (1909–92) was born in Dublin, but spent most of his life working in London. When his work was first shown in 1945, few imagined that he would later be acclaimed as one of the greatest artists of the late twentieth century. He was not formally trained and did not begin painting until his early 30s. His main influences were the horrors of the war years, such as the Holocaust and the atomic bomb. His early work *Three Studies for Figures at the Base of a Crucifixion* (1944) depicts a crucifixion, but not a Christian one. It is one for a secular age, from a nightmare in which figures appear like tormented beasts. It is the first of many disturbing works which suggest menace, hysteria and a darker side to human nature. When it was first shown in London in 1945 it caused outrage and has, since then, lost none of its potential to shock.

His later work showed a fascination with the movement of the human body and is homogenous in style. His subjects were friends, lovers and sometimes himself. There are frequent suggestions of inner torment and violence in his figures. Men in suits sit formally, their smudged heads screaming. Naked figures couple chaotically on beds. Popes are shown isolated and shouting madly. Other pictures use strong, emphatic brushwork to represent bottles, glasses, toilets and sinks, in a type of distorted, grotesquely twisted realism, from which figures struggle to escape.

Bacon is not easy to categorise, as he was open to spontaneous influences which resulted in highly individual pictures. Critical opinion frequently describes his works as disturbing, depraved, intense, cathartic, realistic, austere and occasionally ridiculous. He had several imitators, but no descendants or pupils. However, his originality and style have made his works some of the most highly praised in modern art.

Lucian Freud

Lucian Freud (b.1922), the grandson of psychoanalyst Sigmund Freud, was born in Berlin and brought to Britain in 1932 as a refugee from Nazism. Like Bacon he was largely self-taught and he became well-known for his portraits and figure paintings. These were distinctive, primarily for their obsessive attention to detail. Freud learned to draw not only what he saw, but what he felt about his subjects. This is clearly seen in his works of the late 1940s and early 1950s which show a skilful exploration of the emotions, for example *Narcissus* (1948).

Later he began to make sharp, objective accounts of his subjects, depicting every detail of their physical presence. He represented figures and heads in thick, crusty paint, which although realistic, appear sad, sombre and introverted, for example *Naked Girl with Egg* (1981). During his lifetime his art has changed little. He is often described as a realist; some critics describe him as the greatest, others as the only one alive.

Although their artistic vision of humanity was a pessimistic one, Freud and Bacon both enjoyed flamboyant bohemian lifestyles of heavy drinking and gambling. They led an eclectic social life, keeping company with aristocratic women and criminal gangs. Until they disagreed in the 1970s, the two were great friends and occasionally painted portraits of each other. Many critics believe Freud and Bacon to be among the greatest British painters, not only for their unusual abilities, but also because they have ignored dominant figurative conventions and influences. Instead, theirs are brilliant, intense representations of the human figure in which their subjects are shown as ultimately sad, alone and vulnerable.

Pop art

America continued to have a powerful influence on cultural and artistic life in Britain during the mid-1950s. An exhibition in 1956 at the Tate Gallery, *Modern Art in the US*, featured works by William de Kooning, Jackson Pollock and Mark Rothko. It created a powerful impact, and confirmed public and professional interest in American art and culture.

At the ICA in London, a number of writers and artists were interested in the populist, commercial nature of American culture and mass media. They were known as the Independent Group and included the painter and sculptor Eduardo Paolozzi, the painter and teacher Richard Hamilton, and the architectural historian Reyner Banham.

In 1954 British art critic Lawrence Alloway used the term 'pop' (abbreviated from 'popular') to define the Independent Group's interests. Popular cultural images had a special attraction. They were loud, bright, vulgar and used clichés from the new mass media of advertising and television. They included stars of film and pop, for example 'pin-ups' such as Marilyn Monroe, advertisements for products such as *Coca-Cola* and technology expressed in the styling details of large American cars.

In an exhibition at London's Whitechapel Gallery in 1956 entitled *This is Tomorrow*, Hamilton showed his work 'Just what is it that makes today's homes so different, so appealing?'. It was an important moment in British art, when the first significant 'pop' picture received public exposure. It is a collage, composed of a variety of images cut out of magazines, which together depict a living room. A picture of a body-builder poses in the foreground. The ceiling is filled with a photograph of the planet Earth in space. A naked girl poses on the sofa in front of a giant tin of ham. A picture taken from a comic strip hangs on the wall. In the background, a diminutive woman hoovers the stairs in a scene taken from an advertisement. The picture focusses on the fantastic images of the world of advertisements and mass communications, uniting them in a playful way. It was a distillation of American commercial culture. It reflected 'pop' themes and became known as 'pop art'.

Its influence grew quickly and soon afterwards many other artists began creating pop art, such as Peter Blake, Joe Tilson and Richard Smith. The content of their work was gradually influenced by the Abstract movement of the period: it became less clearly defined and more subjective in appearance. Later, during the early 1960s, artists began to use shaped canvases, instead of the more conventional rectangular ones, which emphasised the work itself as subject and object.

British art in the 1960s and 1970s

By the mid-1960s a generation of pop artists had become established in Britain. Their influence had extended to America, where Andy Warhol was combining pop art with commercial art and Roy Lichtenstein was creating giant pictures based on comic-strips. Pop art became internationally recognised as optimistic, vibrant and easy to enjoy. But many conservative critics argued that it was not a committed, serious art because it was too cool, detached, superficial and apolitical, and described it as a 'disinterested presentation of trivia'.

Despite its critics, pop art later moved from the canvas into other formats. One of the first was record packaging. Pop artist Peter Blake designed the cover for the Beatle's album *Sergeant Pepper* (1967) and the Rolling Stones commissioned Andy Warhol to design several of their record sleeves. Colourful pop art posters became fashionable and improvements in printing methods made them cheap and abundant. With new techniques in graphic design and screen printing, it was also mass-produced on numerous other items, such as T-shirts, stickers, cups and plates.

The extended use of pop art was helped by the development of photography as a new art form. Compact cameras and fast films allowed informal, natural photography which was more spontaneous and revealing than the traditional 'posed' styles. This was slow to be exploited as an art in its own right, but was quickly put to use in fashion and advertising, where Anthony Armstrong-Jones, Patrick Lichfield, David Bailey, Terence Donovan and Terry Duffy were some of the first photographers to receive critical praise for their innovative new styles.

With these developments, the influence of pop art became more widespread and accessible, and some artists were attracting the attention of a wider, non-specialised public, such as David Hockney and R.B. Kitaj. Both entered the RCA in 1959 and later developed a variety of styles. Their work has been consistently popular and critically admired, and Hockney is one of the few British artists whose work has become familiar to the general public.

David Hockney

Since his early success with a series of etchings, *The Rake's Progress*, completed while a student at the RCA, David Hockney (b.1937) has become one of the most widely known and appreciated British artists. Unlike many of his RCA contemporaries, he did not become closely associated with any particular school or movement. Instead, *Demonstrations of Versatility* (1962), an early piece, aptly describes his life and work. During his career he has painted conspicuously attractive pictures in a variety of styles and his eclectic influences have found expression in drawing, the design of opera sets, photography, book illustration and fine portrait work, such as his detailed but economic study of the poet W.H. Auden (1968).

Some of Hockney's most publicly admired works were completed in the late 1960s when he moved to California and developed an increasingly naturalistic style of painting. He depicted beach houses, swimming pools, grass and palm trees in elegant, spacious, scenes of pleasure and leisure, for example *A Bigger Splash* (1967). He used bright, sunny colours to create an atmosphere of comfort, well-being and hedonism. He seemed to paint to please, which made some critics comment that he was too light and unserious in his attitude and subject matter.

In 1987 he opened the 1853 Gallery, a converted textile factory in Saltaire, near his home town of Bradford in Yorkshire, where he regularly exhibits some of his works. He has been the subject of several major retrospectives, and his attractive and accessible style has made him consistently popular with critics, collectors and the general public.

R.B. Kitaj

An American expatriate, R.B. Kitaj (b.1932) ignored the Abstract tendencies which became widespread in the United States. His initial interests were in Marxist history. This was reflected in his early art which expressed human struggle and suffering, but mixed its seriousness with humour. He often employed diverse styles in the same picture, for example *The Ohio Gang* (1965), which remains one of his most representative earlier pieces. He later turned his attention to a wide range of subjects and has not confined himself to the everyday subjects of popular culture. People from

Figure 8.1 David Hockney, 'Mr and Mrs Clark and Percy' (1970–1). The photographer Ossie Clark and his wife are shown at their Notting Hill home.

politics, poetry, theatre and Jewish history have also appeared in his works.

In the 1970s he returned to figurative work, and began to do traditional charcoal drawings of female nudes. In 1976 he organised the exhibition *The Human Clay* at London's Hayward Gallery, where he was joined by Bacon, Freud, Hockney and others. All were close friends who had returned to figurative work and Kitaj defined the term 'School of London' to refer to their alliance.

Kitaj later developed a new style of painting using large brush marks, bright colours and hard edges, which give his subjects sharp definition and is demonstrated in *In the Sea* (1993) and in his portrait of the American president Bill Clinton (1996). His painting *If Not, Not* is a complex composition of images from the twentieth century. A seven-metre square tapestry has been made of it, the largest of its kind this century. It hangs in the British Library in St Pancras, London.

The moving image: op art and kinetic art

In the United States, pop art began to experiment with visual perception, producing exciting new styles of 'optical' or 'op art'. Bridget Riley became the best-known British exponent, who became known for her mathematically precise black-and-white stripes which produce vibrations and

165

rhythms across the canvas. When her work was first shown, it was so bright and intense that some gallery attendants wore sunglasses against the glare and to her irritation, she became known as the 'Queen of Op Art'.

The optical effects which op art introduced became physical movement in 'kinetic art'. Some examples were suspended figures which moved in currents of warm air, known as 'mobiles'. Others were motorised, or responded to the movement of water or the effects of gravity. The constructed nature of kinetic works also began to mark a convergence of painting and sculpture into works known as installations. Sculpture's growing experimentation with colour also emphasised its changing nature.

Sculpture

British painting has been characterised by a number of different movements which sometimes occurred simultaneously, but sculpture has developed in a relatively linear way. During the 1930s and 1940s, Henry Moore (1898–1986) provided the main influence with large smooth forms in stone, bronze or wood. His larger, monumental works were often influenced by the landscape of his native Yorkshire, while smaller figures often incorporated influences from around the world, in particular those of pre-Colombine America. These were often inspired by natural shapes found in nature and projected a gentle, feminine sensibility.

Moore's sensuous style contrasted with 'geometry of fear' sculpture, which appeared after 1945. The main exponents were Reg Butler and Lynne Chadwick, whose characteristic thin, angular, contorted, expressionist shapes suggest pain and suffering. Their tormented mood was inspired by the horrors of war and particularly the destructive potential of nuclear weapons.

Anthony Caro's abstract sculptures provided a major progression. Caro had worked as an assistant to Henry Moore. He had traditionally worked with clay and plaster on Moore's monumental sculptures. But in 1963 he visited America and was excited by the new art which he saw there. On returning, he began welding steel shapes together to make flat, abstract forms, imitating the paintings of Abstract Expressionism. These were then painted in bright, lively colours, to make the cold dark metal appear graceful and attractive. Brightly coloured works had not been seen before in sculpture and were referred to as New Generation work. Gradually they became widely imitated, in a style known as Heavy Metal, in which pieces were cut, twisted, combined into abstract shapes and then painted. This was a new development. It emphasised that instead of the traditional materials such as wood or stone, a sculpture could be made of anything.

The movement marked an increasing convergence between art and sculpture, a process which had been taking place since the 1950s. Initially, conventional figurative paintings had become abstract and then were given a surface texture. Later some artists had begun creating larger works, which they moved off the wall and onto the floor, to create corridors or scenes. With op art the image became unstable, and with kinetic art the work became a process. In a movement known as 'earth art', Richard Long gathered some stones from the countryside and exhibited them on the floor, and by the mid-1970s it was impossible to distinguish clearly between art and sculpture.

Minimalism

Art and sculpture's convergence was also facilitated by their increasingly minimal nature. Many works of the period were simple, abstract forms, often composed of boxes or cubes, with an absence of expression or content. The effect was a cool silence between the work and the viewer, with no meaning, message or ideology. Critics often complained that minimalist works were too independent, free of tradition and history, and therefore socially irresponsible. The movement united critics and the general public in the belief that art was becoming too remote from society and, at the same time, incomprehensible.

This reached its apotheosis in 1976, when the Tate Gallery revealed it had earlier bought *Equivalent VIII*, a minimalist work by the American sculptor Carl Andre. It consisted of 120 fire bricks, arranged on the floor to form a rectangle. At a time of high unemployment and strikes, there was shock and ridicule in the media that public money could be spent on something which a builder's labourer could have done.

The press began a witch-hunt of modern artists. A pile of blankets by Barry Flanagan, Mary Kelly's dirty nappies exhibited in glass cases and Michael Craig-Martin's glass of water called *Oak Tree* were all ridiculed. Cartoonists, columnists and amateur art critics attacked modern art in general and the Tate in particular, alleging a shameful waste of public funds. The bricks seemed to touch a raw nerve of the nation. They entered the popular consciousness, remembered as a symbol of what modern art should not be.

Minimalism never became well established in Britain. But in America it was closely related to the development of New Age music. It later influenced other arts, such as design, fashion and interior decoration, with an emphasis on smooth surfaces, an absence of detail or decoration, and inconspicuous colours such as black and grey.

Conceptual art

In contrast to the absence of content in minimalism, conceptual art placed great emphasis on the importance of ideas. Its origins are in America of the late 1960s and early 1970s, and its development in Britain was largely due to the influence of Victor Burgin, who had studied in the United States. He used pictures taken from advertisements, texts from newspaper reports,

167

maps and other texts which together began to create new associations, references and meanings. The aim was to break existing languages of communication and create new ones by mixing signs and symbols.

Conceptual art quickly became more expressive and adventurous. Traditional ideas about lines, colour, form and content began to disappear, as artists created works with gases, liquids and even bodily substances. But their art could not be easily understood or evaluated by the public, the critics, or potential art buyers, who frequently described it as anarchic and self-indulgent.

Performance art made this distance even greater. Its origins were in 1930s America, but during the late 1960s and early 1970s it became popular in Britain where it took the form of 'events' or 'happenings'. Galleries, studios or even the street became locations for their art. But performances often had minimal content and an obscure, ritualistic nature. The routines could be dull and repetitive, requiring considerable public patience. Its characteristics made it difficult to categorise and as it could not be marketed as a commodity, it was popular only for a short time.

The mid-1970s was a time of disillusionment for many artists, who felt that creative possibilities had become exhausted, and that an established elite had become lazy, tired and decadent. Others felt the art world had become too commercialised and dependent on satisfying conventional critical standards. The response to this predicament was to shock, to rebel against accepted standards and conventions, and provoke the public and critics by breaking the barriers of acceptability and good taste.

'Prostitution'

In October 1976 a show entitled 'Prostitution' was held at the ICA in London by a group of artists known as COUM Transmissions, led by the theatrically named Cosey Fanni Tutti and Genesis P-Orridge. Exhibits included pornographic magazines which were mounted and dated in glass museum cabinets, a Venus De Milo plaster figure with a tampon hanging on each arm and a box of live maggots which evolved into flies. The public was shocked and outraged. Tabloid newspapers began a hysterical attack on the exhibition and its organisers. Questions were asked in Parliament and the Arts Council was forced to publicly deny any involvement or funding.

No single movement or ideology dominated, as the style or 'language' of art was created by artists themselves. The avant-garde disappeared and the art world began to talk of 'post-modernism'. This described new works which mixed a variety of older styles and influences, often in a playful, unconventional way. But the new styles were not popular with more established artists, such as David Hockney and R.B. Kitaj, who proposed a return to figure drawing and more publicly accessible art. Neither was it popular with the general public, who could not understand it, nor had seen anything like it before.

Art of the 1980s

In 1984 a prestigious new prize was introduced by London's Tate Gallery to promote adventurous, innovative new work. The Turner Prize is the art establishment's annual accolade to the avant-garde and has become the best-known award for modern British art. It publicises artists who have most impressed the jury during the previous twelve months. The work of the four shortlisted candidates is shown in the Tate before the winner is chosen by a jury of art patrons, critics and the Tate director. In 1991 an upper age limit of 50 was introduced for candidates, while some critics cynically remarked that there should also be one for the judges.

With the publicity provided by the sponsorship of Channel 4 television, the award has done much to promote modern art to the general public. But critics complain that it has made artists too concerned with winning its generous prize money and attracting subsequent sponsorship, commissions and media exposure, than with the traditional concerns of social issues, artistic problems and solidarity among the artistic community.

After the fragmentation of the late 1970s, no particular style or school prevailed and art works became more personal and individual. Abstraction, figurative and portrait paintings, social satire, critical realism and feminist painting all found expression. But by the early 1980s, a new vitality began to appear under the growing influence of Neo-Expressionism, a movement which had been developing in America, Germany and Italy.

The trend towards Expressionism also drew attention to art in Scotland, where the tradition has always been strong, and where the work of John Bellany, Ken Currie and Adrian Viszniewski became more widely known. Working within an Expressionist style, they used dark, melancholic shades which reflected their pessimism over the industrial decline of Glasgow.

During the 1980s there were attempts to develop the identity of Scottish art with several new exhibitions, such as the 1987 exhibition *The Vigorous Imagination: New Scottish Art* at the Scottish National Gallery. These became more frequent as Scotland began to gain more political autonomy in the late 1990s. However, the centralised nature of the art world means that most young artists need to be in London and responding to metropolitan influences in order to develop their careers.

In England, New Image painting became influential, characterised by a potent use of colour and a strong, spontaneous treatment of figures and images. It aimed to express its subjects clearly, rather than study or analyse them. Several mature artists who had traditionally worked in an

Expressionist style began to receive renewed recognition, such as Ken Kiff, Gillian Ayres and Paula Rego.

Portuguese-born Paula Rego studied at the Slade art college and has lived in Britain for many years. Her work was almost non-existent between 1968 and 1988. But later in her career, she began to produce highly praised paintings. She is widely acclaimed as a sharp observer whose characters often express clearly defined feminine qualities, such as *The Maids* (1987). Other pictures show women asserting themselves over men, such as her 'animal' paintings from the early 1980s, which often include bizarre sexual elements. *Going Out* (1995) is a milder, more humorous work, which shows a girl putting on lipstick while her dog stares indignantly in the opposite direction, in anticipation of an evening alone.

The work of several other women artists began to receive recognition. Mona Hatoum was born in Lebanon, but has lived in Britain since 1975. She has experimented with different formats which have included performance art, video and installations, which combine elements of sculpture, painting and other materials. In *Under Siege* (1982) she was enclosed in a small glass case, naked, slipping and falling while covered in wet clay. Revolutionary songs were played, accompanied by radio news reports in French and English. But it was not until the 1990s that she won recognition as a major artist, with works such as *Corps Etranger* (1994), a video work using a surgical endoscopic camera that moves over and inside her body.

One of the few works by black artists to receive public attention was Sonia Boyce's *Lay Back, Keep Quiet, and Think What Made England Great* (1986). It consists of four panels in which a black female is presented as an English rose, a metaphor of the black British woman who inherits a history of resistance and oppression. But black female artists are few. Critics argue this is because art institutions are overwhelmingly white and male. Moreover, black arts have been dominated by male works, which has further impeded the development of feminist art and styles of expression.

The early 1980s also saw the emergence of a humorous post-modern style of sculpture, sometimes called New British or New Object. It was varied and highly imaginative, using rejected household objects such as old fridges, plates, light shades and elements of old-fashioned technology. These were assembled into eccentric and unconventional shapes, such as a map or a toy machine gun. Tony Cragg and Richard Deacon have both exploited this style. Cragg's *Britain Seen from the North* (1981) uses reject materials to construct an image of Britain which emphasises the north at its centre and the south to its (political?) right.

Anish Kapoor (b.1954) was born in India, but has studied and worked in Britain. Through his work he became associated with New British sculpture, but he does not use common materials or images. Instead, he uses the more traditional wood, stone and plaster to create elegant, complex, sublime works which often suggest aspects of the human form.

Many of his sculptures are huge pieces of rough stone with smooth, highly polished cavities and interiors. *Void Field* (1989) is one of his most famous works, a collection of stones with hollow, polished interiors. *Ghost* (1997) is a huge black, rectangular block of granite. The outside has rough edges, and one face has been hollowed out and polished. Inside, a column of light hangs in the air like a flaming torch. *Holocaust Memorial* (1995) was created for a London synagogue. It is a vast rectangular stone block. A doorway is carved out on one side, in the polished interior a hazy, inverted image of the viewer hangs in the air. In 1991 he was awarded the Turner Prize for his highly praised work.

Gilbert and George

In contrast to the inanimate, New British sculptures are the 'living sculptures' of the duo Gilbert and George. In the late 1960s they began posing as a quaint, formal, serious pair, dressed in collars, ties, old-fashioned suits, and with painted hands and faces. They appeared in strange, shocking situations and in the 1970s they became involved with conceptual art. Their early pieces reflected an innocence and comical naivety. In *Floating, Slipping Glasses* and *Gordons Made Us Drunk*, Gilbert (b.1942) and George (b.1943) combined separate photographs to provide a complete work which illustrated their inebriation. They occasionally did work as 'singing sculptures', repeating a song until the words and music become meaningless and the viewer is aware only of the performers as sculpture.

However, their later works began to suggest a darker side to their nature. In an attempt to communicate less conceptually and more directly, they produced works with titles such as *Prostitute Puff*, *Shag Stiff* and *Wanker*. These were composed of graffiti, photos and paint, and were more generally related to themes of power and oppression. In the mid-1980s, their photographic compositions were increasingly composed of young men, depicted as unemployed and working class, but at the same time proud and heroic. These were collected together for their exhibition *Pictures 1982–86* and were awarded the Turner Prize in the same year .

Later works included *The Naked Shit Pictures* (1995) in which Gilbert and George appear naked, surrounded by bodily fluids and substances, lost in a mixture of theatrical homosexual absurdity. Not surprisingly, they have attracted controversy and censure. Critics accuse them of pushing their art to the edges of poor taste and pornography, and say the titles of some of their works are their strongest elements. But others claim their art demonstrates the increasingly serious and conservative nature of art criticism, and that all great art was initially received in a similar way.

Warehouses as galleries

During the mid-1980s works of art became popular investments and privately owned galleries increasingly showed work by promising new artists. One of the largest in London is the Saatchi Gallery, opened in 1985 by Charles Saatchi who has since become a major patron of young British art. Other major London galleries include the Marlborough, the Mayor, the Lisson, the White Cube, Leslie Waddington and Anthony d'Offay. They specialise in modern work and offer opportunities for artists to show and sell their art.

But there were many young artists who did not like depending on the gallery owners and powerful institutions for opportunities to become established. They began to look for sites where they could exhibit their own work and soon afterwards improvised shows were held in basic, unpretentious locations. Among the most popular were empty warehouses, sometimes without water or even electricity. The move represented a form of empowerment, freedom from the art establishment; an enterprising if not entrepreneurial D-I-Y ethic, in perfect harmony with the spirit of the times.

Damien Hirst

The freedom and opportunity of artists to exhibit their own works helped promote a vigorous eclecticism and one of the most successful artists to emerge from this creative ferment is Damien Hirst (b.1965). In 1988 he organised the first warehouse show, *Freeze*, in London's Docklands, together with sixteen other students from Goldsmiths College. Since then he has produced unusual, memorable pieces which have attracted as much controversy as publicity.

In a later warehouse show he exhibited *A Hundred Years* (1990), which represents the life cycle. It consists of two large glass cases (vitrines) connected by a tube, each measuring six feet square. In one is a dead cow's head, with flies, maggots and an insectocutor. The other remains empty, except for the flies. A larger version was subsequently made and renamed *A Thousand Years* (1990) and attracted huge publicity. Other works form a series of sculptures collectively known as *Internal Affairs*. One of these, *The Acquired Inability to Escape* (1991), again comprises two vitrines: one with a table, chair, cigarettes, a lighter and cigarette stubs, while the other remains empty.

The minimal style and attention to spatial relationships are also charac-teristic of his well-known *Natural History* series. The most dramatic work here is *The Physical Impossibility of Death in the Mind of Somebody Living* (1991), which represents fear, death and the unknown. This comprises a fourteen-foot shark, suspended in a tank of formaldehyde solution. From the same series, *Mother and Child Divided* (1991)

Figure 8.2 Damien Hirst, 'Some Comfort Gained from the Acceptance of the Inherent Lies in Everything' (1996) comprising two cows cut into twelve pieces

comprises a bisected cow and its calf. The four halves are displayed in two separate tanks of formaldehyde. These are placed side by side, allowing the viewer to pass between the divided animals. Many consider the work disturbing and repulsive. Others consider that it produces a melancholic empathy.

Hirst is also well known for his 'dot' paintings, which resemble coloured pills or sweets on the white canvas and have names such as *Alphaprodine* (1993), and his more recent 'spin' paintings, produced by throwing paint onto a horizontal, revolving canvas. More recently, *Pharmacy* (1998) consists of an installation of shelves with packets of tablets and medicines arranged as in a chemist's shop. Critics comment that it provides a unity to his works, which illustrate the processes of death in animals and its postponement in humans.

Hirst continues to be one of the most acclaimed artists of his generation and was awarded the Turner Prize in 1995 for *Mother and Child Divided*.

The 1990s and BritArt

In the early 1990s traditional School of London painters continued to work in their established way. Themes were often sentimental and included neighbourhoods and family: Freud's *Paddington*, Auerbach's *Primrose Hill*, Kossoff's painting of his uncle, Hockney's paintings of his mother. Their work continued to command respect and high prices in an influential art market.

But a significant development has been the arrival of a 'new wave' of young artists, which emerged after the warehouse shows of the late 1980s. The resemblance to the popular music scene has led to its description as 'BritArt', in imitation of 'BritPop' in popular music. Their work is often of a conceptual nature and ignores the traditional figurative styles found in painting and drawing. Works which are unconventional and provocative predominate, in which concerns are often not with figures, but with life and the human body.

Helen Chadwick (1953–96) pioneered the use of body parts and organic material. Her provocative conceptual works had titles such as *Meat Lamps*, which featured photos of raw steak on light bulbs, while *Piss Flowers* comprised plaster casts of urine in the snow and *Bad Blooms* consisted of photographs of flowers suspended in household fluids.

Many artists contemplate and document life experience, bodily rhythms, or flesh, and their work is often composed using a variety of art forms. Feminist painters such as Eileen Cooper, Amanda Faulkener and Gwen Hardie have taken the rhythms and life of their bodies as their subjects. Christine Borland's 'artistic pathology' uses forensic evidence presented as sculpture, such as a bullet-holed suit or a plastercast of foot-prints. And Tracey Emin (b.1963) uses intimate topics from childhood and adolescence to create compositions with confessional themes, such as *Everyone I've Ever Slept With* (1995), a small tent with details of the suggestive title sewn inside.

The work of Sarah Lucas concentrates on people's basic habits and desires, often in a playful, imaginative way in works with titles such as *Sex Machine* (1996) and *Two Fried Eggs and a Kebab* (1992). But critics have observed that, as with punk music, these and other works sometimes display more energy and attitude than content or technique.

In contrast, the work of Rachel Whiteread is often nostalgic and senti-mental. She makes casts of objects which allow them to be seen in different ways. Her early works were plaster casts of bodies and personal memen-toes including childhood blankets. In 1988, her first exhibition included several personal pieces such as *Shallow Breath*, a cast of the space under a single bed, and her best-known early work *Closet*, a cast of an ordinary wardrobe covered in black felt. Later she developed interests in architec-ture. *Ghost* (1991) was a cast of the inside of a room and *House* (1993), a cast of the interior of a terraced house, won the Turner Prize of that year.

Critically praised and widely appreciated, her recent work has included a Holocaust memorial in Vienna.

Anthony Gormley is a more conventional sculptor. In the late 1990s his *Angel of the North* (1998) became one of the most publicly discussed works of the decade. This was not a gallery exhibit, but a major public sculpture. It is a tall dark figure with its arms held horizontally to make the shape of a cross. Many thought it bold and confident, but others found it sinister and Germanic. It is situated at the side of the A1 road near Gateshead in the north-east of England, which, critics have observed, now has the world's biggest angel, as well as one of Britain's biggest shopping centres.

During the 1990s, the creation of installation works of mixed media to create interactive exhibits with sounds and images became common. One of its main exponents is Gillian Wearing. In several works she has used photographs, audio recordings and videos to examine the fears, fantasies and secret aspirations of ordinary members of the public, in which the voice recordings of some speakers were superimposed on the videos of others. The results show old men talking like young adolescents, teenage boys like older women, and so on. Wearing's interest in the ways in which 'realism' can be manipulated was apparent in her video work *60 Minutes Silence* (1997). It shows rows of police in a group photograph. The viewer looks back at them with curiosity, questioning their authority, wondering if they were really policemen, if they posed for one hour and so on. Her video won the Turner Prize the same year, one in which all the shortlisted candidates were women.

In 1997 the varied and brave new works of young British artists captured the public imagination in the Royal Academy's summer exhibition *Sensation*. The title emphasised that exhibits were more about feeling and emotion than the intellect and rational thought, and did much to broaden the appeal of young artists to a wider audience. It included some 1,500 in diverse formats, including multimedia and varied types of installations, and was seen by over 300,000 members of the public. Exhibits reflected a variety of interests which included abstraction, popular culture, feminism, racism and identity politics. They excited great interest and comment, particularly among younger, non-specialists. One of the most controversial was Marcus Garvey's portrait of the child murderer Myra Hindley. The work was damaged by some protesters, while others angrily lobbied visitors to the exhibition.

Controversy began when some members of the Academy resigned at the decision to promote the young artists' work. Critics said many works exploited bad taste, and that a concern with the body and with death was more worrying than stimulating. They argued that such works were so unconventional there were no criteria for their evaluation and they did not deserve attention. They said many works were more like clever publicity than serious art. But others said all great works were originally received in this way and that it is the purpose of art to provoke and probe the limits of acceptability. They spoke of the authority, intelligence and beauty of the work on show.

The RA's exhibition brought British art into public view, and attracted media attention, large audiences and public comment. It caused considerable enthusiasm and excitement among a young, often non-specialised public, something which had rarely been seen before. It also indicated the absence of any clear differences between 'high' specialised art and 'low' popular art.

But in spite of growing public interest, the mass media still offer relatively little explanatory or comprehensible discussion of current trends, especially when compared to their coverage of other arts. Furthermore, the scene continues to be highly centralised in London, and many regional and ethnic artists have yet to gain the recognition they deserve, with the exception of the black artist Chris Offili, who won the Turner Prize in 1998. It continues to be overwhelmingly studied, practised, commented upon and commercialised by a predominantly white, English, middle-class community. Public taste remains highly conservative, often seeing art as something to hang on the wall – as something which depicts traditional portraits, still life or landscape scenes. Consequently, new movements and works are often received with attitudes ranging from indifference or suspicion to mocking disdain, and many British artists have become better known abroad, where the public and media are often more receptive to new developments.

Discussion topics and activities

1   Summarise the major figures and artistic developments in Britain since St Ives.
2   What differences do you see between modern art in Britain and that of your country?
3   Do you think art should confront and shock, or should it comfort and reassure?
4   What pictures did your parents have on the wall when you were a child? What did they represent? Would you have them in your home now?
5   Should the government encourage artists with grants and prizes? What could be the advantages and disadvantages?
6   Choose either an individual British work or an art exhibition with which you are familiar, and write a review of it for a magazine or newspaper. Say what you like/dislike about it and why.

Suggested further reading

Books

Biggs, L. and Elliot, D. (1987) *Current Affairs: British Painting and Sculpture in the Eighties* Oxford: Museum of Modern Art.

British Art in the 20th Century: The Modernist Movement (1987) London: The Royal Academy of Arts.

Collings, M. (1997) *Blimey* Cambridge: 21.

Hayes, J. (1991) *The Portrait in British Art* London: National Portrait Gallery.

Hughes, R. (1991) *The Shock of the New: Art and the Century of Change* London: Thames & Hudson.

Lucie-Smith, E. (1988) *The New British Painting* Oxford: Phaidon.

Russell, J. (1993) *Francis Bacon* London: Thames & Hudson.

Spalding, F. (1986) *British Art Since 1900* London: Thames & Hudson.

The Vigorous Imagination: New Scottish Art (1987) Edinburgh: The Scottish Gallery of Modern Art.

Journals

Of several journals dedicated to modern British art, *Art Monthly* is the oldest surviving periodical. It is particularly strong on young British art and is intelligent, witty and up to date.

9

Architecture and interiors

Introduction

Britain has been a heavily urbanised society since the late eighteenth century and now more than 90 per cent of the population lives in towns and cities. Small, old terraced houses stand in the shadow of high-rise modernist apartment blocks. Post-modern offices tower over neo-classical banks. Churches, windmills and warehouses are transformed into fashionable flats. However, many people believe a superior quality of life exists in the countryside. Some of the most desirable and expensive styles of housing are farmhouses and rural cottages in villages whose architecture goes back several centuries. Street names such as Oak, Elm, Willow and Birch are all common, even in areas without trees, while imitation rustic interiors are found in all types of homes.

In both the city and the countryside there is a strong preference for traditional styles of architecture and conservation is a common practice. Historic and unusual buildings are protected by two public organisations: one is the National Trust, the other is the English Heritage. The NT is a charity. It was created in 1895 to protect and preserve historic buildings and countryside areas of natural beauty, and its properties include hundreds of palaces, country houses, gardens and monuments which can be visited by the public. English Heritage is a government agency which advises and assists the government in matters of conservation. It currently 'lists' (protects) around 450,000 buildings and monuments, many of which are private houses. All relatively original buildings erected before 1700 and most others built before 1840 are automatically listed. Also included are buildings with special features and recent works by influential architects. The owner of a listed building must obtain municipal permission for any alterations, but this is very difficult to obtain and severely restricts what can be done with the property. In Scotland, buildings are listed by Historic Scotland and in Wales by Cadw (Welsh Historic Monuments).

The conservation movement has co-existed with the slow, painful, introduction of new styles. During the 1960s and 1970s many new buildings were designed using modernist principles. However, they were deeply unpopular with the public and their characteristics brutally contrasted with other, more traditional styles of architecture. Modernist office blocks and apartments have profoundly changed the appearance of Britain's cities. But they have also provoked public involvement in design and planning, which is now an integral part of urban development.

Public interest in architecture is sustained by wide media coverage. Newspaper articles and television programmes on design, conservation and town planning are frequent. They contribute to a more open discussion of public space and an increasing involvement with architects and their work.

Movements and influences

During the industrial revolution of the eighteenth and nineteenth centuries, Britain's cities quickly grew in size and architectural styles such as Gothic and Georgian were common. The elegant, symmetrical Georgian style, which originated during the reign of Kings George I–IV (1714–1830), is still one of the most popular with the public. Its main characteristics are uniformity and symmetry in relatively low, red-brick buildings with tall windows of many panes, which together project an air of dignity and calm.

But in around 1850 architects began taking inspiration from earlier styles instead of creating new ones. Reinterpretations of the classical architecture of Greece and Rome were commonly used in the design of many civic and institutional buildings. To make them more individual, features from more recent styles were added, such as Georgian windows or Gothic arches. This became known as neo-classical architecture, whose imposing appearance made many town halls, railway stations, courts, banks, stock exchanges, schools and hospitals look like cathedrals of earlier centuries. But in more recent times they were a proud declaration of civic wealth, strength and pride. Today, they are some of the most distinctive and admired buildings of numerous British towns.

However, by 1900 most cities were dirty, overcrowded and chaotic. They created what the novelist Charles Dickens called an 'unnatural society' and the government began to introduce legislation to control their expansion. With the 1909 Housing and Town Planning Act, urban growth was more strictly managed. The law reflected a better understanding of

Figure 9.1 Vermuyden School, Goole; a fine example of Georgian-style architecture. However, this is mock-Georgian; it was built in 1909.

social needs and led to the planning of parks, libraries, street cleaning and other public services. But it gave the municipalities more projects to finance and consequently civic architecture became less extravagant and elaborate, and more modest and functional.

Today, Britain is a heavily urbanised society. However, most people prefer to live not in the city centre, but in the suburbs. These areas near the edge of the city began to develop as residential zones in around 1920. Rail and road communications had improved and many families wanted to escape the dirt and ugliness of the central zones. Thousands of new houses were built in the green, leafy suburbs, where it was possible to live in a peaceful, detached way, far from the noise, dirt and squalor of the city. Suburban properties were generally smaller than older, central residences, as women were having fewer children and the introduction of household appliances reduced the need for servants. Many houses were built in twos, in a style known as 'semi-detached', with a garden at the front and rear. However, their design generally shows little invention, flair or imagination, and many estates are dull, monotonous, conformist and genteel.

The detached units known as bungalows offer more architectural interest. These single-storey houses were based on those found in the Indian province of Bengal (the name comes from the Hindi word *bangallo*, meaning 'of Bengal'). The first British examples appeared in 1869 in the county of Kent, where they were often built in coastal areas as a second

181

home. But in the early 1920s they became more common, although their unconventional style attracted much professional criticism. However, their detached individuality makes them one of the most desirable forms of housing in Britain today.

The next major period of construction began in 1948, following the loss of many public buildings and some 2 million homes during the Second World War. One of its earliest expressions was in the public exhibition of new styles of architecture, announced in 1951 with the Festival of Britain.

The Festival of Britain

In 1851 the first international exhibition of arts and exotic merchandise was held in the enormous Crystal Palace in London's Hyde Park. The Great Exhibition showed to the world the finest treasures of the British Empire. Its novelty captured the public imagination and the spectacle continued to live in folk memory. A century later, the Festival of Britain was organised on the bank of the River Thames at Battersea in London to commemorate the event.

The symbol of the festival was the Skylon, a tall, elegant, futuristic obelisk, but the focal point was the Royal Festival Hall (1951), which was surrounded by pavilions containing exhibitions of colourful new designs in furniture, painting, pottery and sculpture. A Dome of Discovery contained numerous other artifacts of interest and was decorated by leading artists. It was an exciting, romantic vision to a generation, many of whom had not seen outdoor café tables with umbrellas, had a foreign holiday or even seen any fresh, coloured paint.

The Festival gave architecture and design a new vitality. Futuristic materials were introduced for furniture and decoration, such as nylon, plastic, formica and linoleum. But the most significant change was the preference by public architects for new, modernist design principles, in which the design of a building had to reflect its purpose. Enthusiasts argued that it was a natural response to the demands of modern living. Instead of symbolising power and prestige with imposing, elaborate designs, buildings would be created to meet people's needs. Planning by experts was a common feature of many areas of life in post-war society. There was a strong socialist ideology which demanded equality and progress in health, education, transport and housing. Rationally designed buildings for an equal and informed population seemed to provide the government with the ideal architectural solution.

The modernist influence

In Britain during the early 1950s people demanded both social change and new buildings and, in a massive programme of reconstruction, government offices, hospitals, schools and even entire new towns were planned. But

Figure 9.2 The Royal Festival Hall, South Bank, London

public housing was a priority. Many houses which were still standing had been built in the previous century for factory workers. These 'slums' were badly built, dark and damp. They had no heating and the toilet was often outside the house. Many people could not afford to buy new houses, so cheap, rented 'local authority' housing was provided on a large scale.

Tall, imposing, modernist apartment blocks were quickly erected in parks and gardens around Britain. Among the best known were the Alton Estate at Roehampton, London, and the Hyde Park Estate in Leeds. These were amazing structures compared to the small, old nineteenth-century houses nearby. They were heated and spacious. They had baths and indoor toilets. Outside they offered streets in the air, recreating the street life of children's games, gossip and community. Their modernist design aimed to promote physical health and bright, airy flats were built with balconies for exercising and sunbathing. In their splendid isolation, these concrete-and-glass monuments looked down on the tiny terraced houses they were built to replace.

Modernist architecture and design became established in northern and central Europe in the late 1800s. Its most influential exponent was Charles Edouard Jeanneret (1887–1965), a humanist artist and architect whose nickname was Le Corbusier. The preferred construction materials were steel, concrete and stone. Surfaces were flat and featureless. Interior design reflected the functional needs of the occupants. Plastic and linoleum were

183

introduced. Heavy furniture and curtains were rejected. Inside and outside, decoration and adornment were considered superfluous. The functionality and efficiency of a building made it like a machine. In the words of Le Corbusier, it was 'a machine for living in'.

Many architects and planners also saw modernism as a social movement. They believed that with good architecture and design, it was possible to change not only how people think, but also how they behave. In this way it became a manifesto for social change. Winston Churchill once commented that 'we shape our buildings and thereafter they shape us'. Over the next twenty-five years the British people were severely tested.

Within Britain, modernist design has been expressed in different ways. During the 1960s many new apartment blocks and public buildings were built in a style known as New Brutalism, which is generally attributed to the British couple Peter and Alison Smithson. Theirs was a type of anti-aesthetic approach and is exemplified in a group of municipal apartment blocks, the Park Hill Estate (1961) in Sheffield. But despite initial optimism, there were problems when residents began to complain about the cold, austere, aggressive atmosphere and the poor quality of the materials and finish. The plain, rough, concrete exteriors had no decoration or features and marked badly in the rain. They also required a lot of maintenance and repairs, which the municipal authorities could not always finance.

Living in a high-rise tower was a new experience for many Britons and it soon became unpopular. Residents found them dangerous, depressing and anti-social. They missed facilities such as shops, cafés and cinemas, and the British weather also meant that balconies were superfluous for most of the year.

But during the 1960s architects continued to design numerous public buildings in a similar style. It was a time of expansion for higher education and exposed concrete towers, expanses of red brick, plate glass and ceramic tiling are characteristic features of many new campus buildings, such as those at the Universities of York and Warwick. In London, important new arts buildings were also designed in a similar style. Municipal architects designed several Brutalist buildings for the visual and performing arts as part of the South Bank complex. They comprise the Royal Festival Hall (1951), a multipurpose auditorium; the Hayward Art Gallery (1968); the Purcell Room and the Queen Elizabeth Hall (1967), both used as concert halls. The National Theatre (1976) completes the ensemble, to which were later added the National Film Theatre and the Museum of the Moving Image (MOMI).

Although they are dedicated to the visual and expressive arts, these buildings are cold and serious. They have few windows, no clear entrance and the exposed concrete blocks of the exterior mark badly in the rain. They also have many critics, among them Prince Charles, whose outspoken views on modern architecture have become well known. In a televised documentary in 1988, he described the National Theatre as 'a clever way of putting a nuclear power station in central London without anyone noticing'. But the South Bank has also had its fans: since the 1970s it has become a popular meeting place for young skateboard enthusiasts.

In spite of public hostility towards modernist buildings, some large-scale works were successful. London's enormous residential complex known as the Barbican Estate (1979), designed by Chamberlin, Powell and Bon, is well built and its cold, oppressive exterior is softened with ornamental lakes and waterfalls. It is also provided with local amenities such as bars and restaurants, and its major arts centre is a prime attraction for many visitors to the capital.

However, while New Brutalism was expressed predominantly in public buildings, many private offices, shops and houses were designed using a weaker expression of modernist style. Some of the most common examples are found in new suburban housing estates of box-like red-brick houses. They have plain rectangular exteriors, with large windows and low roofs. They are bright, clean, warm and well insulated, although the public often finds them uniform, clinical and charmless.

The rebuilding of Britain in the post-war years gave several young architects the opportunity to become prominent and respected for the originality of their designs. One of the most admired of the post-war period is James Stirling (1926–92). His early work included several designs for higher education: the Engineering Faculty at Leicester University (1959), the History Faculty at Cambridge University (1964) and the Florey Building at Queen's College, Oxford (1966). These are imaginative, unconventional buildings which exhibit a variety of influences. But Stirling's work was more appreciated abroad than in Britain, where his three designs for museums in the German cities of Dusseldorf, Cologne and Stuttgart brought him international recognition. His works were not always expressed in the modernist style, but were often hybrid and highly individual, incorporating traditional and modern elements of design. The Neue Staatsgalerie (1984) in Stuttgart demonstrates his unique approach and became one of the most highly praised buildings of its time. In 1981 Stirling received architecture's most prestigious international award, the Pritzker Prize.

Richard Seifert claimed he had changed the face of London more than any architect since Sir Christopher Wren in the seventeenth century. But unlike Wren's Baroque churches, such as St Paul's Cathedral, Seifert's designs were mainly temples to commerce – office blocks that later became the subject of property speculation. Centre Point, the imposing modernist building which stands in central London on the crossroads by Tottenham Court Road underground station, was much admired by designers but heavily criticised by the political left when it remained empty in the interests of property speculation during a time of housing crisis in the early 1970s. Nat West Tower (1981) is another of Seifert's London landmarks and is situated in the financial and legal district known as the 'Square Mile' or simply the 'City'. Until the completion of Canary Wharf Tower in 1991, it was Europe's tallest building at 183 metres. Its imposing silhouette – which suggests a castle turret – remains a familiar part of the city skyline.

Denys Lasdun was another of the professionally most respected architects of the period. One of his best-known works is the National Theatre (1976). Later he became informally known as 'concrete's best friend' following his preference for the material and the rigorous, austere Brutalist style he essayed in the university buildings at Liverpool, London, Leicester and East Anglia.

New towns

In spite of public criticism, architects and planners continued to implement their modernist designs. But there was no co-ordinated attempt to create more convenient, desirable or architecturally harmonious cities. Instead, the government encouraged migration to the country with the creation of several new towns there.

The notion of a better quality of life has always been associated with the countryside, symbolised by rural and pseudo-rural domestic architecture. During the nineteenth century, when several wealthy landowners and industrialists with strong religious convictions wanted to improve conditions for their workforce, they removed them from the horrors of the industrial cities and offered them education, health and work in newly built countryside communities, such as Milton Abbas in the English Midlands, Saltaire in West Yorkshire and New Lanark in Scotland.

The village of Bourneville in the English Midlands is a good surviving example. It was built in around 1900 by the chocolate-making Cadbury family. The Cadburys were Quakers, a Protestant denomination with a strong belief in social reform. They wanted to house their workers in an environment that would serve, not oppress its inhabitants. They built a paternalist paradise of solid semi-detached houses with large gardens, each with a minimum of six fruit trees. Alcohol was seen by the reformers as the source of many social and domestic problems, and – to the disappointment of some residents – the village was built without a pub.

In the twentieth century, more secular solutions to the problem of overcrowded cities resulted in the construction of Letchworth (1903) and Welwyn (1920). The results were popular with the public: the author G.B. Shaw once described Letchworth as 'heaven near Hitchen' (a nearby town). Between the early 1950s and mid-1970s the government financed fourteen more new towns in attractive areas of green countryside. Milton Keynes is a more recent example, built between 1976 and 1979. The architect Derek Walker took inspiration from 1960s Los Angeles and designed low-rise buildings of uniform height and design. Although it has been slow to gain popularity with the British residents, it has proved attractive to executives from local Japanese and American business corporations.

The new towns offered a high quality of life. They had a low density of population and allowed an easy flow of traffic. They appeared clean and classless, reflecting the architects' belief that they were creating a new social order. But they lacked the entertainments and facilities of a big city. They also lacked a sense of history and community, and critics described them as sterile, grey, bleak and empty, with neither charm nor character. Several became 'dormitory towns': places in which to sleep but not to live and work. This was especially so with towns near London, for example Stevenage and Harlow. Enthusiasm for new towns' bland uniformity declined and, towards the end of the twentieth century, government policy began to focus on improving the quality of life in more established centres of population.

Attitudes to modernist architecture

The British public has been highly critical of the brave new modernist architecture. Many projects were considered ugly, badly designed, badly constructed and poorly integrated into their environments. Other buildings needed regular attention and expensive maintenance, which they rarely received. And in the case of the tall new housing estates, they were frequently blamed for increasing social problems, high rates of crime and the loss of community. Their negative image was hardened in the public mind by several cases of corrupt local politicians and greedy developers who collaborated in their development, such as the notorious case of Newcastle City architect John Poulson, who was jailed for corruption in 1974.

But architects argued that modernism was not a style, it was a logical, rational way to build in the mid-twentieth century. They emphasised that the problem was not the design, but the cost. Many controversial modernist architects received their commissions from cost-conscious organisations such as central government, municipal authorities or the universities. If costs were the main consideration – and with public projects they usually were – then a brick-and-concrete box would be the probable result. Furthermore, the need for speed of construction allowed little time for research and cheap, charmless tower blocks and towns were seen as the solution to Britain's post-war housing problems.

To public satisfaction, some modernist works were prematurely demolished due to poor construction. But ironically, architectural societies have demanded that early and unusual modernist buildings be preserved as part of Britain's architectural heritage, for example Cluster Block (Denys Lasdun, 1955), an early apartment tower in Bethnal Green, East London.

The sense of public revenge even acquired a humorous dimension, when in the late 1980s Bristol's Arnolfini Arts Centre held a competition to find Britain's ugliest postcard. The winning entry showed a Brutalist concrete underpass in the heavily urbanised area of south-east London, while another prize-winning card showed a modernist recreation centre in Milton Keynes which resembled a brick bunker.

Innovation and experiment: architecture in the 1970s

During the 1970s architectural design began to look for more publicly acceptable interpretations of modernism. One of the most innovative practices of the time was Arup Associates, which has become one of the most successful practices in Britain. Founded by Sir Ove Arup, a British-born Dane, it began to integrate the roles of architect and engineer. These were traditionally separate, with the engineer showing the architect how to realise his project. But Arup's approach recognised that the building's form and function are inseparable and must be worked on together. Some of the most notable works engineered by Arup are found outside Britain, for example the Sydney Opera House (1974) in Australia, the Hong Kong and Shanghai Bank (1986) in Hong Kong and the Pompidou Centre (1977) in Paris.

New techniques of building were proposed by an experimental group of architects called Archigram. Theirs was a flexible and imaginative approach to construction. Instead of constructing the walls and roof brick by brick, parts of a building were preconstructed and then joined together. It became known as 'plug-in' architecture. The Pompidou Centre (Richard Rogers and Renzo Piano, 1977) was the first building to be completed in this way. The Lloyds Building (1986) in the City of London, also by Rogers, continued this experimental trend. During the 1970s Richard Rogers and Norman Foster began to emerge as major influences in architectural design. They have become prominent for original, high-technology styles that often resemble spaceships or machines.

Richard Rogers

Richard Rogers (b.1933) is one of the most admired among contemporary British architects. He is part of an architectural movement working with advanced building technology and his works are some of the most highly praised in modern British architecture. He began his career at Yale University in the United States, together with the British architect Norman Foster. Later they became partners in a practice known as Team 4, which specialised in adventurous, stylish designs.

Many of their early designs were for houses and industrial buildings, but Rogers later worked with the Italian architect Renzo Piano to design a futuristic looking arts building in central Paris, the Centre Georges Pompidou. The exterior is one of the most impressive aspects of the building. The escalators are carried in transparent tubes on the outside. Other tubes are colour-coded and carry water, air and electricity. The design allows convenient access for maintenance, repairs and improvements of service equipment. These are practical features, which mean it can be adapted quickly and easily to technical change. When it opened in 1977, it soon became the most talked about building in Britain and France, and began to rival the Eiffel Tower for attention.

The heart of London's financial district is home to another of Rogers and Partners' most celebrated works. The Lloyds Building (1986) is a tall, impressive, machine-like edifice and became an icon of the advanced 'high-tech' style. It has a stainless steel exterior, supported by a web of tubes. The lifts and service equipment, such as air-conditioning units, are kept on the exterior. They provide a highly distinctive visual display and, as technology improves, improvements can be made quickly and easily.

The location makes it difficult to appreciate the whole building, which fits tightly into central London's medieval street pattern. But inside there is a sense of space, where open floors are designed around a central interior patio surrounded by escalators. The design produces a dramatic effect, in which the building's occupants become actors. The Lutine Bell – symbol of the Lloyds Company – is at the centre. The building established Rogers as a leading British architect and introduced high-tech post-modern architecture to London's financial district.

In the late 1990s he began to collaborate on architectural matters with the newly elected Labour Government and his design for the dome covering the Millennium Exhibition site at Greenwich in London has quickly become a national landmark. Rogers is now known as Lord Rogers of Riverside, after the site of both his office and his wife Ruth's Michelin-starred restaurant, the River Café in Hammersmith.

Norman Foster

Innovative, high-tech projects have made Norman Foster (b.1935) one of Britain's most distinguished architects. After studying in Manchester and the United States he worked with Richard Rogers in the innovative practice of Team 4. But his independent designs during the mid-1970s for an arts centre at the University of East Anglia near Norwich and the Willis Faber office building in Ipswich quickly brought him public attention. These are light, elegant, minimal structures inspired by his interest in aviation. They are visually distinctive and technically advanced buildings which are well integrated into their environment. The Willis Faber building was so highly praised that it became a listed building within thirty years of its completion.

As Foster's reputation grew, he received a growing number of commissions from abroad. One of the most notable was for the Hong Kong and Shanghai Bank (1986). The floors of this high-rise building hang from eight towers and make the building one of the most spectacular in the former colony. Its success confirmed him as a major British architect and one of world renown.

His most recent commissions in Britain have been mostly in or near London and include new galleries for the Royal Academy, a passenger terminal under an umbrella roof at Stansted Airport and a grand pedestrianisation scheme to connect Parliament Square with Trafalgar Square in central London, and together with Rogers, Foster is one of the few British architects well known to the British public.

The conservation movement

The mid-1970s was a time of disillusionment for British architecture. The design and appearance of apartment blocks, theatres, civic centres, shopping malls and small, angular, box-like houses were all strongly criticised. Feeling was especially strong in the rustic market towns, where neither shape nor materials harmonised with the local architecture and environment.

The economic crash in the winter of 1973–4 stopped most projects in the public sector. However, the absence of finance for new projects created interest in renovating older buildings. In the private sector, it resulted in diverse, imaginative new styles and influences, for example the renovation of barns and warehouses for use as flats. It also introduced a new way of thinking about the environment and soon there was a movement for the protection of historic and unusual buildings. At the same time, municipal planning offices began to insist that the height, shape and surfaces had to harmonise with the environment. Local materials had to be used wherever possible. Many old, unusual, historically interesting structures became 'listed', that is, protected by law from demolition, alteration or extension. Moreover, the owners had to accept responsibility for their maintenance.

A significant victory for the conservationists occurred in 1979, when the London landmark of Covent Garden was given official protection. Developers had planned to demolish the buildings of the old fruit-and-vegetable market and construct office blocks and hotels there. But the local residents formed a community action group to resist them and, after a long battle, the Conservative Government decided to protect and restore the market area. Soon there were outdoor cafés, boutiques, specialist food shops and street performers, which today make it one of the most popular areas of London for entertainment and commerce.

The decision to conserve and redefine Covent Garden broke with a post-war planning tradition of demolish and rebuild. It was also significant because it recognised that buildings and spaces needed to meet the needs of the public and the environment. Since then, planning and designing have become increasingly influenced by public preferences and conservation is now a common practice in almost all areas of Britain.

Winds of change: architecture and Thatcherism

The 1980s was a turbulent period when civic architecture experienced radical changes. The Conservative Government elected in 1979 introduced more cuts in public spending and the recession in the construction industry continued. During the decade of individualism that followed, architects' plans were influenced more by private clients than by public commissions.

Some of the most characteristic styles of contemporary architecture were created in response to changes in technology. The introduction of sophisticated computer systems and air conditioning for energy-efficient buildings required deep floors and low ceilings to accommodate miles of cables and tubes. The need for change intensified when London's Stock Exchange closed in 1986. Instead of buying and selling shares in person, trade had to be conducted on computerised systems. Consequently many wealthy private companies, such as investment and banking firms, urgently needed headquarters which would accept the latest high-tech equipment.

City buildings only twenty years old, such as Seifert's Centre Point, were already out of date. Their design had not anticipated the technology of the future. They could not be adapted economically and were unlettable. To satisfy demand it was necessary to contract several American architects, such as John Burgee, Philip Johnson and Cesar Pelli. They were experienced at quickly constructing high-tech buildings and applied 'fast track' techniques. These use large, steel-framed structures, with the characteristic materials of glass, steel, aluminium and chrome, with tubes, cables, nuts and bolts all openly exposed. The building with all its elements clearly visible, openly expressing its structure, is a common feature of the postmodern style.

Inside the new buildings, the strong visual contrasts of metal, glass and concrete are softened by attention to the lighting and a generous distribution of 'rainforestry' and modern sculpture. Many are designed around an atrium: a glass-covered central courtyard, or interior patio, which brings light into the centre of the building. This is a practical feature in areas with a high density of office blocks, where little light can enter through the side windows, and became a fashionable characteristic in designs of the mid-1980s.

The advanced technology and futuristic appearance is known as 'high-tech post-modern'. One of the first buildings in this style was by Arup Associates in 1984, called simply 1 Finsbury Avenue. Its enormous, imposing, glass-covered courtyard won extensive critical praise and design awards. London's financial and legal district – the City – welcomed the new styles and between 1985 and 1993 the number of offices in the City area doubled. In the past, some of the most visually impressive, futuristic and innovative buildings were built as religious monuments. In the last century they often expressed civic grandeur. In the 1960s and 1970s they were built as tributes to the arts. But in the 1980s it was the commercial spirit which was embodied in futuristic, high-tech cathedrals to capitalism.

Not only individual buildings and factories but also whole areas were rapidly redeveloped in many parts of Britain. The most spectacular of these is Docklands, an area of two square miles in the east of London on the River Thames. Between 1967 and 1980, the old docks began to decline as the more modern port of Tilbury grew in size and importance. But as the old port died, the government offered financial incentives to redevelop the area and the most technically advanced and futuristic buildings ever erected in Britain began to emerge from among the mud and weeds.

Some of the first businesses to arrive were from the print industry. Many of the old buildings in London's Fleet Street could not be easily adapted to accept the new computerised print technology. They were also badly sited in central London for the distribution of newspapers to other parts of the country. Rents were high too, and the print unions were strong and numerous. Moving to Docklands resulted in reduced costs, a smaller labour force and faster, reliable, more economic systems of production and distribution.

A new landscape began to emerge from the dirt and dust of the old port. Low-rise offices, leisure buildings and luxury houses and flats were built in a post-modern, high-tech style. Many exteriors are colourful, angular-shaped and often finished with darkened glass. But there are contrasts too. In order to conserve some of the character of the old port area, several warehouses were preserved and converted into luxurious living-accommodation with swimming pools, tennis courts and saunas. Access to the heart of London is facilitated by a driverless light railway and the whole area is punctuated by the massive, square, thick, 244-metre-high Canary Wharf Tower (Cesar Pelli, 1991).

Critics of the new architecture called it arrogant and extravagant, symbolising the excess of the 1980s. But it was the most ambitious ever seen in Britain and began to influence architecture around the country. Many small and medium-sized firms followed the Docklands example and moved to more suitable premises and locations. Old buildings in city centres were often unsuitable and maintenance costs were high, so specially constructed business parks and industrial estates appeared on the edges of many cities. The radical, futuristic designs offered many practical and financial advantages, and have proved popular with the business community.

Community Architecture and Prince Charles

Not everyone was enthusiastic about the diverse new styles of architecture which were emerging around Britain, and during the 1980s there were many individual attempts to design buildings which reflected people's needs and wants more than those of the architects. These initiatives came

Figure 9.3 Canary Wharf, Docklands, London

not only from the public, but also from royalty. Since 1984, when he criticised a proposed post-modern design for an extension at the National Gallery as 'a carbuncle on the face of an old, much-loved friend', the Prince of Wales has been a vocal critic of modern architecture. He later made frank criticisms of London's Festival Hall architecture. His interventions in 1987 led to the demolition of some of the modernist office blocks around St Paul's Cathedral, giving an improved view of Wren's baroque church.

In 1988 he gained more popular support when he made *A Vision of Britain*, a film for the BBC *Omnibus* programme (an arts documentary series), in which he again attacked modernist architecture and its ugly urban offices and apartment blocks. In their place he advocated more programmes of Community Architecture, with their popular neo-classical and neo-vernacular styles. The programme was seen by millions of viewers and a large majority agreed with his conservative, common-sense opinions.

Public amenities

The credit boom and economic confidence of the mid-1980s affected many other areas of architecture and design. There was strong competition among shops and leisure services for a new generation of consumers who had more money available for pleasure and recreation, and architects were increasingly commissioned to design commercial interiors.

Public houses and restaurants began to attract customers not only with their food and drink, but also with their looks. Until the 1980s most pubs were traditional in design and decor. They were generally quiet places with seating designed to promote privacy and intimacy, and often had several smaller rooms where meetings could be held. Children were not allowed to enter and many women found the atmosphere disagreeable. Opening hours were restricted: pubs had to close before 11 PM, conforming with laws introduced to ensure safety and sobriety among the workforce during the First World War. But during the 1980s the demand for novelty saw the appearance of exciting new styles, which sometimes seemed more like stages, as the emphasis changed from privacy to public display. They were often given long curved bars which allowed customers to see and be seen. The colours, materials and styles of lights, tables, chairs and other furnishings were integrated into their surroundings. Theme pubs became common, such as the 'Irish' pub or the 'fun' pub with games, videos and music.

More people began eating out and restaurants started competing with design and decor, rather than with food and prices. Earlier, during the 1960s, if diners wanted elaborate dishes and refined surroundings it had usually been necessary to go to a good hotel or perhaps a French restaurant. But later in the 1960s and early 1970s many cheap ethnic restaurants opened to serve the newly arrived immigrant communities in cities around the country. A new generation of adventurous British diners were attracted by modestly priced, exotic alternatives to bland British dishes and by the 1980s a cosmopolitan restaurant culture had become established. Interior decor often reminded diners of the owners' origins: the dim lights and 'flock' wallpaper of a colonial British officers' club in Indian curry houses; the paper lanterns and murals of the Great Wall of China in Chinese eateries; the crab pots and fishing nets of numerous Greek tavernas. But they were popular with a new generation of consumers, who revelled in their novelty.

Although a strong and increasingly sophisticated consumer culture emerged in the 1980s, the middle years of the decade saw high levels of unemployment, with some 3.3 million people out of work in 1985. In some areas, such as the industrial centres of the north and north-east England, the level was much higher than the national average. Many municipal authorities, especially those on the political left, began to commission more public amenities, such as leisure centres for sport and recreation. They believed the social consequences of recession would be much greater if the unemployed had nothing to do. The provision of sports facilities also coincided with a growing interest in health and fitness, and many urban areas benefited, even though public funds were scarce.

As well as sports centres, many new art galleries and museums were opened to encourage tourism, recreation and study. By 1986, Britain had over 2,000 museums, of which half had been established since 1971. In recent years these have made imaginative efforts to offer more active, 'living' representations of the past. There has been a growing interest in 'heritage' culture – popular artifacts and representations of British history. The Burrell Gallery, situated near Glasgow, was designed by Barry Gasson (1971–83) has won many awards for its individuality of design and presentation.

The new galleries introduced exciting new ways of presenting material. Previously, interior designers had favoured large, bare, open spaces to show works. But these had been appropriate only for large, modern exhibits. Smaller pictures and more traditional works were unsuited to them and such galleries were not popular with the public. However, smaller more intimate rooms were gradually reintroduced to popular satisfaction, often with interactive exhibits and imaginative displays.

Domestic architecture and interiors

At the beginning of the 1980s, financial restrictions were relaxed on mortgages (loans to buy residential property). Credit was easy to obtain and property prices rose rapidly. But in contrast to the futuristic, high-tech styles found in offices and public buildings, people demanded more traditional styles of housing. Among the most popular styles was Georgian, often called 'mock-Georgian'.

The architect Quinlan Terry is noted for his designs of Georgian-style houses. The Richmond Riverside Development (1988) in west London is a well-known and much-admired example of his work; it consists of rows of offices hidden behind a neo-classical façade. His buildings make use of contemporary materials and components, and are highly popular with the public. However, some critics argue the results are often too elaborate and decorative, and do not have the grace and simplicity of the originals. Furthermore, it is argued that the houses represent a step backwards, not forwards, in the architecture of towns and cities. But others interpret the style as an architectural expression of traditional conservative values, in perfect harmony with the spirit of the 1980s.

There is an important characteristic which much contemporary housing shares with the neo-classical architecture of the past. This is the common desire to make a new house look old. For centuries the opposite was the case. The public wanted their houses to look new and impressive. Britain is full of medieval farmhouses with later, Jacobean façades, Tudor mansions with later, classical ones, and Georgian houses with later, Victorian features. But in the mid-1980s the trend was not to modernise, but to make the house look older and more traditional, using features from an earlier period.

In the mid-1980s when house prices rose quickly and many people wanted to buy their own homes. They believed that if they didn't, property would quickly become too expensive. Owners became highly sensitive to the value of their property and looked for ways to improve it. Special loans were available to adapt buildings such as churches, windmills or warehouses for living accommodation. Soon it became fashionable to live in unconventional types of building and an interior-design industry grew to meet demand. Many large stores flourished, selling modern and traditional materials, accessories, furniture and fabrics at affordable prices together with all the notes and instructions.

For some, property renovation became a full-time occupation. For others, the hobby known as 'do-it-yourself' (D-I-Y) became popular. Porches were added, arches installed. Inside and out, walls were covered with a rectangular stone known as 'cladding'. When central heating became a popular addition during the 1960s, fireplaces were removed or covered. But in the 1980s they became desirable again as decorative or functional features. Conservatories were another popular addition. These traditional extensions of glass and wood were originally added to large Victorian houses to display exotic plants from remote parts of the Empire. They created space and united house and garden. But in the 1980s they became a valuable house extension in which it was possible to live and entertain.

Between 1985 and 1989 average house prices doubled and many owners chose to renovate and sell, in order to buy more expensive properties and repeat the exercise. D-I-Y became the second most popular leisure activity in Britain. Those who could not or did not want to, could commission the services of a newly arrived expert: the professional interior designer.

Building new Britain: architecture in the 1990s

Strong support has continued for neo-classical architecture. This has been influenced by the Community Architecture movement, which proposes small-scale housing which meets the needs and expressed wishes of its users. Architects must work in the communities for whom they are designing and are required to consult widely with their clients. The critics call it 'toy town' architecture. But the results have been enthusiastically received by the public. The main impact of Community Architecture has been felt in London and the south, where some of the most notable examples have been achieved in London with Jeremy Dixon's designs in Docklands, in St Mark's Road in North Kensington and in Lanark Road in Maida Vale.

Prince Charles' interventions have been a powerful incentive for change, but the profession of architecture remains a traditional, male-dominated one. All the past presidents of the Royal Institute of British Architects

(RIBA) were male, as are over 90 per cent of current practising architects. The related professions of engineering and building are also male-dominated. Some critics argue that the nature of much building work is masculine: it is dedicated to creating monuments of strength that reflect power and prestige, in which power is exercised predominantly by men.

However, a current architectural issue is the changing nature of the cities and how to adapt them to people's needs. It is argued that women use the city environment more than men, spending more time walking and interacting there, and so understand its problems better. Furthermore, it is said that women architects are better able to communicate with clients and have a better understanding of their needs. So architectural practice may become less male-dominated in the future.

One of the most highly regarded female architects is Eva Jiricna. Born in Prague, she has worked in London since 1969. Her stylish monochrome interiors of shops, bars and restaurants have been widely imitated. Some of her most notable work has been in Mayfair's Le Caprice restaurant (1981) and the interior of the Lloyds building (1985–6). Zarah Hadid from Iraq is also widely respected for her designs, and in Tyneside, north-east England, Jane Derbyshire has designed a number of popular projects including schools, council houses and hospices.

Architecture and design in the late 1990s was characterised by stylistic variety from minimal to classical. Many young architects are involved in a range of projects, such as designing interiors for fashionable restaurants, bars, city-centre apartments and working with local communities to improve some of the less attractive boroughs of Britain. Interiors and exteriors of commercial buildings have become less brash and imposing, indicating an exhaustion with novelty, ostentation and excess. Minimal decoration, pale colours and natural materials are preferred, in a style which has become increasingly common in a variety of establishments, from Indian restaurants to insurance offices, not just in Britain but around Europe too.

The decade was often called 'the caring 1990s' and environmental or 'green' issues acquired a new importance. The universities have traditionally offered opportunities for architects to express themselves in the most progressive, avant-garde styles of the period and in the mid-1990s many design awards were won by campus buildings, for example 'Green Building of the Year' was won by De Montfort University (1995) and Anglia Polytechnic University (1996), and the Royal Fine Art Commission's 'New Building of the Year' by the Universities of Sunderland (1995) and Salford (1997).

During the economic recession of the early 1990s, building activity declined once more and there were few new developments. But after the election of the new Labour Government in 1997 the cranes returned and construction activity increased again. Leading design continued to be influenced by Norman Foster and Richard Rogers. The latter became more

197

closely involved with the newly elected Labour Party, which has a keen interest in rebuilding Britain in more than just the architectural sense.

Plans for Millennium celebrations have renewed public debate about architecture, just as they did in 1951. After initial caution, the public became enthusiastic and responsive to projects such as Rogers' huge Dome, covering the Millennium Project's main site in Greenwich. The 50-metre-high structure is the largest ever constructed, having a diameter of 320 metres and a circumference of one kilometre. Nearby, the Millennium Village at Greenwich, designed by Ralph Erskine and Hunt Thompson, is a futuristic housing complex which incorporates the latest design practice: insulated energy-efficient buildings designed around communal gardens, with a recycling of water and other waste materials.

Housing became a major issue in the mid-1990s, as the government estimated that between 4 and 5 million new homes would be needed by 2016 due to increasing longevity and a greater number of single-occupancy dwellings. The new schemes were welcome, but attitude surveys repeatedly showed that the British prefer older houses to new ones. A view persists that older houses have more character, are less uniform and are better built. This is in spite of the fact that modern buildings are more efficiently heated, insulated and plumbed, are easier to clean and maintain, and have more security features. In 1996 Britain had the oldest housing stock in Europe, with some 25 per cent built before 1914. However, these still sold more easily than many new ones.

Responding to public demand, some of the most modern and desirable small houses built in the 1990s were designed in a neo-vernacular style. Many resembled simple terraced houses for Victorian labourers, while the most fashionable, detached properties looked like conversions of an old farm or barn. Sometimes old bricks and tiles were used to make the wall appear more 'authentically' old. Some houses and estates even began to resemble film sets for a historical drama.

Other major projects which reflected design practice included several schemes to promote public transport and movement. Nick Grimshaw's design for the Eurostar Terminal (which links Britain with France) at Waterloo Station in London incorporates the features of a nineteenth-century railway station. Like the Millennium Dome, it has been described as 'tasteful but anorexic', since it appears light and graceful but seems to lack strength and substance. Similar comments were made about Norman Foster's design for a new bridge over the Thames from the new Tate Gallery in the converted Bankside Power Station. In central London, Foster planned to connect Trafalgar Square and Parliament Square, two of the city's most emblematic places, with a grand pedestrianisation scheme; gradually the citizens were reclaiming their city in preparation for the new Millennium.

The growing number of public projects was helped by a new source of funds from the National Lottery. There were numerous new football stadiums as many clubs moved from their old grounds in the city centre to modern new ones on the edge of the city. In London, Wembley Stadium is to be redeveloped into a national 'superstadium'. Elsewhere in Britain, new museums, galleries and other sports facilities are planned. With over 80 million visitors to museums around Britain in 1998, it seemed the government had finally realised the historic potential of the British Isles.

Towards the Millennium, architecture became more varied and responsive to public needs, and there were many voices which influenced design. Individual buildings and environmental space in the town and country are now public and political issues and as a consequence there is more open discussion of the type of public spaces the public wants to observe and occupy.

Discussion topics and activities

1 Summarise the main stylistic influences in British architecture since the mid-1950s. Do you think Britain is too concerned with protecting its architectural past?

2 How has architecture changed in your town/country in recent years? What changes and influences can you identify? Are they similar to those in Britain. Do architects build what people want and like?

3 Refer to the text and other sources to explain the following: neo-classical / suburbia / Le Corbusier / New Brutalism / neo-vernacular / Docklands.

4 How do you think environmental design can affect people's behaviour?

5 Should successful new cities be created artificially, or should they be allowed to develop naturally? Which type would you prefer to live in?

6 Imagine you have to write about a building you know well for a 'quality' newspaper. Say what you like/dislike about it and why.

Suggested further reading

Books

Durant, D. (1992) *Handbook of British Architectural Styles* London: Barrie & Jenkins.

Glancey, J. (1991) *New British Architecture* London: Thames & Hudson.

HRH, The Prince of Wales (1989) *A Vision of Britain: A Personal View of Architecture* London: Doubleday.

Hutchinson, M. (1989) *The Prince of Wales: Right or Wrong? An Architect Replies* London: Faber & Faber.

Jencks, C. (1988) *The Prince, the Architects and New Wave Architecture* London: Rizzoli International.

Moffat, N. (1995) *The Best of British Architecture 1980–2000* London: E & FN Spon.

Walker, D. (1982) *The Architecture and Planning of Milton Keynes* London: Architectural Press.

Watkin, D. (1979) *English Architecture* London: Thames & Hudson.

Journals

The *Architectural Review* was started in 1896 and is the leading British architecture magazine. It appears monthly and has contributions by prominent British architects.

The *Architects' Journal* covers topics of current importance, carries news and reviews, and pays attention to conservation issues. It appears weekly.

Details of each building listed by English Heritage can be found in some 2,000 volumes. They are now available on a computerised database and can be consulted at the offices of the Royal Commission on the Historical Monuments of England, in Swindon and London.

Name index

Subject index